MW00861584

MARTHA STEWART'S GARDENING HANDBOOK

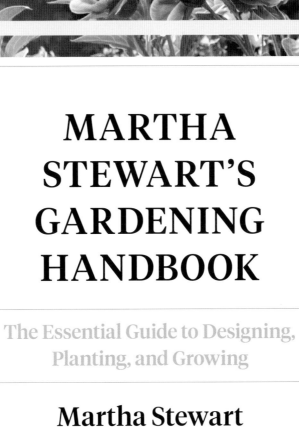

MARTHA STEWART'S GARDENING HANDBOOK

The Essential Guide to Designing, Planting, and Growing

Martha Stewart

HARVEST
An Imprint of WILLIAM MORROW

MARTHA STEWART'S GARDENING HANDBOOK. Copyright © 2025 by Martha Stewart Living Omnimedia, LP. All rights reserved. Printed in Canada. No part of this book may be used or reproduced in any manner whatsoever without written permission except in the case of brief quotations embodied in critical articles and reviews. For information, address HarperCollins Publishers, 195 Broadway, New York, NY 10007.

Page 368 constitutes an extension of the copyright page.

HarperCollins books may be purchased for educational, business, or sales promotional use. For information, please email the Special Markets Department at SPsales@harpercollins.com.

FIRST EDITION

Designed by Laura Palese

Library of Congress Cataloging-in-Publication Data

Names: Stewart, Martha, author.
Title: Martha Stewart's gardening handbook / Martha Stewart.
Description: First edition. | New York : HarperCollins, 2025 | Includes index.
Identifiers: LCCN 2024033462 (print) | LCCN 2024033463 (ebook) | ISBN 9780063323285 (hardcover) | ISBN 9780063323292 (ebook)
Subjects: LCSH: Gardening—Handbooks, manuals, etc. | Handbooks and manuals.
Classification: LCC SB321 .S678 2025 (print) | LCC SB321 (ebook) | DDC 635—dc23/eng/20241104
LC record available at https://lccn.loc.gov/2024033462
LC ebook record available at https://lccn.loc.gov/2024033463

ISBN 978-0-06-332328-5

25 26 27 28 29 TC 10 9 8 7 6 5 4 3 2

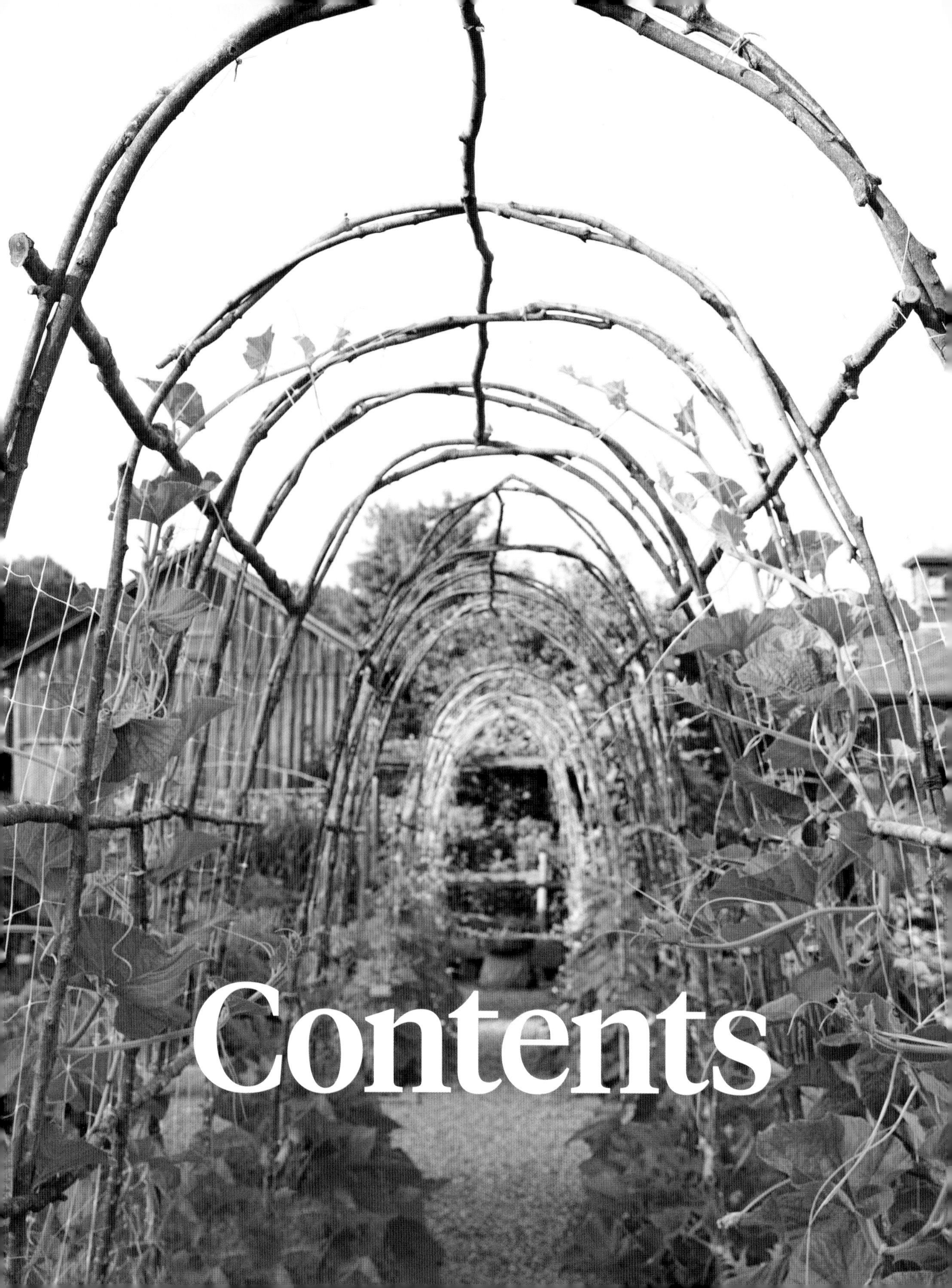

Contents

Introduction

Gardening is an ever-evolving relationship, making it both immediately gratifying and a source of long-term awe and enjoyment.

Those bulbs you planted in the brisk days of fall emerge once the ground thaws in spring and continue to do so year after year. A thicket of scrawny saplings grows into sturdy trees, casting shade, sporting blossoms, or yielding fruit (or all of the above). Nursery-bought perennials and shrubs settle in, take root, and become big and bountiful. Tiny seeds sprout, send up shoots, and provide delicious sustenance or showy flower heads. It all unfolds gradually, and there's great pleasure in checking on each plant's progress.

Or as celebrated British horticulturist and garden designer Gertrude Jekyll sums it up: "A garden is a grand teacher. It teaches patience and careful watchfulness; it teaches industry and thrift; above all it teaches entire trust."

This book is designed in that same spirit, offering encouragement, hands-on instruction, helpful tips and techniques, and inspiring glossaries and photographs. As a trusted guide, it provides lessons for every stage of your gardening journey—from idea to implementation to iterative delight. Hence, the organizational structure of the sections and chapters.

Gardening Basics, which could also be called Getting Started, begins with planning considerations, namely your garden zone and foundational elements such as soil, sunlight, and rainfall. "Right plant, right place" is a worthy mantra to remember. A concise yet comprehensive plant primer explains flowers (annuals vs. perennials and biennials), climbers, ground covers, and other categories, with an emphasis on native plants. Stocking up on supplies, composting, and gardening methods are also covered.

The next section focuses on design principles, including choosing the palette and planting for year-round interest and common garden types—border, perennial, cottage, habitat, shade, rose, container, vegetable, cutting-flower, and xeriscape (for drought-prone areas). A section on preparing and planting discusses the importance of amending the soil, buying plants, and following planting guidelines (including layering bulbs for maximum effect). Jekyll's "industry and thrift" comes into play with a discussion of propagating as a way to grow plants economically and efficiently, whether from saved seeds, divisions, or cuttings. Think of it as "shopping" your garden! Finally, a section on nurturing and maintaining ensures your plants thrive via careful watering, fertilizing, and controlling weeds, disease, and pests, along with winterizing in cold climates.

An entire part is devoted to Trees and Shrubs, approaching these two garden mainstays with the deference they deserve—both as the "backbones" of the landscape and for their critical roles in helping the environment and supporting wildlife. Here, you'll get time-tested guidance for selecting specimens based on site conditions, function, and visual interest; planting for long-term success; and pruning to improve the plants' health, flowering, or appearance.

Third in line is Specialty Gardens, which delves into nine examples, with tips for glossaries illuminating favored plants—including cutting roses for a Rose Garden, hostas for a Shade Garden, and plants with different blooming times for a White Garden. Step-by-step how-tos for hanging baskets and climbing hydrangeas round out the pages.

Finally, Grow Your Own spans vegetable gardens, berry patches, and fruit trees to produce homegrown crops, walking you through site selection, plot design, and maintenance. Handy charts provide at-a-glance instruction for planning a steady harvest and timing your plantings based on vegetables' ideal temperature ranges. Oh, and For the Love of Tomatoes shows you how to reap this summer favorite in spades—and make the most of a bountiful yield, with separate sidebars on pickling and making jam to preserve flavor long after summer fades. Greenhouses, cold frames, and hoop houses are other ways to extend the season. There are even tips on raising backyard chickens, who will welcome all your scraps and excesses!

"The love of gardening is a seed that once sown never dies, but always grows and grows to an enduring and ever-increasing source of happiness."

—GERTRUDE JEKYLL

And should you be dreaming of an endless supply of blooms for indoor bouquets, this section culminates with a deep dive into creating a cutting-flower garden, complete with stunning spotlights on dahlias, peonies, and lilies, with a primer on flower arranging.

No matter your motivation for gardening—be it to reconnect with nature and the land, beautify your landscape and boost your curb appeal, provide food and habitat for your local wildlife population, help save the planet, or live more sustainably by producing your own food—this book will be your trusted companion throughout the journey, year in and year out.

1

Gardening Basics

A thriving garden cannot be rushed. Careful planning and patience are prerequisites, as is gaining familiarity with the components of a vigorous ecosystem that will support the plants (and local wildlife) and satisfy your aesthetic goals. Learning the basics is where every gardening journey begins, and a natural launch for this manual. The starting point is, of course, the soil—the bedrock of the landscape. Knowing how to nurture it for optimal fertility will serve you well, as will appreciating the different types of plants and gardening methods. This running-up stage is ripe with discovery as you explore the flowers, foliage, trees, and shrubs to plant in your own yard. And understanding design tenets will allow you to create a harmonious, year-round display.

Planning

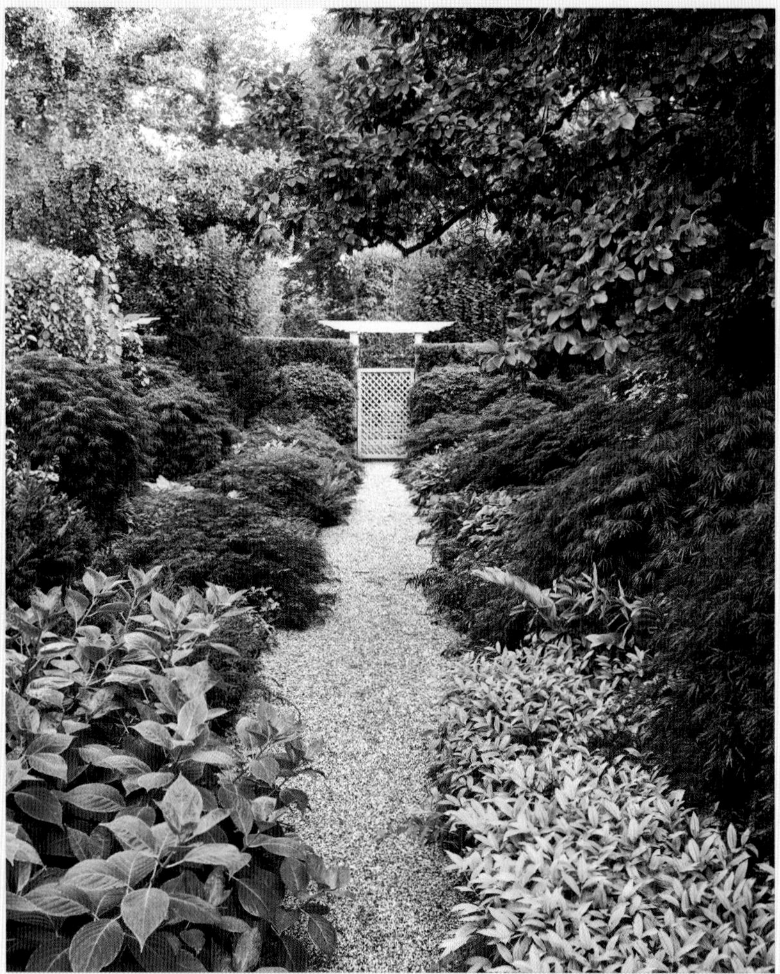

Gardens serve many purposes, so start with this helpful prompt: What do you hope to achieve? A beautiful, serene vista outside your kitchen window? Or are you motivated by sustainability concerns in converting patches of high-maintenance lawn? Perhaps your top priority is supporting your local wildlife. Many people may check “all of the above”—because a garden can be many things at once.

Whatever the answer, a little planning will ensure you end up with the garden of your dreams. It’s one thing to fall in love with a tree, shrub, or flower, and quite another to figure out whether it will fail to thrive in a particular spot—or thrive too well and take over.

Of course, it’s your garden, so you should grow what makes you happy. Don’t overthink it, but do try to stay away from invasives in favor of native plants that help promote a more sustainable environment.

“Go to nurseries and find something you love, and just start digging and planting. You’re bound to make mistakes—I make lots—but you’ll learn from them, and you can always dig up a plant and try again.”

Laying the foundation

▶ **Follow the mantra:** Right plant, right place. This commonsense advice originated from English gardener and garden designer Beth Chatto, who suggested gardeners look to their environment first and then to match plants to the conditions. Some extraordinary plant is bound to grow in practically every part of your landscape. An optimal growing environment is a blend of temperature, moisture, nutrients, and sunlight. The following groundwork takes away the guesswork.

Know your garden zone

Every gardener's go-to guide, the Plant Hardiness Zone Map by the United States Department of Agriculture (USDA), divides the country into 13 zones based on average winter temperatures and frost dates, with each zone representing a 10°F temperature change and further subzones with 5°F ranges.

Recognizing the overall warming of the country due to climate change, the USDA released an updated version in November 2023, the first such update since 2012. The 2023 map is based on 30-year averages of the lowest annual winter temperatures at specific locations. You can search the map by zip code online (see Helpful Online Resources, opposite).

Plant labels, seed packets, and gardening catalogs always reference which zones a plant is deemed to be "hardy" in, meaning it will survive local winters. When shopping online, you can often filter your search by your particular zone. Note that a plant described as "hardy to" zone 6 or zone 5, for example, will generally survive in zones with higher numbers, too.

Think of the zone map as a guardrail rather than a roadblock—you can still have a favorite tropical shrub or ornamental tree that's not hardy for your zone, though you may want to experiment with only one or two. Growing from seed, bulbs, or cuttings (say, from a friend or neighbor) is a low-cost way to incorporate showy specimens into your landscape.

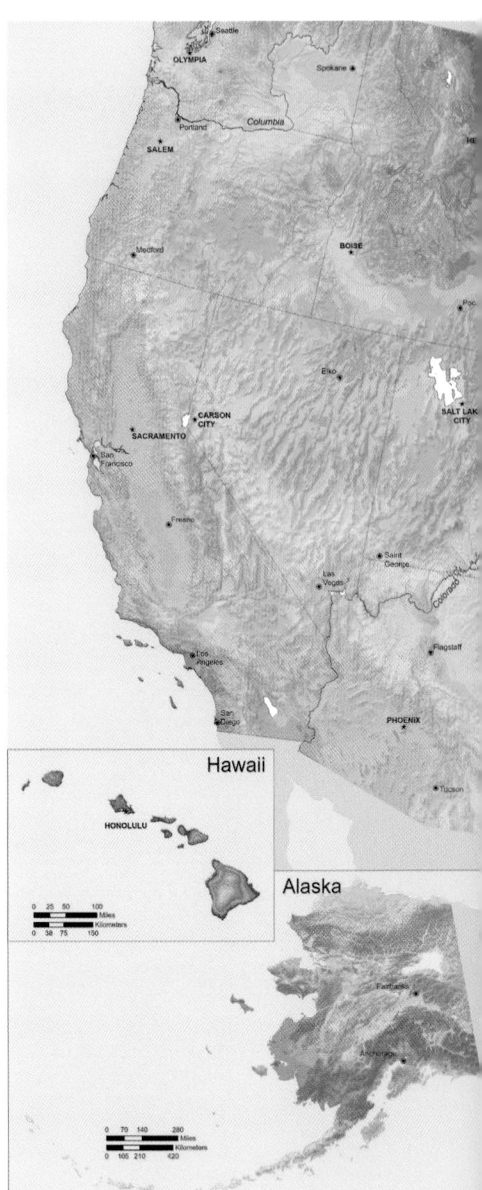

Helpful Online Resources

Here's where you'll find the sources mentioned on the following page.

USDA Plant Hardiness Zone Map
planthardiness.ars.usda.gov

Environmental Protection Agency Ecoregions
epa.gov/eco-research/ecoregions-north-america

National Wildlife Federation Native Plant Finder
nwf.org/Garden-for-Wildlife/About/Native-Plants/keystone-plants-by-ecoregion
nwf.org/nativeplantfinder

Xerces Society for Invertebrate Conservation Native Plants Lists
xerces.org/publications/plant-lists

National Audubon Society Native Plants Lists
audubon.org/native-plants

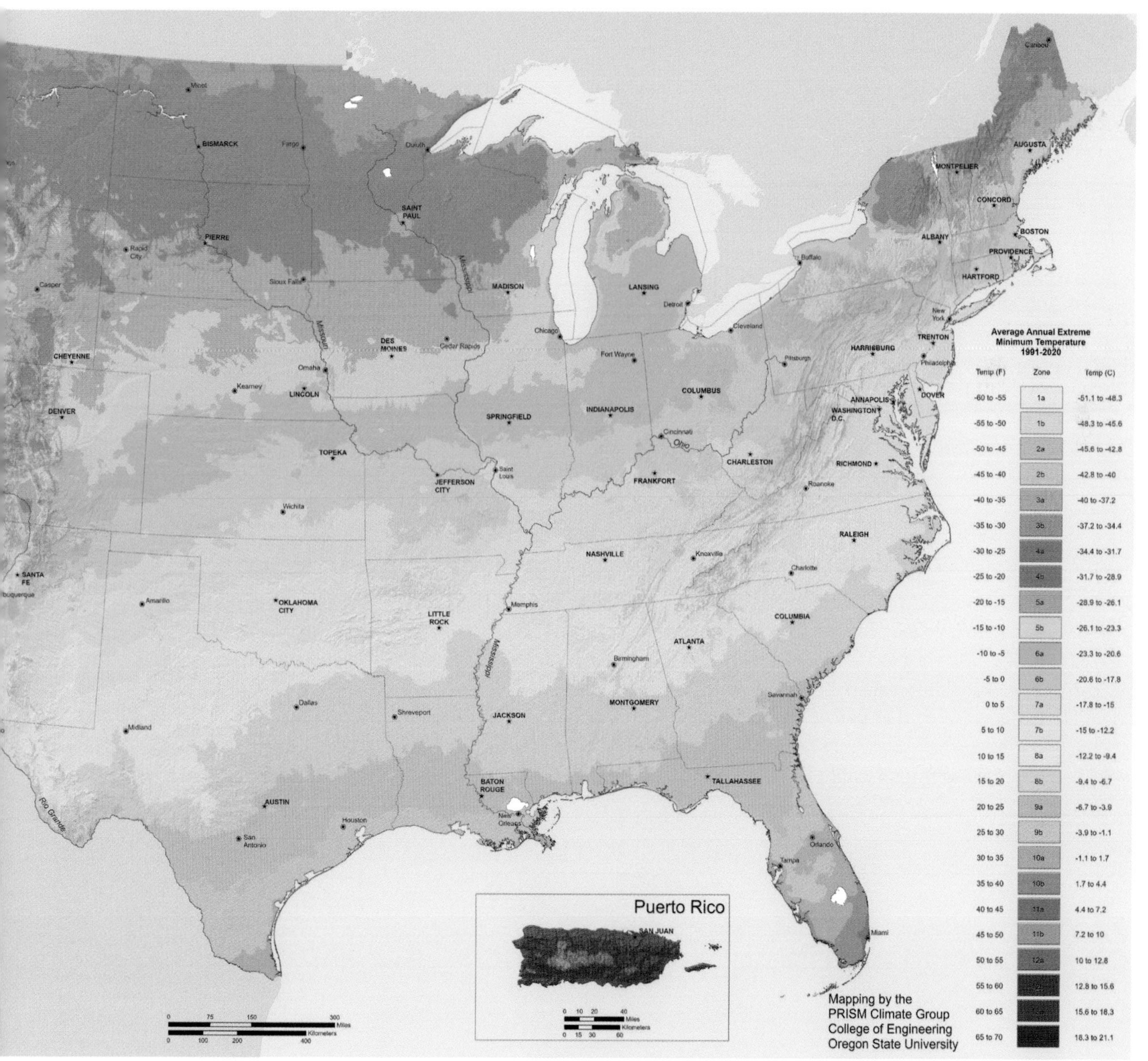

Growing Native Plants

Native plants are the heart of a healthy ecosytem, removing carbon from the air, providing shelter and food for wildlife, and promoting biodiversity.

A plant that is native to an area grows there naturally, without any cultivation. It is also cold-hardy for the area, though that same plant is not necessarily cold-hardy in other areas within the same zone or region where it is not native. Picture the vastly different natural landscapes in Utah and Kentucky (both in zones 5–7) or Montana and Maine (zones 2–5)—or even a rural, inland county versus coastal towns in South Carolina (zones 8–9). Numerous studies have shown that native plants support more species and larger numbers of bees than non-native plants, too.

When growing native plants and supporting pollinators, look past hardiness zones to your particular "ecoregion," according to the Environmental Protection Agency (EPA; see Helpful Online Resources, page 15). Specifically, you can learn about "keystone" plants—the top native plants used by pollinating butterfly and bee species, without which the ecosystem and wildlife would suffer.

North America has been divided into 15 broad "level I" ecological regions with 50 level II and 182 level III ecological areas. The ecoregion maps can be hard to decipher—instead, focus on keystone plants for each level I ecoregion on the National Wildlife Federation's Native Plant Finder, which also lets you search by zip code (see page 15). The Xerces Society for Invertebrate Conservation is another excellent resource, with convenient downloadable one-page plant lists, or you can search by zip code via the National Audubon Society (see page 15). You can also consult your local nursery, botanical garden, or cooperative extension to learn about native plants that will thrive in your area.

Native Plants

Here is just a sampling of some native plants that thrive in Pennsylvania. Consult your local nursery to learn what will flourish in your garden.

1. **Rattlesnake master (*Eryngium yuccifolium*)**
2. **Goldenrod (*Solidago speciosa*)**
3. **'Little Henry' sweet coneflower (*Rudbeckia subtomentosa* 'Little Henry')**
4. **Butterfly weed (*Asclepias tuberosa*)**
5. **Hubricht's bluestar (*Amsonia hubrictii*)**
6. **Tennessee purple coneflower (*Echinacea tennesseensis*)**
7. **'Autumn Bride' coral bells (*Heuchera villosa* 'Autumn Bride')**
8. **Muhly grass (*Muhlenbergia capillaris*)**
9. **Aster Spp.**
10. **White snakeroot (*Ageratina altissima*)**
11. **Blue wood aster (*Aster cordifolius* syn. *symphyotrichum cordifolium*)**
12. **'Proud Berry' coralberry (*Symphoricarpos orbiculatus* 'Proud Berry')**
13. **Joe-pye weed (*Eupatorium dubium*)**

1
2
3
4
5
6
7
8
9
10
11
12
13

Know your soil

First, it helps to know what soil is not—and that's dirt, though it does contain dirt, which is basically broken-down rocks. Soil, on the other hand, is a living ecosystem teeming with friendly fungi, bacteria, microscopic roundworms (called nematodes), protozoa, earthworms, and tiny insects and mites (aka microarthropods). Together, these elements decompose organic matter and release nutrients. Armed with this intel, you can better appreciate how soil is the life force of any landscape—it grounds and nourishes plants and fends off pests and disease. Therefore, the health of your plants depends on the health of the soil they are inhabiting.

How can you tell if your soil is healthy? It is if your garden is lush and robust. It isn't if you use synthetic fertilizers and pesticides, nor if your garden is riddled with weeds, pests, and failing plants. When plants have all the nutrients they need, they aren't as susceptible to the usual nuisances. The good news: You can—and should—boost soil health with amendments, notably compost or other organic matter, as discussed on page 44.

And a note of caution: When planting vegetables or other edibles in the ground, the general advice is to perform a special soil test for lead and other heavy metal contamination, especially if children might be exposed (including by helping out in the garden). See page 86 for more information.

Besides general health, you'll want to determine the following important soil traits.

COMPOSITION

The texture of soil is based on the proportion of three particles: sand, silt, and clay. And this composition determines how workable your soil will be, how it handles water and nutrients, and how well aerated it is—in other words, how fertile it will be.

A soil test (described in detail below) will provide the most accurate profile, though you can also tell a lot with a simple hands-on approach: Dig up a little soil and then rub it in your hands. Since soil makeup can vary on a single property, you'll want to do this for each bed or plot.

- ***Sandy soil,*** common in coastal regions, feels gritty and doesn't hold together. While easy to dig and well drained, sandy soil requires more frequent feeding to maintain nutrients; it is also prone to weeds and an overrun of self-seeding plants.
- ***Chalky soil,*** which consists of limestone and is widespread in the Midwest, feels more like flour and is slightly moldable. It tends to be highly alkaline, prone to drought, and in a shallow layer atop solid rock.
- ***Clay soil*** is dense and clumps together; the higher the clay content, the more moldable it is, and the more fertile, too, because nutrients cling to clay particles. Drainage can be a problem, however, unless the soil is amended with organic matter.
- ***Loamy soil***—the most desirable soil for the garden—has a nice balance of silt, sand, and clay, holding together when dampened but not in big clumps.

DRAINAGE

This is the soil's ability to absorb moisture and let excess water drain away, which is critical for plants that don't like to have "wet feet" (often indicated on the plant label).

How to test drainage:

1. Dig a 12-inch-deep hole that's about 12 inches wide.
2. Fill it with water and allow the water to drain away.
3. Soon after the hole has emptied, refill it, and this time note how long it takes to drain.
4. Calculate the rate of drainage by dividing the total depth of the water (12 inches) by the total number of hours it took for the hole to empty.
5. For a quicker alternative, measure the water level drop after 15 minutes, then multiply that number by four to determine the drainage rate.

Well-drained soil has an average rate of 1 inch of water lost per hour; this is the best medium for most garden plants.

Sharply drained soil dries out more quickly than 4 inches per hour; unless enriched with water-retaining compost, it is suitable mainly for drought-tolerant plants.

Poorly drained soil has a drainage rate that is markedly slower than an inch per hour; this will probably drown the roots of all but bog-loving plants.

PH LEVEL

Plants are generally divided into three types: those that thrive in acidic, alkaline, or neutral growing mediums. The pH levels of soil are measured on a scale of 0 to 14, with a pH of 7 considered neutral. As the number decreases to 0, the acidity in the soil gets higher; and as the number increases to 14, the soil gets more alkaline. Most plants require a pH level between 6 and 7.5, which is also the best pH range for earthworms and microorganisms.

The best way to determine your soil's pH level is by conducting a soil test, preferably by sending a sample to your local cooperative extension (considered the most accurate method); some nurseries also provide this service, so be sure to ask. You can also use a simple at-home test, available at garden supply stores. Alternatively, a digital or analog soil pH meter, which provides an immediate reading, is another at-home option; these affordable tools are also reusable.

It's a good idea to test different garden beds or areas of your yard, since the soil pH can vary. The pH level can also change over time, so you may want to retest it every two or three years, or if you notice plant failure in a particular spot. Do this at the same time each year, preferably in the fall or early spring before planting, when you have time to make the necessary amendments—or to choose plants that do well at that pH level.

Know the sunlight quotient

You can amend your soil, but you have less control over how much sun a location gets, so it's a principal factor when matching a plant to each site.

- ***Full sun*** plants need at least six hours of direct sunlight daily. These do best on south- and west-facing sites, where they will get strong afternoon sun.
- ***Partial shade*** plants should get no more than three to four hours of direct sunlight; in general, morning sun is better than harsher afternoon sun—so put these on north- or east-facing sites. Or plant them where periods of direct sunlight alternate with periods of shade, or where the sunlight is filtered by a canopy of branches or a trellis overhead.
- ***Full shade*** plants mean just that—they thrive where the sunlight never penetrates, such as under shade trees or in the shade of dense evergreens or solid man-made structures, such as a high wall or a porch roof.

Know the rainfall

Choosing plants that will be satisfied with your area's rainfall will make gardening that much easier, economical, and eco-friendly—without the need for additional irrigation.

If you are in a particularly drought-prone area, choose native plants or check with your local extension agent to see if it has a list of suitable plants. Indeed, planting specifically to avoid watering out of environmental concerns is catching on across the country, particularly in the arid Southwest. As temperatures continue to rise and weather patterns become less predictable, implementing this practice is a good idea no matter your region. And if you live in an area with above-average rainfall, you'll want to avoid plants like succulents and certain shrubs—such as Pieris, rhododendrons, and azaleas—that prefer drier soil, or put them in pots that you can move under cover as needed.

FOLLOWING PAGES: This Vermont garden was created in an area that was smothered with roses and brambles. For an easy design, it contains two sections: one for edibles and the other for flowers, which is further divided into four smaller rectangles separated by mown-grass paths. Fast-growing poplars block strong winds and make the garden feel more intimate; the thickly packed flower and shrub beds don't need as much weeding as a more sparsely planted garden.

Gardening methods

▶ **There's no one-size-fits-all approach** to gardening. The method you choose—in the ground, in raised beds, or in containers (i.e., pots)—depends on how large or small your yard is, or if you have no yard at all. You might also be swayed by the soil quality, climate, aesthetics, and your energy level, as well as what you'll be growing and what your goals are. Each approach has pros and cons, but ultimately, it's a matter of personal preference.

In-ground

Many gardeners appreciate how this maximizes growing areas—and are willing to do the proper prep work.

Pros

- It's the most economical option, requiring nothing other than a spade and shovel.
- You can plant wherever you like—including on slopes and rocky areas where a raised bed wouldn't work.
- This also lets you fill in spots in the landscape too small for a raised bed.

Cons

- You're working with the soil you have, which may require testing and amending to become fertile. It can take years to regenerate unworked soil, if necessary.
- Ground-level soil is more prone to weeds, pests, critters, and poor drainage.
- It can also take longer for the soil to warm up in the spring if you live in a colder climate.

Tip

One way to get around these downsides is to create slightly raised rows where the planting soil is mounded a few inches higher than the surrounding soil level. This allows plants to develop deeper roots; raised rows also drain better.

Raised beds

If your yard has challenging conditions—hard or rocky soil, uneven terrain, limited space—raised beds are a convenient work-around.

Pros

- They offer more flexibility: You can plot them wherever you want, fill them with any blend of soil, and plant them more densely than a regular garden, which means fewer weeds.
- You can line them with hardware cloth to keep burrowing critters out.
- They have better drainage and deeper rooting for a higher yield.
- They warm up quickly in spring, so you can start growing earlier.
- You can also use row covers to extend the growing season in the fall.
- A raised garden bed is easier on the back and knees, and allows for a more accessible gardening experience for people with mobility issues. For example, wheelchair-accessible raised beds are available to purchase online.

Con

- Raised beds are more expensive to set up and fill, though there are affordable DIY kits and alternatives to cedar boxes (such as galvanized metal or resin). But after that up-front cost and occasional soil replenishment, the beds will pay you back with productivity.

Containers

Many plants will do just fine (or even better) in a vessel as long as you provide them with the extra attention they need.

Pros

- No yard? You can grow flowers, vegetables, herbs, and even small trees in pots; they'll be happy on a balcony or rooftop deck in the city.
- Container plants are also a nice way to "accessorize" a landscape teeming with in-ground or raised garden beds.
- You can use vessels of varying materials, textures, shapes, and heights to create an arresting display on a porch or patio.
- Containers can be moved easily, such as to provide the plants with the right amount of sun and shade or to shield them from a severe thunderstorm or heavy winds.
- Plants grown in containers also require much less weeding.
- Grown in pots, invasive plants are less likely to spread into unwanted areas or push out existing plants.
- Some plants—notably drought-tolerant geraniums, begonias, coleus, and succulents—can be easier to grow in containers than in the ground.

Cons

- The types of plants you can grow are limited; larger shrubs or trees will have root systems too large for pots.
- The high plant-to-soil ratio means more frequent watering and fertilizing.
- You'll need to relocate some plants indoors if they are not hardy for your region.
- The cost of the vessels, potting soil and fertilizers, and plants can add up.

How to Build a Raised Bed

Whether you build a raised bed from a kit or from scratch, the following four steps will ensure that it will perform year after year.

1. **Size it:** Scout out your yard and decide what you want to grow, then plot a bed where it will get the right light; for example, many vegetables and herbs need at least six hours of sun. The length of the box will depend on your space, but width is important: You want to be able to weed and reach plants without stepping in and crushing them or compacting the soil. Keep it under 2½ feet wide if it's against a wall or fence, or 5 feet wide if you can reach in from both sides. Plan for each bed to be at least a foot deep.
2. **Frame it:** Although raised beds can be constructed with stones, bricks, or other materials, wood planks are the most common material and the easiest for beginners. Choose untreated lumber, such as rot-resistant cedar, cypress, or black locust. Avoid pressure-treated boards, which have been preserved with chemicals that can leach into your soil—this is especially important if you plan to grow food.
3. **Line it:** If your ground soil is healthy, leave it exposed. If you live in a city where soil contamination from lead or other chemicals is a concern, or want to plant on a patio or another concrete surface, staple heavy-duty landscape or weed-blocking fabric across the bottom of the bed before you place it. This water-permeable cloth holds off the bad stuff and keeps your soil from washing away. You can also choose a bed with legs that stands well above the ground, which makes working in it easier on the knees and back, too.
4. **Fill it:** Pour a mixture of topsoil and compost into your box (ask an expert or consult your county's cooperative exchange for advice on the right ratio), leaving about an inch of space below the top of the frame. A bed that is 6 feet by 4 feet and 13 inches deep, for instance, will need approximately 1 cubic yard of soil (for a handy calculator, go to gardeners.com). Remember to top off your beds every year with more soil and compost.

Plant primer

▶ **The plant world** is vast and varied, so appreciating the different categories and their uses in the garden will allow you to create a robust, biodiverse environment outside your own back door. Peruse seed catalogs, browse local nurseries, stroll public gardens, and hike in woodland settings to see what strikes your fancy—and grows where you live.

Flowers

Flowering plants can be divided into three categories based on their life cycle. Many gardeners prefer to have a mix of all three, with perennials as staples and annuals and biennials as intermittent enhancements.

ANNUALS

As their name suggests, these plants sprout from seed to plant to flower and back to seed in just one year, leaving only the seed to grow the next generation (which you can collect and sow in the spring).

- With their long flowering season, annuals are superb at garden edges, in bountiful containers, to fill in gaps between perennials, and for creating colorful groupings.
- Popular varieties include cosmos, zinnias, marigolds, petunias, pansies, fuchsia, geraniums, sunflowers, and calendula.

BIENNIALS

Biennials produce foliage in the first year, then require a cold dormant period before blossoming in the second, after which they die.

- Many vegetables, such as cabbage, beets, and chard, are actually biennials, as are showy flowers like foxgloves (shown opposite), hollyhocks, forget-me-nots, and sweet William.
- Plant these pollinator-friendly flowers as fillers while waiting for perennials to reach maturity. They also work at the garden's edge along with annuals; taller varieties look great along a fence line.
- If you find one you like, plant new seeds each year to have a continuous resupply of foliage and flowers every season. (Or wait until they drop their seeds before removing spent plants.)
- For the best display, pinch off any buds that appear in the first season to encourage more volume in the second.

Deciduous vs. Evergreen

Perennial plants, shrubs, and trees fall into two main categories: deciduous, meaning their foliage dies at the end of the growing season, or evergreen, which is just that—their foliage retains its hue in winter.

Planting some of each is ideal so you have lush greenery when little else is on display and a riot of blooms during the growing season (deciduous plants, which go dormant to store up energy for next year's buds, are the showy ones). Plus, the leaves of deciduous trees and some shrubs change color before falling, putting on a gorgeous spectacle in autumn.

PERENNIALS

Like annuals, these plants also go from seed to seed each year, but perennials come back again and again for decades or much longer.

- Herbaceous types die back to the underground roots at the end of each growing season and put out new growth in the spring.
- Evergreens retain foliage throughout the year, as do some other perennials grown in warmer climates.
- Because of their long life cycles, these are staple plants against which you can plan annuals and biennials and should form the backbone of your garden designs.
- Of the countless varieties are peonies, anemones, asters, astilbe, daisies, salvia, nepeta (catmint), delphiniums, hellebores, rudbeckias, echinacea, lilies, hostas, yarrow, bleeding hearts, and sedum (shown opposite).
- Note that certain "tender perennials" are grown as annuals in colder regions. Most, like dahlias, begonias, calla lilies, and caladiums, are grown from bulbs, tubers, or corms (see right).

All About Bulbs

Most flowers grow from seed, but there are many reasons to explore those that grow from bulbs—namely, their extraordinary beauty and diversity.

The term "bulb" encompasses a few non-seed-growing plants:

- **true bulbs** (daffodils, tulips), which look like onions
- **corms** (gladioli, crocuses), which are rounder than true bulbs with the same papery protective skin
- **rhizomes** (irises, canna lilies), which grow horizontally near the surface and produce a series of buds that develop into foliage and flower stems
- and the two categories of **tubers**—root tubers (dahlias) that look like large roots, and stem tubers (begonias), which are swollen underground stems similar to rhizomes

Choose wisely and you can plant bulbs that put on a dazzling show come spring, from the first appearance of snowdrops peeking up through the earth followed by crocuses, grape hyacinths (Muscari), fritillaries, daffodils, and, by spring's end, tulips gracing your otherwise barren lawn. Indeed, drop-and-grow daffodils can be planted in the grass to transform your yard into a wildflower meadow. Alliums flower in early summer, while dahlias, agapanthus, canna and calla lilies, begonias, cyclamen, and ranunculus emerge later, when other flowers are on the wane, and can last until the first frost. They all make gorgeous cutting flowers, extending the season indoors and out.

Ornamental grasses

Comprising true grasses and grasslike sedges, ornamental grasses are a relatively easy-care way to weave interesting colors and wispy, billowy texture throughout your landscape, with some varieties soaring to well over six feet tall. They are especially popular in border gardens in combination with perennials and annuals.

- Choose among steely blue, dark red, and every shade of green foliage, as well as grasses that feature sprays of oat-colored, golden, or pink-tinged flowers in the summer (and a few types that put on a display from spring through fall).
- Though botanically different, sedges are grasslike plants that have true leaves (as opposed to hollow stems) and are often grouped with grasses at nurseries and in home gardens.
- Most ornamental grasses are perennials, though some live for only one growing season because of their natural growth habit or because they are not cold-hardy for the location.
- It's worth buying perennials for year-round interest, with a mix of evergreens for color and deciduous types for eye-catching structure and seed heads.
- True grasses tend to prefer sunny sites with well-drained soil and are a good choice for areas with little rainfall, as established plants can be drought resistant.
- Sedges, on the other hand, grow anywhere—in wet or dry soil, sun or shade—and don't tempt deer. Both do well in gravel gardens, too.
- The growth habits of grasses and sedges are either clumping, meaning they tend to be taller than their diameter and are good for filling in gaps, or spreading. Care must be taken when planting spreading grasses and sedges, which expand rapidly and may overtake desirable plantings.

Grow-Anywhere Carex

The genus *Carex*, a member of the sedge family, has over 1,000 different species. These mop-tops are a gardener's dream—they thrive in any kind of soil or sun and are vigorous and long-lived. There's one for every situation; here are seven to choose from.

1. *Carex morrowii* var. *temnolepis* 'Silk Tassel'
2. *C. siderosticha* 'Variegata'
3. *C. laxiculmis*
4. *C. oshimensis* 'Everillo'
5. *C. flacca* (or *C. glauca*)
6. *C. conica* 'Snowline'
7. *C. oshimensis* 'Evergold'

Ferns

Often called the fillers of the garden, ferns are non-flowering "vascular" plants that have roots, stems, and leaves (which in ferns are called fronds).

- Besides being among the oldest plant species, ferns are the second-most diverse type of vascular plant, with over 10,500 living species, including variegated options like the Boston (tiger) fern or the 'Red Beauty' Japanese painted fern, which sports silvery fronds and deep-burgundy stems and veins.
- Many ferns offer fragrance as well as good looks.
- Unlike flowering plants, ferns do not reproduce through seeds but asexually via spores, like mushrooms and other fungi, or as vegetative growth, with buds growing on fern fronds (similar to certain mosses).
- Some ferns (like ostrich fern and common horsetail) are creeping rhizomes with a single fern spreading to form large colonies. As with grasses, creeping ferns should be planted with care to avoid pushing out other plants.
- Deciduous ferns will lose their fronds in the fall; however, all ferns are perennials that will survive through winter, and creeping ferns send up new fiddleheads from the rhizomes in the soil come spring (note: not all are edible).
- Because they occur naturally on forest floors, ferns do best in moist soil and dappled shade, such as the open shade of mature trees or the north side of a house or wall—wherever you want to lend a woodland accent (and scent) to your environment.
- Be sure to leave them over the winter, too, as habitat and food for wildlife.

Succulents and cacti

The group of plants collectively known as succulents, which includes the cactus family, are prized for their exotic look and low-maintenance qualities. All are easy to grow—just give them plenty of bright light and very little water.

- Many people grow succulents (including cacti) as houseplants, but these drought-tolerant sun seekers also thrive outdoors, given the right conditions—and not just in the arid Southwest.
- They are like the camels of the plant world, storing water in their fleshy stems, roots, and leaves. In severe drought, the plants can shut down active growth and become dormant.
- Some succulents have spikes on the edges and tips of their leaves, which act as a defense against predators.
- Cacti differ from other succulents because they have pad-like buds, called areoles, out of which grow sharp spines. These spines detach easily, protecting the plant from harm. But because most cacti grow primarily in the desert, the main purpose of the spines is to collect and condense moisture, dripping it onto the ground for the roots to absorb.
- Succulents and cacti are available in a variety of exotic forms. Some succulents look like smooth stones, while others display perfect rosettes or resemble strings of bold, green beads. Still others—notably cacti, with their columnar shape and branching arms—are more architectural.
- The plants thrive in many climates, but gardeners across Texas, Arizona, New Mexico, Nevada, and southern Utah and California can grow them with abandon, both in the ground and in containers.
- If you live in colder regions, you may want to limit the plants to containers that can be brought inside during winter.

Climbers

Of the many reasons to grow climbing plants, their beauty is just the beginning. Growing vertically allows you to increase the number of plants without taking up space.

- You can use climbers to hide unsightly fences or other structures or enhance those you want to draw attention to, such as arbors, pergolas, stately trees, or stone walls. And there's nothing more lovely than a plant covering the side of a house or scrambling up a brick chimney.
- Understanding how they climb—some wrap, some curl, and some adhere—will ensure you match the right plant with the proper support. For example, tomatoes and pole beans won't naturally climb a lattice; morning glories and hops can't grab onto a pole.

Ground covers

Whether you are looking for a sustainable, no-mow alternative to a grassy lawn or for plants that can grow on banks and slopes, ground covers can be a smart, easy-maintenance choice. Make that *choices*, as the wide variety spans herbaceous, woody, evergreen, deciduous, annual, perennial, and so forth.

- Basically, any plant that grows out rather than up qualifies as ground cover, and you can use it to provide year-round interest, whether in full sun or part or full shade.
- One of the best applications of ground covers is as "green mulch" to choke out weeds, protect the roots of neighboring plants from extreme weather conditions, and control soil erosion. In this vein, ground covers can yield long-term cost savings by replacing the need to purchase wood chips or other types of mulch as a top dressing in the spring and fall.
- Many types can withstand heavy foot traffic, too, making them great for filling in spaces around stepping stones or for flanking a walkway.
- Many creeping plants, such as thyme and phlox, are used for trailing over rock walls or blanketing the ground in a showy display of purple or white flowers each season (summer for thyme, early spring for phlox).
- Sweet woodruff is another flowering variety that sends up whorls of white blossoms in spring, while sapphire indigo clematis (named for the shade of its blooms) can be allowed to scramble sideways.
- Sedums and other succulents, such as hen and chickens, can thrive in drought-prone areas. Some low-lying grasses and sedges (such as carex, see page 34) can also serve as ground covers.
- Moss is an especially low-maintenance grass alternative that can be trampled on, stays green all year long, and requires no weeding, watering, or fertilization.

Steppable Ground Covers

There are dozens of low ground covers and creeping perennials resilient enough to withstand being walked on—in fact, some thrive underfoot. Tucked around stones or pavers, these plants, which might get lost in a larger garden bed, become focal points, softening otherwise utilitarian spaces.

1. Blue moneywort (*Lindernia grandiflora*)
2. Cobweb houseleek (*Sempervivum arachnoideum*)
3. Motley mazus (*Mazus radicans*)
4. Woolly thyme (*Thymus praecox* 'Pseudolanuginosus')
5. Mossy stonecrop (*Sedum lydium*)

1
2
3
4
5

Shrubs

Rather than being a botanical classification, "shrub" is a general term for plants that have multiple stems and a spreading growth habit; they generally range from a mere foot (or less) to no more than 15 feet tall.

- How to differentiate shrubs and trees is a common question, so here's a simplified answer: Trees have a single woody stem, from which branches grow to form a crown, whereas the branches of shrubs arise at ground level, forming a crown without a stem.
- Shrubs tend to be hardy plants that, once established, need little maintenance, though some benefit from regular pruning to keep their shape and promote blooming the next season (for flowering types).
- They can be employed in various forms and ways, such as an allée of boxwoods flanking a driveway or as a border for a perennial garden.
- Other flowering shrubs offer colorful blooms from the first days of spring (forsythia and lilac) right on through fall (hydrangea and double-blooming viburnum). In fact, they're a great way to ensure you have blossoms before, during, and after perennials and annuals come and go—including in the midsummer lull.
- As with other plants, shrubs vary in their preference for sun, shade, pH level, and drainage, so be sure to read the label and choose the right shrub for a specific spot. For example, azaleas (shown on pages 38–39) prefer partial sun and acidic soil. Indeed, there's a shrub for (almost) every site, especially if you are looking to fill an awkward gap in your existing gardens.
- With that in mind, be sure to note the height and width of the mature plant as well as spacing recommendations—shrubs have vastly different spreading habits.

  Keep ground-hugging shrubs (such as heather and creeping juniper) in mind for edging beds and borders.

  Low-forming varieties (including some hydrangeas, dwarf fothergilla, and 'Minuet' weigela) bring midlevel height to gardens and soften a stand of taller shrubs or trees.

  Columnar (fastigiate) shrubs that grow taller than wide (such as numerous cypress, sky pencil holly, or columnar yew) inject drama anywhere and always.
- For more information on shrubs, see the section starting on page 210.

Trees

Trees are hard to resist, especially given their incredible variety. They can be tall and majestic or shorter in stature; have wide canopies for shade or a compact profile; boast smooth or exfoliating barks; and yield ornamental blossoms or edible fruit or nuts. Some sprout up quickly, while others take years to fully mature.

If you inherited established trees on your property, you no doubt appreciate their place of importance in the landscape. But even the most avid home gardeners shy away from the idea of adding new trees, citing the permanency, cost, and unfamiliarity with the upkeep.

Yet walk through any forest and marvel at how trees manage to thrive without human intervention. Indeed, taking the forest as inspiration, you don't need to overthink things—just embrace trees' graceful beauty and fortitude.

- That said, because of their long life cycle and large-scale stature, it's important to pay attention to the potential size, shape, and color of each tree to avoid a mistake that might be hard to remedy.
- Beware of spreading root systems that can wreak havoc with driveways or structures. Same for branches that might end up breaking a window if too close during heavy winds.
- You can mine the diversity of trees for four-season foliage and flowers. Early ornamentals like magnolias, dogwoods, flowering cherries, pear, crab apples, and eastern redbuds usher in spring, while maples, ginkgoes, tupelos, crape myrtles, oaks, hawthorns, and so many more (including dogwoods) put on a kaleidoscopic display come fall.
- Evergreens aren't the only option for winter interest; you can fully appreciate the sculptural beauty of a barren weeping cherry, Stewartia, paperbark maple, or birch tree's branching structure and textural bark.
- Another reason to plant more trees: They are unquestionably important to our environment, releasing oxygen, helping combat climate change, and providing nutrition and habitats for wildlife, among many other virtues.
- Perhaps the best part of planting trees, then, is what you are doing for future generations and the planet—though you can enjoy their grace, beauty, and fortitude in the meantime.
- For more information on trees, see the section starting on page 178.

"I strongly believe in reforestation and protecting the environment, and try to plant new trees every year. Some are native species like maples, oaks, and pines. Others have been a bit more exotic, including beeches, lindens, katsuras, ginkgoes, and Camperdown elms."

FOLLOWING PAGES: A pair of deciduous trees frames the garden pathway and forms a natural arbor, casting welcome shade.

Composting

▶ **Avid gardeners share** a secret weapon: At-home composting, nature's very own circular economy, transforms spent plants, grass clippings, fallen leaves, and other vegetation into "black gold," a potent substance that revitalizes gardens and adds nutrients back to the soil. Making your own compost is financially smart—buying it by the bag or even in bulk can quickly add up, especially if you have multiple raised beds to fill and lots of growing areas to maintain. And it doesn't require expensive equipment or scientific expertise. Instead, you let nature take its course, breaking down biodegradable matter into a soil treatment that's packed with moisture and nutrients that you can administer to your plants.

You don't need a field or even a sizable space, either. Follow the guidelines here to produce a steady supply.

The benefits of composting

Nutrients aren't the only benefit; here are several other reasons to adopt this practice.

- ***Reduces soil erosion:*** Compost acts as a sponge, absorbing almost five times its weight in water, meaning it can lessen the impact of stormwater runoff; it also acts as a filter for pollutants, improving water quality in local watersheds. What's more, compost protects against drought conditions and reduces the need for watering in general.
- ***Boosts overall plant health:*** By improving soil quality, compost yields more robust plants that have greater resistance to certain diseases and pests.
- ***Reduces your carbon footprint:*** Food scraps and materials that would have otherwise gone into your garbage are now used to make compost, thus cutting down on the amount of trash (and plastic bags) that ends up in landfills.

"At my Bedford farm, almost nothing goes to waste. We've developed an adaptable composting system that will keep a garden—whether large or small—at its healthiest."

What to compost

Garden compost requires the right combination of green matter (such as vegetable scraps and coffee grounds) and brown material (including leaf litter and cardboard)—typically in a one-to-three ratio. Never add animal waste, meat or fish, dairy products, cooking fats, diseased plants, perennial weeds, treated lumber, or glossy/colored paper to your pile.

GREEN MATTER

This material breaks down quickly and brings nitrogen and moisture to the mix.

- ***Kitchen waste:*** fruit and vegetable trimmings (rinds, seeds, cores, seeds, and stems), overripe or wilted produce, stale bread, spent coffee grounds and tea leaves (avoiding plastic tea tags or those with staples), and eggshells.
- ***Garden waste:*** fresh grass clippings and trimmings from healthy plants.

BROWN MATTER

Paper and other dry materials are slower to decompose, lending structure; the following are rich in carbon, too.

- ***Paper:*** shredded or torn newspaper, brown paper bags, and cardboard, as well as the contents of your security shredder (removing any plastic or foil).
- ***Garden waste:*** dried fallen leaves (discard any diseased leaves or those near plants infested with pests), stems, and twigs.
- ***Other materials:*** hay (for feeding animals) and untreated wood chips.

Where to compost

Choose a space in your yard that is easily accessible year-round, near a water source, and has good drainage. Compost will break down in sun or shade, though partial sun is ideal—too much sun means more frequent watering while too little slows down decomposition.

Next, choose the type of bin or other enclosure to use in keeping out pets and wildlife. You can purchase compost bins at garden centers or by contacting your local cooperative extension. For an easy DIY option, purchase inexpensive chicken wire and form it into a cylinder, using stakes to secure it into the ground.

Increasingly, composting services are springing up that will drop off bins that you fill and then put out on the curb for pickup, similar to trash and recycling. The service processes your scraps and then returns the bins filled with ready-to-use compost. Certain towns and municipalities are also adding compost bins to their trash and recycling drop-off (aka transfer) stations.

How to compost

The decomposition process is simple, but there is a method to getting it started and keeping it going. In addition to greens and browns, compost needs oxygen to support the microorganisms as they work. Moisture is also critical, and while it is naturally found in green plant and food scraps, a bit of supplemental water from a garden hose can help.

1. Before adding your browns and greens to the pile, it's helpful to chop them into smaller pieces so they will decompose more quickly.
2. Start by placing a 4- to 6-inch layer of bulky browns, such as twigs and wood chips or lots of dried leaves, as the base to absorb extra liquids, elevate the pile, and allow air to circulate.
3. Then add a 2- to 3-inch layer of greens followed by three times the volume of browns to the volume of greens.
4. Continue layering greens and browns (like lasagna) in a one-to-three ratio, ending with browns; always make sure food scraps are covered with several inches of dry leaves or other browns. To ensure air circulation, poke holes all the way to the bottom and make the top slightly concave to catch rain (have a tarp or other cover on hand in case of heavy rain).
5. After about a week, as the materials begin to decompose, the temperature of the pile will start to rise, especially in the center. Begin turning and mixing your pile every week or two, using a pitchfork or shovel to turn the outside of the pile inward. As it reduces, keep adding more layers, ending with brown.
6. Monitor the pile for moisture—the materials should feel like a wrung-out sponge. If the pile is too dry, activity in the pile will slow or cease. Add water as needed and turn. If the pile has a bad odor, it may be too wet or need more air circulation. Add more browns/dry material and turn the pile.
7. Monitor the temperature of the pile. A well-maintained backyard pile can reach 130°F to 160°F, at which point any pathogens and weed seeds will be killed. If the pile is not heating up, mix in greens (covering food scraps with browns) and turn the pile.
8. The compost is ready when it is no longer heating up after turning and most of the ingredients have broken down. This can take anywhere from three months to a year depending on how often you turn it. You can separate out part of this pile and let it cure, or finish, for at least four weeks while continuing to feed the remaining pile with new materials.
9. Your finished pile will have shrunk to about one-third of its original size; the compost should look dark, loose, and crumbly and smell like fresh soil. You can sift it through ¼-inch hardware cloth to remove any large pieces, which can be added back into the still-active pile. You can also remove the oldest compost at the bottom to use in the garden and keep feeding the rest, or start over in a new pile—for example, you can have multiple small piles at different stages in the same area, depending on allotted space.

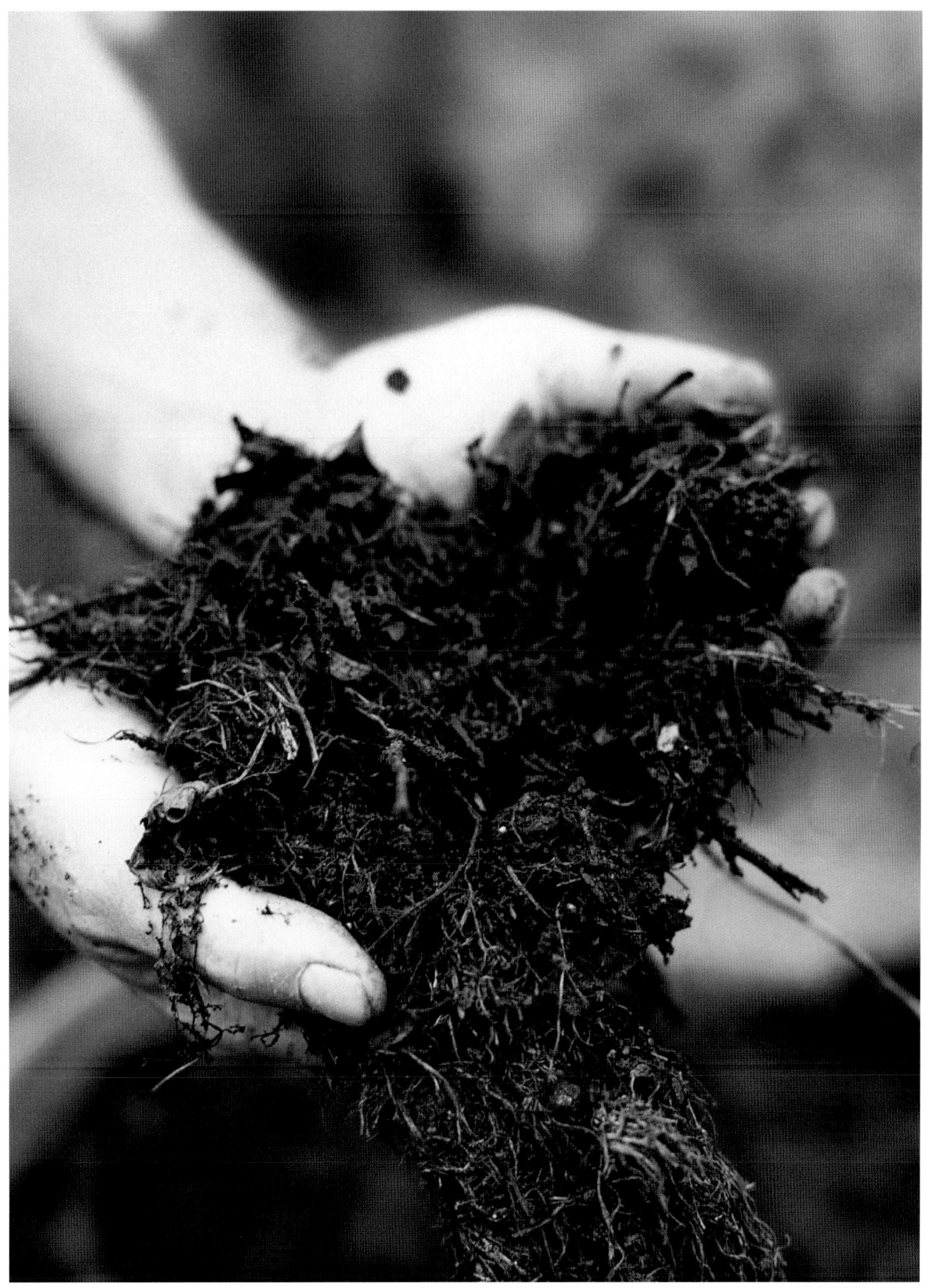

Stocking up on supplies

▶ **You don't need** to buy a lot of tools for gardening—it's better to invest in just a few high-quality ones that will last a lifetime with proper care—but you do want to use the right tool for the job. You'll also want to protect your investment and your garden by knowing how to properly clean, maintain, and store your supplies—and adopt the practice after each and every use.

Hand Tools

1. ***Secateurs*** (or hand pruners): These hand pruners are the workhorse of the garden tool kit. This trusty, versatile item is the one to use for deadheading, cutting back annuals and perennials, and pruning branches up to half an inch in diameter. Look for bypass pruners, which make nice, clean cuts using two curved blades that bypass each other in a scissor-like motion.
2. ***Hand snips:*** With their long pointed blades, snips offer precise pruning and trimming of houseplants and outdoor garden plants and are ideal for removing spent leaves, trimming soft stems, and harvesting flowers and various fruits.
3. ***Hand cultivator*** (or hoe): Used for regular weeding; "scabbing" (lightly scoring) the roots when planting perennials or shrubs; loosening the soil inside a dug hole (when planting) and mixing compost into the backfill; raking debris from around plants; and cultivating the soil between rows in a vegetable or cutting-flower garden.
4. ***Hand trowel:*** A must for smaller digging jobs, such as when planting annuals, smaller perennials, and vegetable seedlings or starts. These tools should be sharp and made out of steel so they can effectively break up the soil.
5. ***Hand saw:*** Use this for pruning jobs when secateurs won't do, including for woody shrubs and smaller tree branches. Foldable models, where the blade tucks inside the handle, are safer than non-folding ones when carrying and storing.
6. ***Japanese weeding hoe*** (or sickle): The clever design of this lightweight tool allows you to quickly scrape across the surface of a bed to remove shallow-rooted weeds in one fell swoop.
7. ***Hedge shears:*** Besides maintaining the shape of shrubs, climbers, and topiaries, these long-handled shears are a nifty alternative to a weed whacker when clipping grass from underneath shrubs and around tree trunks, fences, walls, and other structures.
8. ***Hori hori:*** This Japanese gardening "knife" is a serious (and stylish) multitasker. Use it to slice through weeds in the ground when removing, through plant roots when dividing or transplanting, and through root-balls when planting trees. Look for one with a concave blade with etched digging marks to use when planting bulbs.
9. ***Garden gloves:*** Fit and material are two factors to consider. Ensure the gloves fit your grip comfortably and match the garden task: Long leather gloves will keep you protected when pruning shrubs while a thin, breathable pair is ideal for weeding. Because they will need to be cleaned frequently, having a backup pair (or two) means you'll never be without these protective helpers.
10. ***Watering wand:*** You might get by with a watering can (or empty jug) for container plants on a porch or patio, but this long-necked hose attachment allows you to more easily reach hanging baskets or climbers up high and has a showerhead-like spray.

1
2
3
4
5
6
7
8
9
10
Niwaki. GR 210

1
2
3
4
5
6
7

Heavy-duty Tools

1. ***Bedding rake:*** Also known as a hard rake, this implement has tines that form a uniform line, making it ideal for leveling garden beds and spreading mulch or compost on beds. It also works to level gravel on pathways, patios, or driveways.
2. ***Shovel:*** Use this pointed digging tool when planting larger items or removing sod and also hauling materials such as compost or mulch. Pick one that is sturdy but not too heavy.
3. ***Spade:*** With its straight edge, a spade is designed to cut neat lines, such as when edging beds. It is also the tool for cutting sod when creating new beds, switching to a shovel to lift the cut areas and the soil underneath.
4. ***Spring rake:*** Named for its springiness and not the season, a spring rake has flexible tines that enable it to grab fallen leaves without harming the lawn. Metal tines are sturdier and less prone to breaking than those made of resin.
5. ***Garden fork:*** When prepping in-ground or raised beds, use this to loosen the soil, work in compost, level the soil and spread an even layer of mulch as a top dressing. A garden fork is better than a shovel for lifting plants when dividing. Avoid using it on grass or around shrubs, when the tines might damage roots near the surface.
6. ***Loppers:*** When pruners or a hand saw won't do, loppers can remove hard-to-reach branches, or those that are up to 2 inches thick. It can be tricky to use loppers that are too heavy, so look for a version with lightweight aluminum handles.
7. ***Twine:*** Sturdy jute twine is used for creating supports for climbing plants and marking rows, among other common tasks.

Other supplies

- ***Gardening hat:*** The best shield against the sun's harmful rays is a hat with ultraviolet protection of at least 50 and a three-inch-wide brim. Natural fibers such as palm and straw allow airflow and naturally repel water; like canvas, the woven fibers bounce back when rolled or scrunched up.
- ***Tool bag or belt:*** A multifaceted canvas garden bag (like the one shown, opposite) or a carpenter's tool bag is a convenient and portable way to keep smaller, frequently used tools at the ready.
- ***Wheelbarrow:*** Carting bags or loads of soil, mulch, and compost (as well as gravel for hardscaping) from one spot to another is just the start. A wheelbarrow is also helpful when doing heavy weeding, since you can collect everything and then dispose of it all in one fell swoop.
- ***Seed distributor:*** If you plan to sow lots of annual or perennial seeds, such as in a wildflower meadow, you may want to rely on a handheld or push-model seed dispenser to do the job evenly and efficiently. They come in a range of price points and styles.
- ***Plant markers:*** Noting the plant name on a marker and putting that in each row when sowing seeds (or planting bulbs) will help you keep tabs on what's growing where—which is especially useful in a vegetable garden. Besides ensuring the seeds are spaced evenly, they serve as reminders while waiting for sprouts to appear days or weeks later.
- ***Garden organizer:*** Seed packets and plant labels contain valuable information for planting as well as maintaining; keep these essential aids in binders with plastic sleeves or in storage containers, one for each bed or type of plant.

How to maintain

Keeping all your garden tools clean is a must to minimize the risk of spreading disease among plants. By following a few simple steps, you can extend the longevity of the piece and improve the long-term health of your garden. The process takes only a few minutes, and it keeps your gardening implements in proper working order.

ROUTINE MAINTENANCE

Make a habit of regularly cleaning your tools, especially after a muddy session.

1. ***Disinfect:*** Using the same tools on multiple plants without disinfecting them can spread disease from unhealthy plants to healthy ones. Many pathogens are microscopic and invisible to the naked eye. Disinfecting is especially important after working with a diseased plant.

   Avoid bleach, however—bleach is very hard on metal and will cause it to rust quickly. Instead, use rubbing alcohol or even disinfecting wipes—they make for quick cleanup and are handy for removing sap, bacteria, and fungus.

2. ***Clean and dry:*** While you don't have to clean every tool after each use, you should clear them of dirt and debris on a regular basis (say, once a week) to minimize the transfer of bacteria or rust, which can impair your plants' health. Use a special scouring block (such as a Crean Mate by Niwaki) or medium-grit sandpaper to remove any dirt, sap, or other grime from the blades. Get all the dirt off the metal parts—anything left on tools can attract and hold moisture and cause rust. You can also apply liquid dishwashing soap with a soft- or medium-bristle scrub brush for extra grit. Then rinse your tools and make sure to dry them thoroughly. Once dry, disinfect the tools as above.

3. ***Sharpen:*** Tools such as pruners, loppers, and spades are easier and safer to use when kept sharp, and smoother cuts put less pressure on your arms, hands, and wrists. Making clean cuts also allows plants to heal more quickly and exposes them to less damage from disease, insects, fungi, and weather extremes.

   You'll know when to sharpen a tool if the metal is not cutting well.

   You can sharpen smooth-edged blades at home, but tools with serrated edges, such as pruning saws, should be sharpened by a professional.

   A fine-grain stone such as a whetstone will sharpen the edges of steel tools and implements through grinding and honing.

   - Soak the stone for a few minutes before using—this will help keep the pores of the stone clean, dissipate frictional heat, and ensure smooth sharpening.
   - Rub the stone over all edges on both sides of each blade, holding the whetstone at an angle to sharpen the edges and maintain the existing bevel. (The bevel is what makes a tool sharp, and blades are factory ground to a precise angle that's just right for each tool.)

4. ***Lubricate:*** Keep your tools conditioned and moving smoothly with a thin coat of lubricating oil such as mineral oil, camellia seed oil, or bio-friendly UltraLube.

   - Oil all parts of the tool, especially the metal components, putting a light coat on any part of the tool that moves.
   - Be sure to oil the ratchets and pins that allow blades to open and any exposed crevices, too.
   - After oiling, it is a good idea to open and close pruners, snips, and shears to ensure they work smoothly and evenly.
   - Finish by wiping away any excess oil with a rag.

END-OF-SEASON MAINTENANCE

Do this before storing so your tools are ready to use at the first sign of spring.

For pruners, shears, and loppers:

- Wipe off all soil with a rag.
- Use a wire brush to remove all dirt; when possible, disassemble these tools to get into hard-to-reach places.
- Rub any rusty spots with steel wool.
- Before reassembling, sharpen the blades.

For hand trowels and cultivators, as well as long-handled tools such as shovels, spades, hoes, and forks:

- Scrape stubborn dirt off with a wire brush.
- Use hot soapy water to clean the heads and fiberglass or wooden handles.
- You may want to smooth any rough spots on wooden handles with sandpaper to avoid splintering.

How to store

You can store small tools, such as a hand trowel and hand cultivator, heads down in a bucket of play or building sand mixed with lubricating oil (about five parts sand to one part oil) after cleaning and thoroughly drying them. This will prevent rust from forming between uses.

Larger tools can be stored with their heads in a larger bucket of oiled sand or hung on a shed wall; you can spray the heads with vegetable oil to keep them lubricated. Do not rest shovels, spades, or rakes on their working ends, as this will compromise their sharpness and structure.

Removing Rust

Should your pruners, shears, shovels, or other tools develop rust (say, after inadvertently leaving them outside after a lengthy gardening session), there are a few ways to tackle it using household ingredients—the sooner, the better. Wear protective gloves when handling any rusty metal items.

Distilled white vinegar

For light rusting: Try rubbing the corroded parts with the vinegar and a scrubbing pad or firm-bristled brush.

For tougher corrosion: Fill a jar (for hand tools) or pail (for larger ones) with the vinegar and submerge the tool, blade side down, in the vinegar and let soak for 24 hours. Then rub off the remaining rust with steel wool or a wire brush, disassembling the tool as needed to get at every last spot.

Wash with soapy water, dry with an absorbent cloth, and allow to air-dry completely before storing (or reassembling).

Lemon juice and coarse salt

Sprinkle the rusted areas with salt, cover with fresh lemon juice (add a bit of white vinegar for heavy-duty removal), and let sit for 15 to 30 minutes.

Use the lemon rind as a scrubber to remove light rust, or steel wool or a wire brush for stubborn stains. Rinse off the tool and dry thoroughly.

Potato and coarse salt or baking soda

Cut a raw baking potato in half crosswise (to expose the oxalic acid, which is a rust-busting agent), sprinkle salt or baking soda onto the cut side, and rub over the rusted area. Or insert a rusty hori hori or other gardening knife into the spud and let it sit for a few hours. Rinse off and dry thoroughly.

Garden Design 101

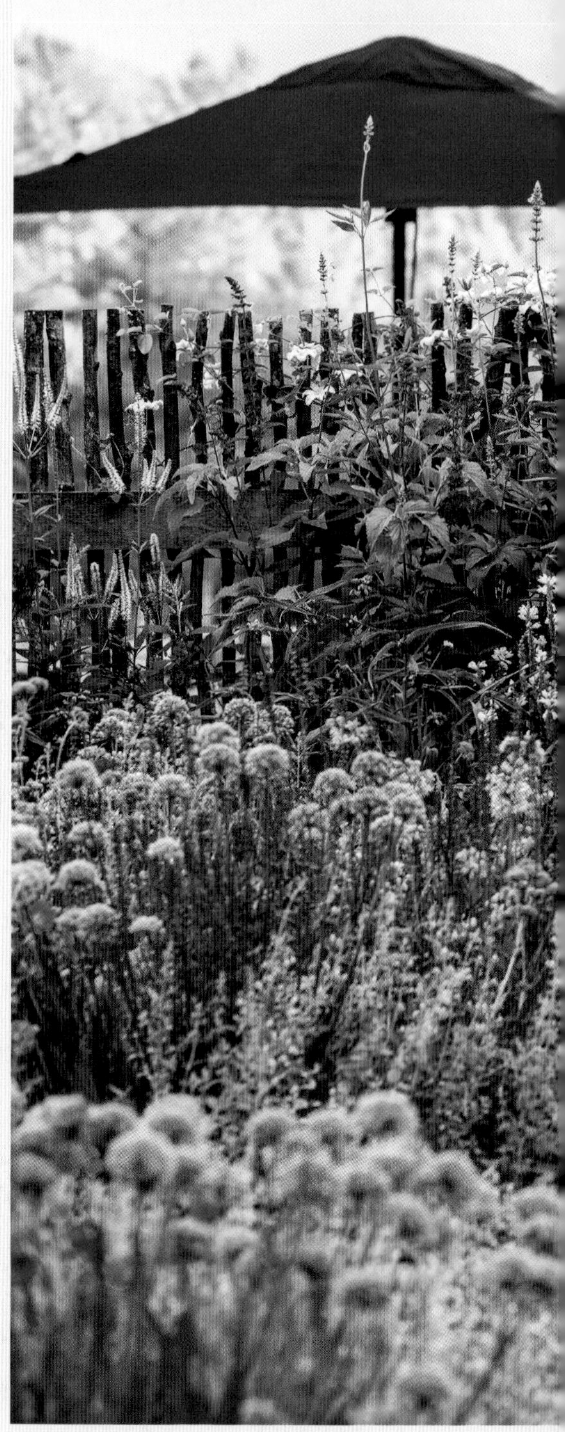

Designing an outdoor space should be just as intentional—and requires as much or more thought—as designing for your home's interior. So before ordering seeds or shopping for plants at the nursery, it's important to plot out your landscape. Even seasoned gardeners delight in this process, taking time to gather inspiration and contemplate what will bring them the most enjoyment, such as creating a garden of paths that wind past dense flower beds to a panoramic lounge, as shown here.

Begin by figuring out what you want from your space, finding your particular style, and planning for year-round beauty. On that last note, it helps to keep the main plant types—flowers (annuals, biennials, and perennials), ornamental grasses, ferns, succulents and cacti, climbers, ground covers, shrubs, and trees—in mind as you go, so you choose varieties that cover all four seasons.

Choose the use

When beginning a new project, landscape designers generally look at what you hope to get out of your garden. This is how you should approach your own yard as well, either when adding new arrangements of plants or starting your design from scratch.

For example, do you like to have large gatherings at your home? Or do you prefer a more reflective area for moments of peaceful solitude? Is your primary goal to live more sustainably by growing your own food?

The answers will be the springboard of almost every design. Keep those questions in mind as you familiarize yourself with the different types of gardens and how they might contribute to your ideal space.

BORDER GARDENS

Named for their location, border gardens hug some element of your lot—the front and sides of your house, a driveway or walkway, a fence, or the edges of your yard, especially the one facing the street (for curb appeal). These eye-catching beds typically feature a mix of annuals, perennials, shrubs, and grasses, with climbers if there are vertical components (like the pergola shown opposite) and smaller trees depending on the size of the bed.

PERENNIAL GARDENS

If the idea of gazing out your window at a field of flowers appeals to you, this is one way to achieve that. The key is to plant a variety of perennials with different blooming times, from early spring through late summer and into fall, and to stick with plants that return year after year.

HABITAT GARDENS

The purpose of these gardens is to attract native and migratory birds, butterflies, and other wildlife seeking food and cover by using flowers and shrubs that are native to your area (primarily keystone plants as described on page 16). That they also happen to be lovely in a naturalistic way is a bonus.

COTTAGE GARDENS

These free-spirited gardens arose in England as a naturalistic alternative to the rigid designs of the Victorian era—and are more recently gaining popularity as a sustainable update to high-maintenance suburban lawns. Dense plantings of flowers and shrubs (prioritizing native, pollinator-friendly varieties) are the rule. Personalization is another hallmark; benches, birdbaths, trellises, and other elements lend whimsy and keep them from being at all cookie-cutter.

ROSE GARDENS

One classic expression of a perennial garden is a rose garden, which can showcase this flower's multitudinous nature—antique specimens, modern cultivars, climbing roses, and so on.

SHADE GARDENS

For areas under trees or in the shadow of a house or another structure, these lush, inviting gardens offer an opportunity to put the focus on foliage, with a smattering of shade-loving flowering plants for seasonal color, and climbers to scale shade-giving trees or walls.

WHITE GARDENS

These monochromatic designs are reminiscent of "moonlight gardens," another century-old trend popularized by Vita Sackville-West at Sissinghurst Castle. Their success relies on having blossoms in a range of white hues—some bright, others creamy, some tinged with yellow or pink—and with varied-colored and -textured foliage. You may be surprised at just how many species fit the bill.

PREVIOUS PAGES: The limestone terrace is surrounded by clumps of blue perennial perovskia and pale-lavender and deep-rose cleome. A blue vitex bush is in flower under the wisteria arbor. White buddleia, hydrangeas, and tall miscanthus grasses form the background. **ABOVE:** A coffee table and hoop chairs create a modern "den" in a shady area of a gravel garden. **OPPOSITE:** Cabbages, alliums, lettuces, and kale are planted in rows alongside dahlias in Martha's Skylands vegetable garden.

XERIC GARDENS

Xeriscaping refers to landscaping that reduces or eliminates the need for watering by replacing most grassy turf with drought-resistant plants and mulch or gravel to aid in water retention. It originated in drought-prone areas but has been embraced by people who are interested in creating a more sustainable home environment.

The core principles—water conservation, soil improvement, and the use of native plants—are part of the same conversation around habitat gardens and rain gardens that's taking place in the context of climate change and its implications.

CONTAINER GARDENS

You don't need acres of land—or any land at all—to cultivate a thriving garden. As discussed on page 23, plenty of plants do well in pots on a balcony, terrace, or rooftop in an urban environment. But a container garden can be an integral part of a design that also includes some or all of the above plantings, providing further opportunities to create inviting vignettes for a front porch or backyard patio.

VEGETABLE GARDENS

For many people, growing their own produce is the only type of gardening they are interested in pursuing. Vegetable gardens can also fit seamlessly into a more comprehensive plan. When combined with flowers that attract beneficial pollinators and ward off pests—such as sunflowers or marigolds—they provide unique visual interest in addition to yielding delicious food for the table.

CUTTING-FLOWER GARDENS

These gardens are for growing flowers—primarily annuals and biennials—specifically for harvesting. Since the plants can be started by sowing seeds or planting bulbs, this is a relatively easy and inexpensive way to enjoy fresh flowers throughout your home. These gardens can be in-ground or in raised beds, depending on how many flowers you desire and how much space you care to dedicate.

Find your style

When you visualize the ideal yard, what do you see? Perhaps you fell in love with a highly manicured garden on a trip to Paris or Florence—or meditative Zen designs during a visit to Kyoto—and long to replicate some elements at home. Or maybe you want to see unruly waves of wildflowers in every direction.

Walking around your neighborhood and visiting public gardens can help you figure out what you want for your own space. Snap photos and take notes on anything that sparks your interest—as well as on things you don't like, because ruling those out can also be helpful.

Ultimately, the garden should relate to the architecture of your home. A whimsical cottage garden, for example, might look out of step with a midcentury modern ranch or a sleek contemporary structure but completely at home for a farmhouse, while billowy grasses and clump-forming sedums share an aesthetic sensibility with the distinctive barn shown here.

"When traveling, I love to visit spectacular places, like the great châteaux in France and the stately homes of England. I'm endlessly fascinated by the vastness of these masterpieces and how the designers could comprehend their visions when they had no aerial photographs of the land they were asked to transform."

Plant for lifestyle

Consider your comfort level with high-, moderate-, or low-maintenance gardening. This includes lawn care; unless you don't mind mowing weekly or biweekly, finding ways to replace grassy turf with other vegetation is a worthwhile exercise.

Low-Maintenance Plants

The safest path to creating an easy-care garden? Seek the guidance of a trusted person at your local nursery. Some online sources also allow you to filter your search based on your desired level of maintenance.

A plant deemed low maintenance in one area might require more maintenance in another, so always consider your climate and soil condition before committing. But the following will generally thrive no matter where you live.

Ajuga	Fern
Butterfly bush	Geranium
Butterfly weed	Grass
Caladium	Holly
Canna lily	Hosta
Catmint	Hydrangea
Clematis	Knock Out rose
Coleus	Marigold
Coneflower	Peony
Coral bells	Rudbeckia
Cosmos	Russian sage
Creeping Jenny	Salvia
Creeping thyme	Snowdrop
Daffodil	Spirea
Dianthus	Spotted laurel
Dusty miller	Tickweed
Euphorbia	Zinnia

Low-maintenance gardens

- Lean into a more naturalistic look with easy-care plants (see left), succulents, hardy shrubs and perennials, and small trees that require minimal pruning and cutting back.
- Arbor vitae and other conifers are good options, especially if you want a fast-growing privacy screen that doubles as wildlife habitat.
- When it comes to vegetables, choose lettuces, greens, cucumbers, summer squashes, and others that don't require much tending and can be planted in-ground or in pots.

Moderate-care gardens

- Focus on high-visibility border gardens with hardy perennials, bulbs, and shrubs and perhaps a few annuals.
- Incorporate some climbers that only need once-a-year pruning (like clematis and trumpet vine), a few specimen trees such as ornamentals (cherries, pear trees, or dogwoods) or sturdy shade trees, and some container plants.
- More extensive in-ground or raised-bed vegetable gardens can fall into this category, too, and include tomatoes, peas, pole beans, and others that need vertical supports.

High-maintenance gardens

- Embrace the full gamut of annuals, tender bulbs and perennials, and needier shrubs and trees.
- Add vigorous, prune-heavy climbers like wisteria.
- Work in hanging baskets, window boxes, and container plants that need to spend winter indoors or in a greenhouse.
- Starting seeds indoors for transplanting outside is another high-labor, high-reward endeavor for a vegetable or cutting-flower garden.

Pick the palette

As an extension of your home, your garden's palette should be considered in the overall context. Is your siding natural cedar, red (or whitewashed) brick, or natural stone? Or is it painted—and if so, in what color? Is there any element that you'd like to bring forth with the landscape?

Less can be more

Mixing lots of different hues is challenging—shades can clash and overwhelm. Instead, you may want to pick no more than three core colors, such as clusters of yellow daffodils blended with deep-burgundy tulips and sweet pink bleeding hearts that jubilantly trumpet spring.

That said, all bets are off if you are planning a wildflower meadow, when a riot of color is a big part of the charm. Plus, a multicolored garden will attract more pollinators.

On the other hand, monochromatic gardens can be striking, whether you cast your entire yard in only one hue or splash that color all over just one section—for example, planting white flowers in a shade garden, where their blooms sparkle at dusk and dawn. (See White Garden, page 256.)

Whatever you choose, start with your favorite color, then play with different gradations of that hue.

- ***Use a color wheel*** to add a secondary color, found opposite the primary shade—orange for blue, or purple for yellow—for contrasting colors that are pleasing to the eye.
- ***For a more subtle contrast,*** look to tertiary colors, which are a combination of two adjacent primary colors. So for blue, those would include teal (made with blue and green) or blue-tinged purples.
- ***Don't forget about foliage,*** which even when green can have different undertones; variegated leaves and those with contrasting veins lend two-tone color and dimension. Some plants are prized for their rust or magenta leaves.

Pretty in Pink

Here's an example of how to mix annuals and perennials for a white, pink, and lavender palette. These flowers all peak during the same time, in mid to late summer, and are available at most nurseries.

1. *Eupatorium* 'Gateway' (joe-pye weed)
2. Angelonia
3. *Miscanthus* 'Little Kitten'
4. *Echinacea* 'Magnus' and 'White Swan'
5. Verbena
6. *Gaura* 'Whirling Butterflies'
7. *Cleome* 'Senorita and 'Senorita Blanca'
8. Perovskia (Russian sage)
9. *Agastache* 'Blue Fortune'
10. *Boltonia* 'Snowbank'
11. Vitex (chaste tree)
12. Japanese anemone 'Robustissima'

3
8
6
4
7
9
11
5
2
12
1
10

Coral Bells

Heuchera, also known as coral bells, has recently become a native-plant all-star for its splashy color, showy foliage, tidy growth habit, and versatility. Easy to maintain, it thrives in sun or shade, poor or rich soils.

Dark Stars

These specimens lend drama to sunny garden beds.

1. 'Bella Notte'
2. 'Midnight Rose'
3. 'Forever Purple'
4. 'Frost'
5. 'Glitter'
6. 'Tapestry'
7. 'Blondie'
8. 'Cherry Cola'
9. 'Peppermint'
10. 'Glacier Falls'

Light and Bright

These lighter-hued options will bring touches of vibrant color to shady spots.

1. 'Southern Comfort'
2. 'Georgia Peach'
3. 'Buttered Rum'
4. 'Solar Eclipse'
5. 'Marmalade'
6. 'Electra'
7. 'Solar Power'
8. 'Ginger Ale'
9. 'Lime Ruffles'

Vary the texture and structure

▶ **Consider the entire plant structure**—leaf, stem, flower, trunk, branches—when settling on your garden designs.

- Find photos of how plants of interest evolve throughout the season—peonies, for example, continue to provide lush green foliage long after their gorgeous blooms fade away.
- Look at all the plant categories to find contrasting textures, from feathery ferns and wispy grasses to broadleaf varieties and those with needles. Succulents are a gold mine of spiky, smooth, rosette-shaped, or other characteristics.
- Try to mix glossy leaves with those that are matte or felted (silvery); variegated leaves add another dimension, as do leaves with darker spines.
- Think about flower gardens the same way you would an arrangement, which should have greenery, focal flowers, and filler flowers.

  Focal flowers are typically discs—flowers with symmetrical petals arranged in a circle around the flower head (like roses). These should be placed closer to the back or middle of your bed.

  Offset the focal flowers with fillers, such as spiky flowers (like snapdragons) and airy flowers (like feverfew), which can be planted closer to the front of your bed.

Foliage for Texture

Velvety, crinkled, scalloped, needlelike—the subtle beauties here offer these and other kinds of visual appeal.

1. Lamb's ear 'Big Ears'
2. Catmint (*Nepeta*)
3. Sweet bay
4. Euphorbia
5. Greek horehound (false dittany)
6. Rosemary 'Tuscan Blue'
7. Teucrium
8. Santolina
9. Dwarf olive 'Little Ollie'
10. Achillea
11. Lavender 'Hidcote Giant'
12. Oakleaf hydrangea

1
2
3
5
4
9
7
8
6
12
10
11

Plant for year-round interest

A recurring theme in these pages is taking a multiseasonal approach to your garden design.

- Choose perennials, shrubs, and trees that bloom at different times and provide showy seed heads and/or fetching foliage after their flowers are spent.
- Leave holes in your garden beds and visit nurseries weekly or monthly throughout the season to add perennials that bloom at different times. That ongoing effort is part of the satisfaction.
- Early bloomers such as hellebores, geraniums, and cornelian cherry dogwoods are lovely harbingers and connect you to what lies ahead. Likewise, having witch hazel, for example, in bloom in November can provide warmth as you hunker down.
- Cobaea, or cup-and-saucer vine, is covered in blooms from late summer until the first autumn frost. Same for sweet autumn clematis, whose tendrils are eternal.
- Evergreens and conifers offer year-round interest beyond their frondescence—the exfoliating bark of a kousa dogwood can be downright sculptural in the dead of winter. Don't overlook cold-tolerant grasses, either, such as quaking sea oats and Cape Rush, as well as natives like prairie dropseed and little bluestem. All are simple to care for.
- Even if having a barren backyard half the year is fine by you, know that early- and late-season plants help support our at-risk pollinator population by providing essential nutrients and nectar when they are needed most.
- End the season with a lavish display of annuals—birds and bees adore asters, sunflowers, ironweed, zinnias, cosmos, marigolds, rudbeckia, echinacea—plus single-flower dahlias and Japanese anemones, which go on forever. Tall sedums (shown opposite) leaf out in early spring in neat clumps that then bloom from late summer into fall in a striking profusion of pinks and purples.
- Heed, as well, the impulse to push fall cleanup until spring. You'll be supplying food, water, and shelter for wintering birds and other wildlife.

March Bloomers: Ephemerals

A harbinger of spring, ephemerals—so named because they come and go quickly, disappearing back to the ground—appear in woodlands each year, offering glimpses of color on the leaf-littered ground. Here's how to plant these wildflowers in your own yard.

Bloodroot, claytonia, hepatica, trillium, Mertensia (Virginia bluebells), dogtooth violets (yellow trout lilies), mayapples, and jack-in-the-pulpits are all common examples—and good companions for ferns, which start poking up around the same time.

- Choose a location that gets partial sun in spring and more shade in summer after the trees leaf out.
- Plant in soil that's moist, well drained, and rich in humus (a nutrient-packed mix of decayed organic matter).
- In the fall, top-dress the area with compost, or mulch it with shredded leaves.

Bloodroot Bloomers

These grow up to 8 inches tall and are found at nurseries specializing in native varieties.

1. ***S. canadensis* f. *rosea***
2. ***Sanguinaria canadensis***
3. ***S. canadensis* 'Multiplex'**

2
3
1

Factor in height

▶ **Grouping plants by height** makes sense. On a practical level, you don't want taller plants obscuring shorter ones, so look at the mature size on the label when designing each bed or container.

But that doesn't mean tall plants must be relegated to the back row. A garden with low-mounding, midlevel, and taller varieties interspersed in the same sight line will be more animated than one with plants all similarly statured, as demonstrated in the garden at left. Here, dwarf boxwoods add a bit of formality in contrast with the more naturalistic plantings within.

For other examples, dwarf trees can be planted amid perennials, or you can add height here and there with a climber on a slender trellis.

Height also matters when deciding what to plant together in pots. Make sure the tallest specimens are in the center and the shortest around the perimeter.

Consider hardscaping

▶ **Whether it's laying** stepping stones winding throughout your garden, installing a patio for outdoor gatherings, or building a decorative stone wall that doubles as a surface for climbing plants, hardscaping can add tremendous visual appeal and functionality to any garden design.

The possibilities are endless and will depend on your budget, allocated space, and goals. If you have multiple planting areas across an expansive lot, for example, pathways will provide a sense of connection between them or to a living wall such as the one at left, which is replicated using modular pocket planters that easily attach to a wall or fence. Here, 'Kent Beauty' oregano and bright-red 'Santa Cruz Sunset' begonia complement the dark-purple 'Trailing Queen' coleus and 'Crystal Palace Gem' geranium.

Paths can also lead to a focal point, such as a fountain, gazebo, or arbor, or to a resting place—like a picnic table or bench underneath a towering shade tree.

Separate patios for firepits are another popular hardscape, as are outdoor dining "rooms" complete with wood-fired ovens and assorted seating areas.

Stone walls are a long-standing feature of gardens both formal and naturalistic, including at Skylands and Bedford.

Draw a garden plan

▶ **Once you've decided** on the style and types of plantings, it's time to capture your ideas in a simple garden blueprint. This step will allow you to try out different locations and groupings before you break ground. Keep these tips in mind as you go:

Start small

If you are beginning from scratch, don't attempt to tackle the entire property at once. You can (and should) sketch the ultimate result to see how everything meshes, designating when each area will be implemented—for example, design A, B, C, and so on. Another reason to take an iterative approach: It creates opportunities to tweak the design to accommodate newly discovered specimens or an evolving aesthetic.

Pick the priority

Relatedly, it's a good idea to focus on what matters most initially, whether it's a border garden out front to improve curb appeal, an allée flanking your driveway for a grand entrance, or a pergola-covered patio with climbers and potted plants for outdoor entertaining. This is also important if you have a limited budget—prioritize whatever will instantly improve your enjoyment or give you a return on your investment.

Gather the data

First, take measurements of your yard (front, side, and back). Locate buried utility lines and drainpipes so you avoid disturbing them. Identify any unsightly objects (HVAC units, gas tanks, utility meters, garbage cans) that you'd like to hide with flowers and shrubs. Make notes on the amount of sunlight each spot gets and the location of a water source.

Draw a general overview

Use those parameters to draw plans—on graph paper, on a blown-up photo, or by using a garden-planning app or online software program—for each major planting area to scale. If sketching over a photo, you may want to consider how the area will look from different angles (overhead or looking out a window) and in different seasons. Label each location—lawn, border garden, shade garden, pathway, patio, and so on.

Make a detailed plan

Once you're happy with the placement of the various components, plot out the precise plantings in each bed or site. Note the spacing between plants based on their label; remember to put taller plants behind shorter ones, and to account for the size of mature plants.

Include succession plantings

When sketching vegetable and cutting-flower gardens, whether in-ground or in raised beds, make note of succession plantings over the growing season (as discussed on page 293). If you've chosen a mix of perennials and shrubs, it's important to recognize that perennials take about three years to flourish; for that reason, you may want to include annuals in your initial designs.

The same can be said for trees, which can take years to reach their full size; you can fill in the space with perennials that will be easy to transplant as needed.

Use odd numbers

To give your garden a natural, less curated look, consider clustering plants of each variety in groups of threes or fives. Pollinators are also more attracted to larger masses of the same flower.

Explore the edges

For border gardens and other free-form beds, you'll need to decide whether to go with curved or straight lines. You can use a garden hose or landscaping chalk to see which boundary you like best. Curved edges, which draw your eye around the space, lend a more organic look. Straight edges, on the other hand, create a more graphic appeal and are well suited for homes that have linear architecture.

Be flexible

A plan is not permanent. Take it with you to the nursery and ask a staff member to help you find the plants. If you see something else that will work in the same spot (many garden centers group plants by sun versus shade), you can swap it in.

After you've planted everything, take photos and reevaluate each year. You can generally transplant perennials or small shrubs if they are not thriving, or if there are any holes that invite an addition or two.

Preparing and Planting

A garden that is easy to maintain—and easy on the eyes—doesn't happen by accident; it is the product of planning. Here, for example, multiple beds are edged with a boxwood hedge and embellished with tuteurs; a surrounding gravel path and container plants complete the design. Whether you are planting a flowering shrub from the nursery or heirloom seeds for a vegetable garden, an attractive, healthy garden must be built from the ground up. Improving the texture and fertility of the soil is fundamental, and always the best way to begin.

Why go to all the trouble? A well-prepared garden will be more resistant to pests, diseases, and weather extremes. It will also ensure your plants prosper—and you spend more time enjoying the fruits of your labor. Sure, proper soil prep takes time and effort, but skipping this step will create more work down the road, and you'll be wasting money on plants that aren't set up to survive. Think of it as laying the foundation for years to come.

Getting started

Much of the time, a "new" garden isn't really new. It's an update of what came with the purchase of a home (even if that was years ago) or the evolution of your own efforts. Either way, before you begin plotting the redesign, decide what you will do with existing plantings and your lawn.

- Mature plantings can be an asset, but not an old tree that's losing its limbs or an overgrown shrub that's at the end of its life. Better (and cheaper) to clear those out and start anew.
- Any healthy perennials, bulbs, and small trees and shrubs can ideally remain in your design, either left where they are or incorporated into your new beds. Remember: Consolidating plants in one large bed will make maintenance far easier than when they are dotting the yard.
- If you are creating garden beds (in-ground or raised) where grass is currently growing, you can employ three options for removing the sod.

  The spade-and-shovel method, where you cut and lift the grass down to its roots, is the traditional option; it is also the most labor intensive and typically used for smaller beds.

  An electric or gas-powered rototiller, which can be rented from a home-improvement store, makes fast work of removing larger areas in strips. (It's important to wear safety goggles in case of flying stones.) Overuse can damage soil structure, so you may want to limit rototilling to the sod-removal stage when other methods aren't practical.

  A popular no-till way to eliminate sod is sometimes referred to as the "lasagna" method: cover the area with flattened cardboard boxes, layer with mulch and compost, and wait for the grass to die. Besides being the least labor intensive, this method results in rich, ready-to-plant soil (and is an effective way to smother stubborn weeds), though it can take months to complete. Starting in the fall will ensure you can plant when spring arrives.
- Finally, try to recycle as much garden waste as you can to put back into your landscape—green matter and twigs can be composted, and larger branches and trunks can be shredded to use as mulch (tree companies can do this for you). When removing sod with a spade and shovel or a rototiller, use it to replace bald spots in your lawn.

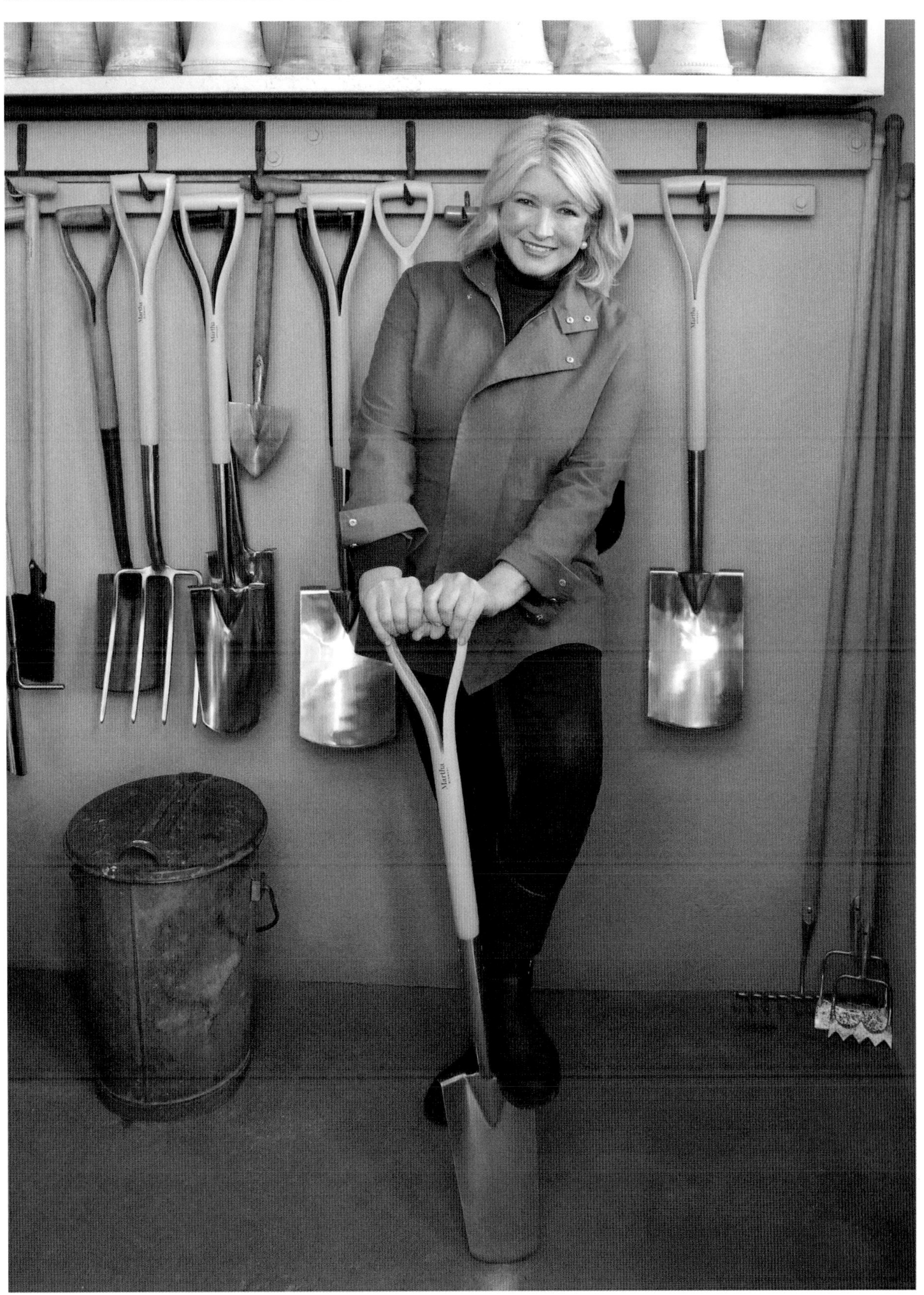

Amending the soil

▶ **A conscientious gardener** is, first and foremost, a soil builder. Plants depend on the soil for most of their nutrients, including the macronutrients nitrogen, phosphorous, and potassium, with three elements (oxygen, carbon, and hydrogen) derived from rainfall and the sun during photosynthesis.

Soil testing

Testing the soil for nutrients and pH levels is the most accurate way to measure its fertility (as discussed on page 19), and you can use the results to guide you in making the appropriate amendments or improvements.

This is especially important for determining any deficiencies in new planting areas, but soil changes over time, so you'll want to continue testing it on a regular basis.

And, because soil composition varies within a single yard, it's best to sample each planting area, such as a perennial border, cutting garden, and vegetable garden.

TO RAISE THE PH LEVEL

- Add lime—either dolomitic limestone for new gardens or calcitic lime for established beds. Mix it into the top 6 inches of the loosened soil following the instructions on the label.
- Add baking soda: Mix 1 tablespoon per gallon of water and pour the solution over the bed to thoroughly moisten. This is a convenient way to maintain a higher pH level around established plantings.

TO LOWER THE PH LEVEL

- Add compost or aged manure, both of which are rich in sulfur: Apply about 2 inches to the area, then work into the top 6 inches of the soil before planting.
- Another option is to work elemental sulfur (often sold as soil acidifier) into the soil at least one month before planting.
- You can amend soil over time as well by using compost or aged manure as a side dressing around plants.

Rather than having to continually amend pH levels, you may want to choose plants that are well suited to your soil's profile, such as planting masses of azaleas in acidic soil (as shown on page 89).

Soil tests will also pinpoint any nutrient deficiencies, which can often be solved with the addition of ample organic matter or by using organic fertilizers.

- All fertilizer products display their NPK ratio, or the percentage of nitrogen, phosphorous, and potassium—the three critical nutrients for plant health—in the mix. For example, a 10-6-4 fertilizer has 10 percent nitrogen, 6 percent phosphorous, and 4 percent potassium.

  So if your soil is highly deficient in one of these elements, you would look for a fertilizer with a higher percentage of that element. But always read the fine print, as too much fertilizer can harm plants, and using the wrong type can create new problems.

  For example, if flowering and fruiting plants get too much nitrogen, they will have excessive foliage and low yields.
- A safe choice is to use an all-purpose fertilizer with a balanced NPK ratio suitable for most plants and gardening tasks, including growing vegetables or flowers.

- If you notice yellowing, browning, or spotting on leaves, or other signs of stress, take photos of the plant and ask your local nursery for recommendations.

For soil to be a good growth medium, it must have the right texture: Healthy, well-drained, loamy soil is teeming with earthworms, which create channels that bring air, water, and nutrients to plant roots and microorganisms. Soil that is the ideal degree of loaminess and rich in organic matter will look almost like chocolate cake.

- Heavy clay soil tends to be poorly drained, while sandy or stony soils have the opposite problem, allowing water to drain too freely, thereby depleting the soil of nutrients.
- Working organic compost—your own made from recycled garden matter, or aged manure or earthworm castings from a garden center—into the soil is the answer to both situations.
- As a general practice, some gardeners add a 1- to 3-inch layer of organic matter to the soil at the beginning of each planting season.
- When preparing new beds, use 3 inches of organic matter to bulk up sandy soils and 1 to 2 inches for clay soils.
- Greensand, which comes from marine deposits, also helps loosen clay soils and stiffens sandy soils. (It's especially recommended for rose growers because it imparts brighter color to the flowers.) A typical application is 5 pounds per 100 square feet, with new applications made every five years. Take care not to overuse greensand—too much creates a harmful imbalance in the soil.
- Keep in mind that if your soil is particularly dense with clay or light and sandy, you may want to consider gardening in a raised bed using an optimal soil mix rather than struggle with what's in the ground.

Mulching, or top-dressing with organic matter, is another way to improve the soil.

- Chipped or shaved wood (pine or cedar), buckwheat hulls, straw, shredded leaves, pine needles, aged manure, and grass clippings can all be used as soil conditioners, improving water retention, suppressing weeds, and releasing nutrients as the matter breaks down.
- Mulch also makes garden beds look neat and tidy—like a fresh coat of paint on your house, giving your garden a finished look and pulling together the different plants into a harmonious whole.
- Apply 2 to 3 inches of mulch at the beginning of the growing season and another layer before winter (at which time using fallen leaves is a good way to go; topping with a little soil or compost will help keep them in place).
- When mulching with pine bark and needles, it's a good idea to balance their acidity with lime. Straw and leaves are good sources of carbon.
- Ground covers double as a more permanent, low-maintenance form of "green mulch" for surrounding plants, especially trees and shrubs.

Acid-Loving vs. Alkaline Plants

The following is just a sampling of common plants. You can also ask for guidance while shopping for plants at a nursery.

Plants that prefer acidic soil	Plants that prefer (or will happily tolerate) a slightly alkaline soil
Azalea	Astilbe
Begonia	Boston ivy
Blueberry	Boxwood
Caladium	Brunnera
Camellia	Buddleia (miniature butterfly bush)
Ceanothus (California lilac)	Caryopteris (bluebeard)
Daffodil	Clematis
Fothergilla	Coneflower
Heather	Coral bells
Japanese anemone	Deutzia
Lily	Forsythia
Magnolia	Geranium
Muscari	Hosta
Pieris japonica (andromeda)	Juniper
Rhododendron	Lilac
Strawberry	Phlox
Trillium	Salvia
	Smoke bush
	Spirea
	Viburnum
	Virginia creeper
	Weigela
	Yarrow

Working the soil

▸ **When planting in existing beds,** it's important to avoid doing anything that will damage the soil structure. Here gardeners have to decide whether to dig or not to dig.

Cultivation gardening

The traditional approach when preparing beds at the beginning of each growing season is to rake any debris and loose weeds from the top, then dig and turn the top few inches of soil over and loosen it with a garden fork or tiller. This is when you would also mix any amendments into the soil.

No-till gardening

Also called no-dig gardening, this approach has been gaining popularity for being easier and more ecologically friendly because it builds up the soil through the application and decomposition of mulch and cover crops. See opposite page for more information.

BELOW: Martha hard at work in her Turkey Hill vegetable garden, c. 1988.

About No-Till Gardening

A garden that's already cultivated doesn't need any digging at all. Instead, no-till gardening replicates how soil is continually enriched in nature.

How It Works

Instead of working compost, lime, fertilizers, or other amendments into the soil, you apply these materials to the surface (in a method called top dressing) and allow them to be gradually pulled into the soil during watering and by earthworms.

Mulch is layered on top to control weeds—no yanking them out and disturbing the soil—and to keep the soil from drying out; it also creates an ideal environment for earthworms and helpful insects. Note, too, that with consistent mulching, you will need to water less frequently; soaker hoses and drip irrigation systems deliver water directly to the roots for less water waste.

You can plant bulbs right through the mulch; when transplanting nursery plants, pull back the mulch before digging the hole, then spread it back around the plant, leaving 2 to 3 inches around the base of trees and shrubs. You will also want to brush the mulch aside when side-dressing with amendments throughout the growing season. At the end of the growing season, you can cover the beds with another layer of mulch, which will break down over the winter.

During the offseason, many no-till gardeners use cover crops—grasses or legumes—in place of mulch to improve soil structure, boost soil fertility, protect against erosion, and crowd out weeds, leaving beds in tip-top condition come spring. The most common types of "green mulch" are winter rye, hairy vetch, red (or crimson) clover, and oats. At least four weeks before the first frost date, scatter the seeds evenly over the soil, cover with straw, and water well to trigger germination. You should see sprouting within a few weeks.

When preparing the beds in the spring, hand-cut the cover crop to 1 or 2 inches and then cover it with mulch (or cardboard) to suppress growth. Do this at least two weeks prior to planting so the cover crops have time to decompose and release nitrogen into the soil to boost healthy roots in the new plantings.

Benefits of No-Till Gardening

- **Protects beneficial organisms:** Tilling can disrupt the many beneficial organisms—bacteria, fungi, and earthworms—in the soil that help plant growth. It can take the entire growing season for the soil to return to normal. By leaving the soil undisturbed, these organisms are allowed to thrive and multiply.
- **Healthier soil:** No-till systems have been found to be more resistant to pests and disease, possibly due to the buildup of beneficial soil microbial activity. Plus, tilling speeds the breakdown of organic matter and causes nutrients to be released more quickly; a gradual release of nutrients is better for plant growth.
- **Less weeding:** Contrary to widespread belief, tilling can bring dormant weeds to the surface where they can germinate, while no-till gardening keeps weed seeds deep in the ground.
- **Less watering:** No-till gardening maintains the integrity of the soil's physical and biological properties—the soil retains water better, reducing the need for supplemental irrigation.
- **Less risk of compaction:** Walking on and digging in the soil can cause it to become compacted—that is, to lose the spaces for root growth and for air, water, and nutrients to flow through. This is especially true for soil that's wet from watering or after rainfall, and even more so for clay soils.
- **Less physically demanding:** Not everyone can (or wants to) maneuver machinery or do the heavy lifting of digging and turning, so no-till methods allow more people to garden, whether they have limitations or not. (And no-till gardening can be done in a raised bed, which requires less bending down.)

Buying plants

It pays to be as thoughtful when buying plants as you are when caring for them. So before you set foot in a nursery or start filling your cart online, do some preliminary homework to know where (and when) to shop, what questions to ask, and especially how to choose the healthiest plants.

Don't just settle for whatever has been set out on the shelves of the local garden center—paying for a lackluster plant that fails to thrive has discouraged many budding gardeners from pursuing their passion. Worse yet, a diseased specimen or one that's infested with pests or insects can destroy surrounding plantings.

Familiarize yourself with the following checklists so when you shop, you can be confident of getting a vigorous specimen that fits your yard and your garden needs.

Also, be strategic in when and where you buy plants, and lean into the knowledgeable staff for assistance.

BUY THROUGHOUT THE SEASON

- Spring is when most people do the bulk of their shopping and often when inventory is at its peak, though it's worth checking back throughout the season if you are looking for a specific plant; many nurseries continually replenish their inventory with what's in bloom.
- Nurseries often hold sales in July and are much less crowded after Labor Day, meaning the staff will have more time to offer guidance; you will also find major discounts at this time of year.
- What's more, in the northern half of the country, September is the best time to plant hardy evergreens, and late fall is the best time to plant many perennials and deciduous trees and shrubs.
- Where winters are mild, in the South and along the Pacific Coast, a late-fall or early-winter planting is ideal for virtually all kinds of garden plants, except heat-loving annuals.

BUY LOCAL

- Nothing compares to strolling the aisles of an independent (often family-owned) nursery and being able to see, touch, and smell the plants in real time. If you establish a relationship with the staff, they may get to know your goals and preferences.
- These retailers can be valuable sources of information on what plants do best in your area; an increasing number are expanding their native plant selections, too.
- And should the plant fail, you can usually replace it at no cost.

EXPLORE ONLINE SOURCES

- Mail-order nurseries offer a greater selection of plants than local garden centers, often at excellent prices. Some specialize in rare species.
- It's best to stick with online vendors within your same region, though many websites allow you to filter your search by zip code to ensure you buy plants that are hardy for your zone.
- Before placing an order, make sure they guarantee their plants in case of damage during shipping—or in case you receive a plant that's diseased or infested. Most have 30-day warranties that you can supplement by paying for an extended one-year period.
- When in doubt, call (or use the chat function) to get the details.

CHOOSE SMALL

- Avoid the (impatient) temptation to buy the largest tree and shrub specimens you can find. More times than not, that proves to be an expensive mistake. Because they have larger root systems, bigger specimens suffer more damage when dug for sale (or when grown in containers and transplanted).
- Small specimens recover much faster from transplanting—and within a couple of years, they commonly overtake the jumbo-size shrubs and trees that cost many times as much.

COME PREPARED

- Bring photos of your existing garden, preferably in different seasons, along with your sketches or designs, including sunlight exposure and drainage for each spot.
- Take the results of soil tests—or carry samples to see if the nursery can evaluate them for you.
- You should also bring any photos of other gardens that you use as inspiration, as well as any swatches or ideas for the color palette.
- Finally, if the nursery lets you create a wish list on the website, it's a good idea to populate it with desired plants and print it out (or have it accessible by phone).

ASK QUESTIONS

- Perusing aisle after aisle of plants can be overwhelming, even if you come prepared with a finite list.
- Start by finding a staff member who can help you find what you are looking for or steer you in the right direction as needed. Share your sketches and goals.

BE REALISTIC

- Consider your skill set and interest in high- versus low-maintenance gardening. If you are not the best at watering, say so—there are plenty of drought-tolerant plants to choose from. If you don't want plants that require staking or regular pruning, be up front.
- On the other hand, if you are looking to stretch your gardening wings with climbers, fruit trees, or other "needy" plants, communicating that will be important.

Reading a Plant Tag

Plant tags provide all the information you need for buying, planting, and caring for individual plants. Knowing what to pay attention to will ensure you end up with the right plant for your garden and your lifestyle. Be sure to keep the tags for future reference.

Photo of the plant: Read the description of the plant to make sure it matches what's shown—including the color of the bloom. Tags can fade, or the wrong tag can get inserted into the plant.

Scientific and common names: The scientific name describes the genus, or group, the plant belongs to and its species; it also includes the cultivar (a plant variety produced by selective breeding) and classifies the plant even further in terms of color and leaf and petal shape. Common names are easier to remember but can be misleading, as they can vary in different areas of the country. Double-check with a staff member.

Hardiness zone: All plant tags include the zones a plant is hardy in. It may also indicate that the plant is annual in certain zones and perennial in others.

Sun exposure: How much a plant needs is usually indicated by a graphic showing full sun, part sun, or full shade.

Water requirements: These are often shown as raindrop icons—one drop for well drained, two for normal, and three for soil that should remain moist.

Bloom time: Sometimes the description might be general and just say spring or summer, while other times it may list the specific month(s). These may vary based on your climate and hardiness zone, so take both into consideration to ensure you are not planting too late or too early in the season.

Size: This is the maximum size the plant achieves in ideal growing conditions and is provided in the following ways:

- **Height:** The plant's mature height can be listed as a range from the minimum to the maximum average height.
- **Spread:** This is how wide you can expect the plant to be when fully grown.
- **Habit:** The habit, or shape of the plant, describes how it grows and its general form. Common habits are mounding, trailing, and upright.

Spacing: Follow the recommendations for how far apart to plant the same species to prevent overcrowding.

Care: This section gives important clues about how to keep the plant looking its best and may suggest pruning, deadheading, or following a specific fertilizer program.

Use: Not every tag has this, but those that do might include recommendations based on popular applications such as in a container or raised bed or as a ground cover.

Features: Other helpful information can include whether the plant is resistant to deer or rabbits (usually by icons of those animals).

Choosing healthy plants

Knowing what to look for and what to avoid is key to picking a strong candidate from the crowd.

INSPECT PLANTS CLOSELY FOR PESTS

- Look at the undersides of leaves and at their bases along the stems, two spots where pests and their eggs are likely to hide.
- Foliage stippled with lighter specks can be evidence of mite or insect infestation.

LOOK FOR HEALTHY FOLIAGE

- Avoid pots with just a few straggly, brown, or yellowing leaves—a sure sign of a poor plant.
- Also avoid weak stems, which are easily damaged during handling and may never rebound.
- Wilted leaves signal a top-heavy, weak-rooted plant.

AVOID PLANTS IN FULL BLOOM

- It helps to buy annuals with at least a few flowers to verify the variety and its true color.
- Vegetable seedlings, however, should not yet be putting out fruit—a premature harvest is a sign of stress.
- Purchase woody plants before or after they flower: Trees, shrubs, and perennials with open flowers are devoting their resources to reproduction, so it's not the best time to transplant them.
- If you happen to buy perennials with open buds, remove them before planting.

CHECK THE ROOTS OF CONTAINER-GROWN PLANTS

- Ask a staff member to gently slip each plant out of its pot—or don't be shy about doing this yourself.
- You should see crisp white root tips emerging from the soil; avoid plants where the soil is encased in a sheet of encircling roots.
- Alternatively, you can examine the underside of the pot. Roots snaking out of the drainage holes likely mean the plant is root-bound.
- Lifting the pot can be telling: The lighter it is, the more likely the plant is root-bound because there's no room for soil or water.

INSPECT THE STRUCTURE OF TREES AND SHRUBS

- Broken branches or a split at the spot where the trunk divides into the major branches are evidence of careless handling and may be entry points for insects and diseases.
- The plant should also have a well-formed and balanced structure; avoid trees that are growing in a direction other than straight.

CONSIDER THE SEASON

- Beware of perennials, trees, and shrubs that are flowering or leafing out earlier than they should in your area.
- That's a sign that they came from a greenhouse or were grown in a milder region and then shipped north. In either case, they may not prove hardy in your garden.

Planting 101

▶ **Once your soil** is amended and you've selected your plants, it's time to dig them into their places according to your garden designs. It's preferable to buy plants (except annuals) the same day they'll be planted; if necessary, keep them in their pots in a shaded spot that's protected from wind and rain until you can get them in the ground.

Although you should always follow specific guidelines for depth and spacing as indicated on the plant label, knowing the fundamentals will ensure you have the underpinnings of success.

Annuals

For annuals to strut their eye-catching abundance of flowers and foliage all season long, they require a little more initial care. Proper planting will ensure they last until the first frost. In this henhouse-adjacent vegetable garden (opposite page), for example, zinnias, dahlias, and giant sunflowers bloom well into fall—and attract pollinators to increase the edibles' yields.

WHEN TO PLANT

Garden centers usually sell annuals that are ready for transplanting in your area, gradually replacing early-spring varieties with those that prefer hotter summer temps. But that's not always the case, so be sure to read the plant tag for planting guidance.

HOW TO HARDEN OFF

Having spent their infancy in the cozy confines of a greenhouse, annuals need conditioning to soften the transition to the stressful outdoors.

1. Begin by setting the seedling packs or pots outdoors for just an hour or two, in a spot sheltered from the wind and with filtered sunlight. If it's spring, wait for a day when the temperature rises above 50°F.
2. Over the next week to ten days, increase the time you leave the seedlings outdoors each day by ½ hour to 1 hour daily.
3. Gradually expose sun-loving plants to more intense sunlight, too. Leave plants indoors on chilly days.
4. By the end of the second week, the plants should be staying out all day and night, and are ready for the move to the garden.

HOW TO PLANT

Before planting, place the pots in your desired arrangement, whether in a garden bed or a container, following the spacing recommendations on the plant tag. Annuals grow quickly, so be sure to give them ample room to reach their full size. If they feel dry, water lightly to moisten their root balls.

1. Use a hand trowel to dig a shallow hole that's slightly larger than the root ball. You may want to sprinkle fertilizer in the bottom of the hole (using the amount specified on the label).
2. To remove annuals from their pots, gently push—never pull. Tilt the pot and cradle the stem with one hand, then gently squeeze the sides of the pot; the plant should slide out. It's okay if some of the potting mix stays behind so long as the roots come out in one piece. Cradle the annual in the hole and backfill with soil, gently tamping around the stem to ensure good contact between the soil and roots.
3. Always water immediately after planting. Use a watering can or the shower setting on a water-hose nozzle to soak the soil gently but thoroughly. Finish with a 2- to 3-inch layer of mulch.

Tip

If you are planting many annuals in one bed, you may want to dig all the holes before planting each annual, or do what professional gardeners do: Stab your trowel, concave side facing you, into the soil, pull the handle forward and back to create a divot, then place the annual in the hole and repeat for the next one.

Perennials

Perennials are truly the superstars of the garden—they come back every year (so you don't have to replant them!), require little maintenance, and draw pollinators to your yard. Although their blooms are short-lived (typically one season—spring, summer, or fall), perennials earn their keep during their annual show, and keep adding interest with foliage long after their blooms have faded away. Wherever you plant them, there are a few basics you need to know to ensure these plants flourish year after year. For best results, stick with those deemed hardy for your region.

WHEN TO PLANT

- The timing varies depending on where you live, but the general rule is to plant summer- and fall-blooming perennials in spring, shortly after they've awakened and once the danger of freezing soil has passed.
- Spring-blooming perennials (and even some early summer bloomers) should be planted in the fall, allowing enough time for the plants' roots to establish themselves before winter.
- The optimal planting season depends on your climate or conditions in specific years.

HOW TO PLANT

Using your garden sketches, begin by placing plants in their designated spots. Remember to check the tag on each one to ensure you're spacing them correctly. Start, as always, with well-prepared soil and match the site to the plant in terms of sunlight.

1. Dig a hole about twice the diameter of the container and as deep as the pot (or as directed on the plant tag), setting the pot in the hole as a guide.
   - Most perennials should be planted at the same depth as when in their original pots.
   - A few exceptions: Moisture-loving plants like to be a bit deeper, while a few plants that prefer dry conditions like to be about an inch above the surface.
2. Score the bottom and sides of the hole with a garden fork or hand cultivator to loosen compacted soil. Add granular fertilizer if desired, mixing it into the soil.
3. Water the plant if it is dry, then carefully slide it out of the pot, cradling the stems with your other hand (do not tug on the stems). Tease a few of the roots free from the root ball with a hori hori knife or a hand cultivator.
4. Place the plant in the hole at the recommended depth. Add compost to the removed soil, then backfill the hole and tamp down firmly all the way around the plant to ensure the roots come in contact with the soil.
5. Water generously, then spread mulch over the soil, leaving space around the base of the plant.

Bulbs

Dig, drop, and wait. That's how easy it is to grow bulbs, which provide a dazzling display all year long—from snowdrops in late winter to daffodils and tulips in spring; dahlias, canna lilies, and gladioli in summer; and colchicums, nerines, and more in the fall.

Most bulbs prefer full sun, though some varieties will thrive in the dappled light of overhead trees.

Regardless of whether planting is formal or random, bulbs look best planted en masse versus in straight lines.

Spring is a great time to assess your bulb plantings and identify gaps. Use wooden markers to indicate where to add more bulbs. Taking photographs of any thin areas is another good way to remember where to plant bulbs that arrive in the fall.

OPPOSITE: A perennial paradise offers wave after wave of flowers from spring through fall. This "garden of variety" in Bedford counts more than 200 different types, including climbing roses, lupines, poppies, hollyhocks, asters, and daisies, to name just a few. Perennials in various border areas complement shrubs and trees—and that is certainly among the more popular ways to put perennials to good use in your own garden.

Daffodils

Sprouting in beautiful shades of yellow, orange, peach, white, cream, and even pink, daffodils—known by their botanical name *Narcissus*—are an early sign that spring has sprung.

Some tried-and-true cultivars are the 'Golden Ducat', 'Rip Van Winkle', and 'Petit Four'—all examples of the double daffodil, featuring one or more flowers to a stem. Another common variety is the trumpet daffodil, which has a center that is as long or longer than its petals. Large-cupped daffodils are defined by their prominent cups, while small-cup iterations have short cups that are less than one-third the length of the petals.

Don't worry about recognizing all the different varieties; just choose what you like from your local garden center or online resource. Because no matter the type, daffodils (and other small bulbs) are so rewarding. The blooms last for two or three weeks in the garden and bring such color to your landscape. They are also low maintenance.

Here are some tips to help you make the most of these perennial crowd-pleasers.

- Daffodils are winter-hardy in zones 3 through 8 and will return to bloom again year after year so long as they are planted in full or partial sun and in any soil that's not soggy.
- If your goal is to have drifts of daffodils, include varieties recommended for naturalizing and forming carpets on lawns and into woodlands. That way, the 100 bulbs you plant this fall will gradually multiply to 300, then 600, then 1,000, and so on.
- When planting en masse, it helps to create a planting "map" in advance on paper that can be transferred onto the ground with granular lime, as Martha does (opposite).
- Daffodil bulbs should be planted about two to three times as deep as the bulbs are high, so if you have one that's 2 inches tall, plant it 4 to 6 inches below the top of the soil.
- When harvesting for arrangements, grasp the stem at the base and pull rather than cutting, as viruses in bulbs can be passed along to other plants when using pruners to trim stems.
- Don't cut back daffodils too soon. Once the flowers bloom and fade, allow the whole plant to die back to the ground to create food for the bulbs so they can multiply.
- After removing spent foliage, apply a balanced 10-10-10 fertilizer over the entire area, and then add a layer of mulch. Fertilize the area again in the fall.

“When I first bought my farm in Bedford, I rebuilt a new stone wall that goes along the perimeter and decided to plant daffodils on both sides. Now we’ve planted close to 60,000 bulbs and they have multiplied and beautified and made a walk up through the garden one of the most beautiful experiences of the year.”

Waves of Blue

When massed together, these miniature spring bulbs make a grand statement over a period of six to eight weeks.

1. Grecian windflower (*Anemone blanda*)
2. Glory-of-the-snow (*Chionodoxa luciliae*)
3. Grape hyacinth (*Muscari* 'Valerie Finnis')
4. Siberian squill (*Scilla siberica*)
5. Woodland crocus (*Crocus tommasinianus*)
6. Grape hyacinth (*Muscari latifolium*)

1
2
3
4
5
6

WHEN TO PLANT

- Most bulbs need to be planted about three months before their bloom dates to ensure they have the necessary cool, dormant period before growth can begin.
- Fall-blooming bulbs are the exception; you can see blooms a few weeks after planting.
- Plant early bloomers in fall, a few weeks before the first frost date.
- Plant summer blooms in early spring, after the last frost date.

BEST SPRING BULBS TO PLANT IN FALL

- Snowdrop
- Crocus
- Muscari
- Hyacinth
- Daffodil
- Fritillaria
- Tulip

BEST SUMMER BULBS TO PLANT IN SPRING

- *Allium giganteum*
- Dahlia
- Gladiolus
- Calla lily
- Canna lily
- Caladium
- Chocolate cosmos

BEST FALL BULBS TO PLANT IN FALL

- Colchicum (and several other autumn-blooming crocuses)
- *Sternbergia lutea*
- *Lycoris radiata*
- Nerine (these can be planted in early spring for summer foliage and fall blooms)

BULB-PLANTING TOOLS

These make short work of planting multiple bulbs in the garden. Choose the one that best suits your situation, making sure the diameter of the hole is larger than that of the bulb.

- ***A cordless drill with an augur:*** The easiest tool by far and one that's often used by landscape professionals when planting hundreds of bulbs (or more) at a time. You can find augur attachments at hardware stores and home improvement centers.
- ***Post-hole digger:*** Designed for fence posts, this tool has two concave metal blades on the bottom that operate by the handles above. Holding the long handles straight, forcefully stab the metal blades into the ground, then pry apart the handles while lifting to remove the soil.
- ***Bulb trowel:*** Like a regular hand trowel but narrower for right-size holes.
- ***Bulb planter:*** This cylindrical tool is slightly wider at the top. Push the planter straight down into the soil, twist with the handle, and lift to remove the soil, tapping it out next to the new hole.
- ***Stand-on bulb planter:*** An alternative to digging by hand, this tool has a ledge atop the cylinder that you stand on to force the cylinder into the ground.
- ***Diver:*** A pointed sticklike tool that you thrust into the ground and whirl around to open the hole a bit before dropping in the bulb.

Favorite Flowering Bulbs

These are some of the more common spring bulbs that bloom in waves, from snowdrops and crocuses through fritillarias and irises, depending on the variety.

1. Iris
2. Fritillaria
3. Muscari
4. Bluebell
5. Snowdrop
6. Crocus
7. Daffodil
8. Allium
9. Tulip
10. Hyacinth

1
IRIS
2
FRITILLARIA
MUSCARI
3
BLUEBELL
4
SNOWDROP
5
CROCUS
6
7
DAFFODIL
HYACINTH
ALLIUM
8
10
TULIP
9

HOW TO PLANT

Bulbs are often sold in bags of 5, 10, 50, or some other round number. Sort through the bulbs and discard any that are soft or rotting.

Be sure to follow the instructions for depth and spacing. Most bulbs need to be buried two to three times their own depth, but others (such as tulips) like to be deeper, and some (like snowdrops) like to be just below the surface.

Group three or five bulbs together in each hole for a more robust display, or plant hundreds (say, on a slope or in a trench) for a naturalistic result.

1. Whether planting in the ground or pots, it's a good idea to set out the bulbs where you intend to plant them, so you find the right arrangement.
2. Loosen the soil in the planting area and mix in compost or prepare in-ground soil to improve drainage, which is necessary for healthy bulbs. This is also a good time to add bulb fertilizer or bone meal to the soil following package directions. Bone meal helps rejuvenate the bulbs so that most of them will come up again and again, year after year.
3. Dig a hole at the appropriate depth and large enough to space the bulbs correctly (usually 3 to 4 inches apart), then place the bulbs in the hole, pointy end up and the basal roots down. (If you're not sure what's up and what's down, plant the bulb on its side.)
4. Backfill the hole with soil and gently tamp it with your hands, being careful not to damage the tips.
5. Unlike other plants, bulbs should not be watered after planting, though always refer to the specific plant guidelines. The general rule is to hold off watering until the first sign of growth breaks through the surface.

How to layer bulbs

An efficient, space-saving way to have a succession of colorful flowers in the same bed or container is to layer bulbs that bloom at different times in the same spot, as shown on the opposite page. When the early bloomers fade away, they will be quickly replaced by the next variety.

STEPS

1. Plant the deepest layer with late-blooming bulbs, spacing them about 2 inches apart (or as directed).
2. Add a layer of soil at least 2 inches thick, then plant a second layer for midseason blooms.
3. Repeat layering with soil and early blooming bulbs.
4. If desired, add a fourth layer of bulbs that bloom within the others as indicated on the packaging.

PLANTING TIPS

- For succession planting, you generally plant bulbs at a depth of three times their height and space them three times their width apart, so they have plenty of room to grow.
- As shown, plant tulips about 8 inches deep, hyacinths 6 inches deep, crocuses 4 inches deep, and snowdrops 2 inches deep.
- Avoid planting two layers right on top of each other to ensure their roots won't be crowded; here, they are staggered.

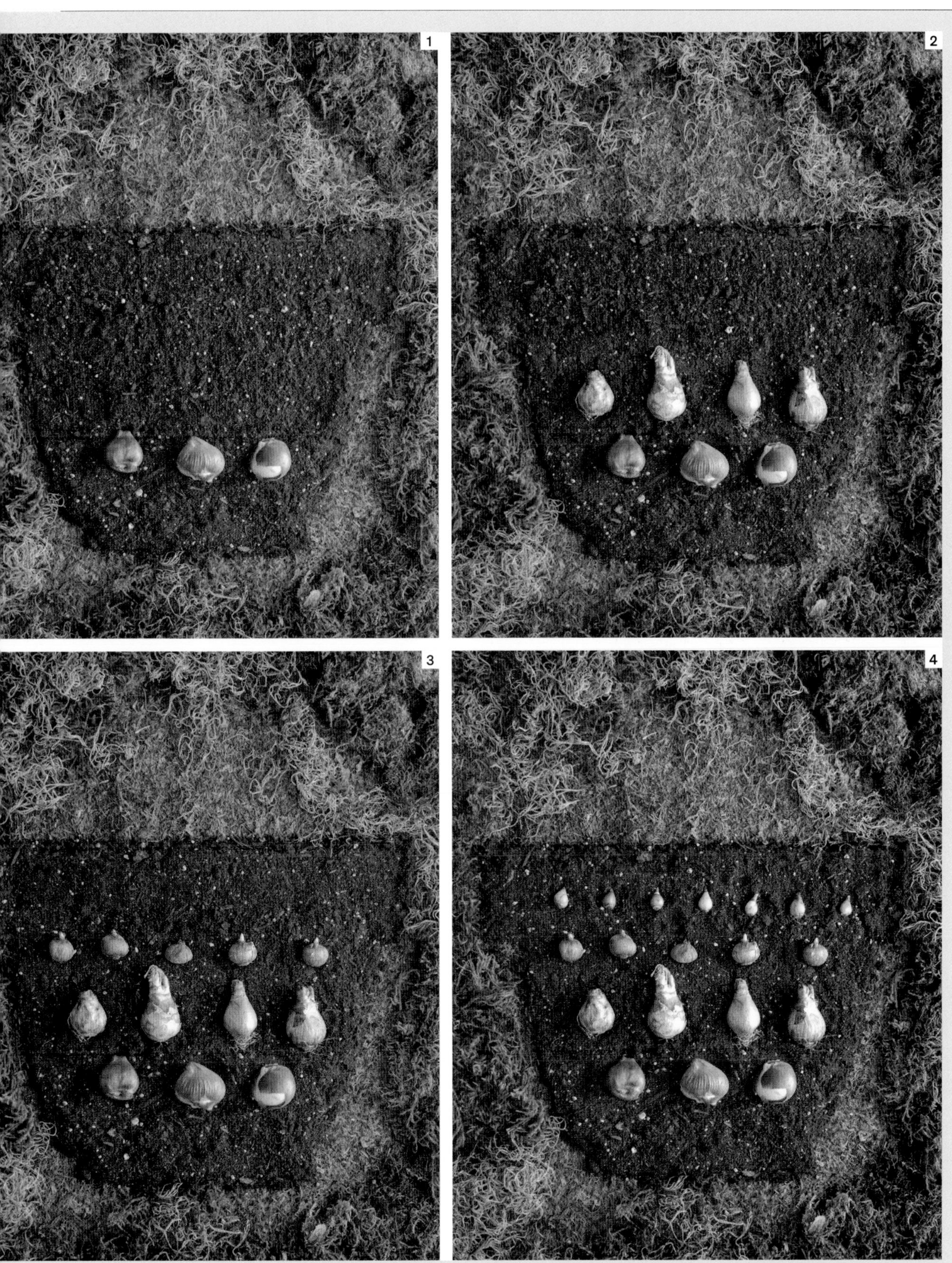
1
2
3
4

Forcing Bulbs

Forcing is the process of speeding up the bulb's development by simulating the conditions of winter and spring for indoor blooms. The most common bulbs to force are daffodils, tulips, hyacinths, crocus, paperwhites (narcissus), and amaryllis.

It takes only a couple of weeks to fill your house with their wonderful beauty and fragrance. Forced paperwhites and amaryllis also make terrific holiday gifts.

The two methods shown here work for all the bulbs mentioned, though soil provides a more complete growing medium with necessary nutrients for the bulb to develop roots and flowers, whereas gravel primarily acts as a support structure to hold the bulb upright while allowing the roots to access water directly.

TO FORCE BULBS IN GRAVEL

This method is especially recommended for bulbs such as daffodils, paperwhites, and hyacinth that can be forced in water. Unlike soil, the gravel acts mainly as a support structure and provides fast results with minimal root development.

1. Fill a bowl, compote, or other attractive vessel with pea gravel. It can be deeper than what is shown here, though you will need to purchase more gravel.
2. Place the bulbs in the gravel with growth ends up, nestling the bottoms in the gravel as close together as you like (they can be touching).
3. Sprinkle more gravel around the bulbs, leaving the growth uncovered. Pour in enough water to moisten the gravel without leaving any standing water in the bottom of the bowl. Cover with moss if desired for an appealing display.

1

2

3

TO FORCE BULBS IN SOIL

The advantage of this method is that the soil is a fertile medium, providing nutrients and water retention.

1. Fill containers with a well-draining potting soil mix. Use only containers with drainage holes. Adding sand or coconut coir to the sterile potting mix will also help keep the roots from getting waterlogged.
2. Place the bulbs in the soil with growth ends up. Large bulbs can be forced singly in individual pots (as shown), or you can plant a grouping of smaller bulbs (as shown opposite).
3. Sprinkle a layer of gravel around the bulbs for a neat appearance, leaving the growth uncovered. Water after planting, and place in a cool, dark spot until green foliage appears, then move to a cool, sunlit location for flowering. Bulbs will rot if overwatered, so water only when the pots dry out completely.

CHILLING REQUIREMENTS

Most bulbs require chilling at an average temperature of 45°F to 50°F to bloom when forced. Paperwhites (narcissus) do not require chilling, nor do new amaryllis bulbs, though these do need a period of cool, dry dormancy to bloom.

The following are the suggested chilling times for each bulb.

- **AMARYLLIS:** 8 weeks (for bulbs you've been growing a few years)
- **CROCUS:** 6 weeks
- **DAFFODILS:** 8 to 10 weeks
- **GRAPE HYACINTH (MUSCARI):** 6 weeks
- **TULIPS:** 12 weeks

1

2

3

Planting in containers

Start by selecting the ideal pots for your space, then match the plants to those containers. Pay attention to how much sunlight the target spot receives, too. See Container Garden, starting on page 272, for more detailed information on choosing the pots and plants.

SPACE PLANTS CORRECTLY

How you space the plants in a single container differs from planting in a garden. For a robust display, you'll want to keep plants much closer together in pots. This also crowds out weeds. In fact, the New York Botanical Garden says that you can grow twice as many plants in a container as you would in the same amount of garden space.

PAY ATTENTION TO PROPORTION

Small containers call for small plants, just as larger containers call for larger plants—you'd never plant a huge tree in a tiny pot, right?

- A plant in a too-small container will become root-bound and eventually dry out; in a too-big pot, the plant may get root rot.
- The soil in smaller containers will also dry out more quickly than in larger pots.
- When you need to transfer a plant to a larger container, use one that is 2 to 4 inches wider in diameter.

USE THE RIGHT SOIL

Potted plants require a different medium than those planted in the ground or in raised beds.

- Use only a good-quality organic potting mix, which you can buy at a nursery or online.
- Or you can make your own by mixing equal parts garden soil (store-bought or dug from a well-amended bed), compost, perlite, and coir. (Or see another formula on page 140.)
- Use a well-draining mix designed for succulents so the roots don't get soggy and rot (or add one part vermiculite to the above homemade mix).

OPPOSITE: A large strawberry pot with pockets on the sides is filled with giant alocasia, purple scaevola, chartreuse creeping Jenny, and trailing silver dichondra.

How to Plant in Containers

This time-tested potting method ensures the specimens will flourish all season long.

SUPPLIES

Bubble wrap

Planters

Pea gravel or clay shards

Landscape cloth

Potting mix

Plants

Hori hori knife

Organic fertilizer

Decorative rocks and pebbles

Spacers

1. First, add a layer of bubble wrap to the bottom of the planters. This will fill the planters so you don't have to add as much potting mix.
2. Next, place gravel or clay shards to help with drainage. Add a layer of landscape cloth on top of that. (It lets water drain but prevents soil from passing through the drainage holes of the container. Plus, it prevents the container from deteriorating.)
3. Add the potting mix, dig in the plants, and use a hori hori knife to push the landscape cloth down into the container.
4. Sprinkle some fertilizer on top and finish with decorative rocks and pebbles.
5. Last, hide spacers underneath the container for extra drainage.
6. Water thoroughly.
7. Continue to water and fertilize as discussed on page 275.

Propagating

▶ **The cost of buying plants** from a local nursery or online source can quickly add up, particularly if you have a lengthy wish list. Fortunately, there are ways to grow plants economically and efficiently, whether from seed or by multiplying existing plants through division or cuttings—the latter of which is like "shopping" your garden for specimens that are proven to thrive in your environment. Besides expanding your own collection, propagating allows you to bestow a plant in the making on a fellow gardener.

Growing from seed

How a tiny seed, planted with care, emerges as a whole new life is one of nature's great wonders. Even seasoned gardeners are tickled by seeing a delicate green shoot pop up through the soil at the first sign of spring.

WHY GROW FROM SEED

- Besides this seeming hocus-pocus, growing from seed is practical—a single packet can contain hundreds of seeds, each capable of sprouting into a distinct plant.
- It also opens up vast new opportunities to experiment and expand your repertoire with rare species. For example, you'll have your choice of maybe three dozen annual flower varieties at a nursery, while there are thousands of varieties of seeds, including the latest introductions. Are you yearning to plant a tomato patch? Many heirloom varieties await discovery.
- Along the way, you may even spark the interest of a child, who will quickly see the magic that seeds hold—and continue to experience such awe for the rest of their life.

SHOPPING FOR SEEDS

The success of any sowing depends on the quality of the seed.

- Buy from a trusted source, either a local nursery or a reputable seed purveyor, which you can access online (though dog-earing pages in a print catalog is a beloved old-school tradition).
- Purchase seeds packed for the current year, which is always marked on the packet. If you've got old ones, you can test their viability by presprouting them in a wet paper towel kept inside a plastic baggie and stored somewhere warm. Most seeds sprout between 2 and 14 days.
- If you have extra seeds in any given year, store them in a cool, dark, airtight place, like a resealable plastic bag placed in the freezer.

7082
CUCUMBER
ROW
BADGER
FLAME
BEET
CENTERCUT
SQUASH
HABANADA
PEPPER
BEAUREGARDE
SNOW PEA

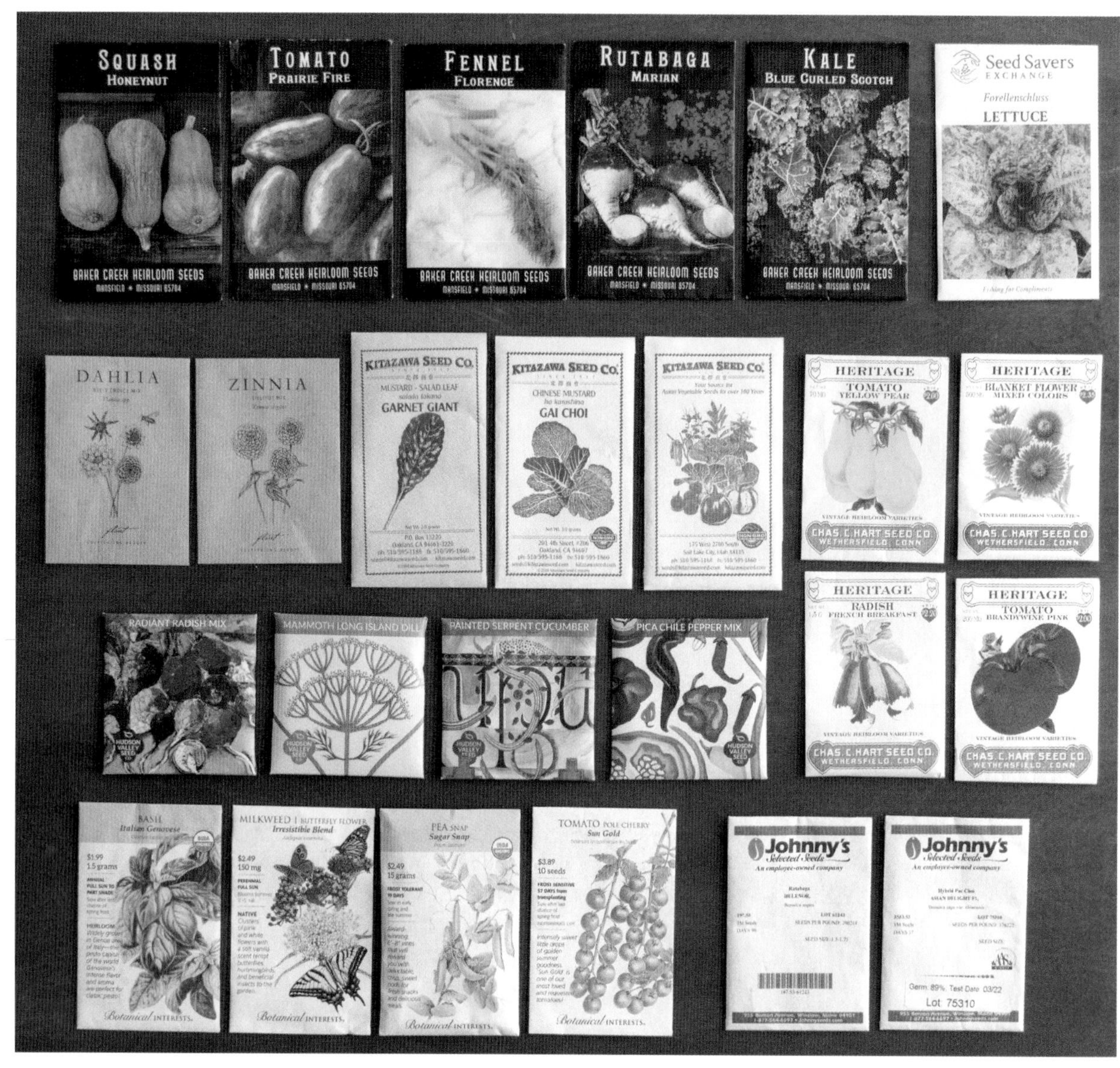

"My father taught me that you can do it all from scratch, starting from seeds or cuttings, and if you nurture them, they will produce. I still do this: I grow trees from saplings and boxwood from rooted cuttings, and pretty much all my flowers are from seeds sown in the greenhouse. I enjoy seeing them develop. I think a gardener learns more this way."

ORGANIZING SEEDS

A seed collection can quickly get out of hand. A few tricks will keep your "library" in check.

1. First, lay out all the packets on a table and sort them by plant type (for instance, annual flowers, perennials, vegetables).
2. If direct-sowing, organize the packets according to their location in the garden, be it the vegetable garden, cutting-flower bed, border garden, and so on, putting them in the order in which they need to be planted.
3. If starting indoors, organize the packets into trays according to how long they take to germinate.
4. Write the name of each plant seed on a wood plant marker, then tuck the marker inside the corresponding packet so you can eventually keep track (either by sticking the marker in the seed-starting trays or in-ground rows).

STARTING SEEDS INDOORS

Starting seeds allows you to control the environment and give plants the best shot of germinating. You can do this in a greenhouse, garden shed, garage, or cellar—or even on an indoor windowsill. Another reason to start seeds indoors is to extend plants' production or harvest cycle, especially in colder regions, where the growing season can be too short for plants to fully mature and bear fruit or flowers between first and last frost dates.

How to start seeds

The process is as easy as plant, water, provide light, and let nature take its course.

SUPPLIES

You don't need any special equipment to start seeds indoors, though the following materials are readily available and inexpensive.

Seed-starting containers

- Any container is fair game for starting seeds so long as it is at least 2 inches deep and has adequate drainage.
- Thoroughly clean terra-cotta or plastic pots before reusing them for seed starting.
- Large clay or plastic pots with drainage holes, also known as community pots, work great for a group of seedlings.
- Biodegradable peat pots, cell packs (or trays), and pellets are naturally sterile and, because they can be directly planted outdoors, they are ideal for plants with delicate roots that might not like to be transplanted. Multicell flats allow you to grow lots of plants closely together and then pull them apart when ready to transplant.

Potting soil

- The ideal medium is a sterile soilless mix made from about 40 percent coir (from coconut hulls), 20 percent composted pine bark, 20 percent vermiculite, and 20 percent perlite.
- Most commercial seed-starting mixes also have enough fertilizer for about two weeks.
- Never use a mix containing topsoil or compost, as these can impede drainage and rot your seeds.

Watering trays

- To avoid disturbing the seeds and provide even moisture, practice "bottom watering" by placing deep-sided plant trays (or sterile baking pans or storage containers) under the seed-starting flats or pots.
- For large-scale sowing, use special two-part seed-starting trays (such as from Johnny's Selected Seeds), which have a multicell flat that sits in a reservoir for self-watering. These come in many sizes and formulations, so choose the right one based on the size of your seeds.

Seed dispensers

- Sprinkle smaller seeds by hand or out of the packet or with a small, handheld seed dispenser, which allows you to set the number of seeds and sow hundreds of seeds in quick fashion.
- Larger seeds are easier to sow with your (clean) hands.

Grow light

- Seeds need light and warmth. Usually, a sunny windowsill in a warm room will do the trick.
- If you live in a light-deprived setting, or if you are growing in a windowless cellar or shed, you will need a grow light to promote germination and healthy development.
- Choose full-spectrum fluorescent lights that can be positioned directly above seeds and raised as seedlings grow.

KITAZAWA SEED CO.
EDIBLE PODDED SUGAR PEA
SUGAR SNAP
CALENDULA

BASIC STEPS

Before you begin, find out the last frost date in your area by checking online. Read the seed packets to learn how many weeks before this date they should be started and when the seeds should be planted outdoors. Calculate your sowing date accordingly. For example, if you live in northern regions, you can begin sowing seeds soon after New Year's so the plants have time to germinate before the ground thaws. Gather all your supplies and seeds before you begin so you can use an assembly-line approach.

1. Prepare the containers

- Pour the seed-starting mix into a large bucket or tub and add hot tap water, a cup at a time, until the mix is evenly moist but not wet, like a wrung-out sponge.
- Cover the drainage holes in clay or plastic pots with a single thickness of newspaper so the seed-starting mix won't leak out; multicell packs and peat containers don't require this step.
- Fill containers to the top with moistened mix, then tamp down the mix so the surface is firm and level, about ½ inch from the top.

2. Distributing the seeds

- Using a pencil, chopstick, or your finger, make holes in the mix according to the depth and spacing instructions on the packet. A handy rule is to bury seeds about twice as deep as they are thick.
- Drop in the specified number of seeds (or two seeds per plug), then cover with the mix.
- Unless seed-packet instructions specify otherwise, cover seeds with additional seed-starting mix, then lightly press on the mix to allow it to come into contact with the seeds.
- Add plant markers with the plant name and date it was sown. You may also want to keep a log with the plant name, sowing date, and germination date.

3. Water

- Water immediately after sowing the seeds and keep the soil evenly moist while the seeds are germinating; check by sticking your finger about 1 inch into the soil mix and water when it feels dry to the touch.
- For best results, water the containers from the bottom by standing them in a plant tray (or a sterile baking pan); add enough water so the moisture rises to the surface of the mix.
- Alternatively, you can gently spray water over the surface of the soil, being careful not to disturb the seeds and adding enough water to reach the bottom of the soil mix.

4. Germinate

- Most seedlings need 12 to 16 hours of light daily. Cover containers with a clear plastic cover (such as an overturned storage container). Place them in a warm, sunny spot.
- If you're using grow lights, place them 2 to 3 inches above the seeds.
- For seeds that require darkness to germinate (noted on the seed packet), use an opaque cover, and set them in a warm spot, such as the top of a refrigerator. You can also use a special heating mat (sold at garden centers) to promote germination.

5. Monitor daily for new shoots

- Keep the seed-starting mix moist—but not soggy—until germination is complete and the emergence of new seedlings slows markedly or stops.
- At this point, remove the covers. If you're using grow lights, leave them on for 14 to 16 hours a day. Continue to bottom-water.
- The first set of leaves that unfold are the cotyledons, with the second set of leaves being the "true leaves." As soon as seedlings produce their first true leaves, begin watering with a balanced fertilizer or fish emulsion diluted to one-quarter strength.
- As seedlings grow, raise grow lights, keeping them 2 to 4 inches above the plants.

Self-Seeding Perennials

The easiest way to propagate from seed requires no effort on your part. Simply incorporate the following self-fertile perennials into your garden, allowing room for new plants to take root around the parent plant, and do not deadhead the spent flowers. For example, you can allow alliums, poppies, lupines, and other flowers to drop their seeds in a deliberately "chaotic" perennial garden. Besides proliferating your flower beds, the seed heads provide food for wildlife and have an elegance all their own.

Here are some popular self-seeding perennials:

Allium	Hosta
Borage	Lady's mantle
Clary sage	Lupine
Columbine	Marigold
Common poppy	Morning glory
Coneflower	Nasturtium
Delphinium	Pampas grass
Euphorbia	Primrose
False indigo	Rose campion
Forget-me-not	Sedge
Foxglove	Solomon's seal
Gladiolus	Sweet alyssum
Hollyhock	Viola

How to transplant seedlings

Make sure your garden bed is well prepared and ready to go. You can do the necessary amendments while hardening off the transplants before they go into the ground. Make sure the temperature is above 45°F before beginning the transition.

1. Before planting, gradually harden off seedlings to prevent transplant shock: Two weeks before transplanting, place seedlings outdoors for a few hours at a time, gradually increasing their time outside until they are acclimated. Leave them inside on chilly days (below 45°F).
2. When transplanting, dig a hole in well-tended soil that's a little larger than the plant's roots and about as deep.
3. Tilt the pot while supporting the soil side with your hand and tap the bottom of the pot with your other hand to help the seedling out. Always hold the seedling by the first two leaves to avoid damaging the stem.
4. Plant the seedling in the hole at the same depth as it was growing in the pot. Fill in with soil to cover the roots. Gently tamp down the soil around the seedling so there's good contact between it and the roots.
5. Water the soil around new seedlings thoroughly after transplanting and continue watering regularly to keep the soil damp but not soaking wet.

DIRECT-SOWING SEEDS

Some plants (such as peas, beans, and nasturtiums) are too delicate to survive being transplanted when started indoors. Many others—sunflowers, pansies, zinnias, cosmos, to name a few—will happily germinate and grow from seeds sown directly in outdoor beds or containers. And because most people have far more space for planting out-of-doors than in, direct-sowing allows you to plant in far greater numbers.

Of course, many gardeners do a mix, starting some annuals indoors and sowing others in the ground.

When to direct-sow seeds

- Always wait until the ground has thawed in spring to begin planting seeds in the garden.
- Beyond that, the exact timing depends on whether you are sowing seeds for cool- or warm-season flowers and vegetables. This information will be included on the seed packet.
- If you are growing a vegetable garden, see page 300 for more details on when to plant different types.
- The idea of succession planting, in which you swap out cool-season vegetables with warm-season varieties and then go back to cool-season types over the growing season (see page 293).

How to direct-sow seeds

Just as when planting seedlings or annuals and perennials from a nursery, you'll want to put the right plant in the right place in terms of full sun versus shade—and ideally, you've already plotted this out in your garden designs.

The following guidance is for general know-how. Refer to the packet for specific instructions.

1. ***Plant at the right depth***
   - In general, the depth is three times the seed's diameter, and no deeper.
   - However, some seeds need more light to germinate and need only to be pressed into the soil surface.
   - Otherwise, poke individual holes for seeds with a chopstick (which can be premarked at ¼-, ½-, ¾-, and 1-inch intervals) or your finger, or you can create a furrow with a handheld trowel.
   - When sowing, gently press on the surface to ensure good contact between seed and soil.
2. ***Space correctly***
   - Plant in rows, usually about 12 to 18 inches apart (again, check the packet), which allows ample space for plants to grow and for you to tend to and harvest them.
   - Note packet guidelines for spacing between seeds, too.
   - Be sure to mark the rows with plant markers—this way you won't mistake a seedling for a weed.
3. ***Water in well***
   - Gently water new seeds in with a watering can to avoid disturbing the seeds.
   - Continue to water frequently to keep the soil moist until the seed germinates, using a drip irrigation or a soaker hose; or put a regular hose at ground level and let the water gently soak the planting area.
4. ***Cover with mulch***
   - Leave planted rows unmulched to allow sunlight to reach the seeds, but spread a 2- to 3-inch layer of mulch—straw or buckwheat hulls work best in vegetable gardens—over the rest of the beds to suppress weeds and help with water retention. Mulch also helps the soil warm up more quickly in cooler climates.
5. ***Don't forget to thin***
   - Thin seedlings as directed on the packet, generally when shoots are 2 inches.
   - Many gardeners skip this step, but thinning allows plants to have space to grow and avoid competing for nutrients.
6. ***Protect from pests***
   - Some pests love seedlings, as do birds, so you may need to use netting or row covers to protect them.
   - Use fencing to keep critters at bay, burying it a few feet underground (for burrowing animals).
   - Other ways to prevent pests include companion planting (see page 293) or natural remedies and applications (see page 275).
7. ***Support as needed***
   - Climbing plants and those with heavy fruit or flowers may need supports.
   - Use bamboo or wood stakes, trellises, tomato cages, or other methods as discussed on page 164.

Sowing Wildflower Seeds

Dreaming of a pollinator-friendly meadow outside your kitchen window? It couldn't be easier to create—just use a high-quality wildflower seed mix, available at many garden centers and online.

Look for mixes that are "100 percent perennials" with no fillers and that are appropriate for your region, including native-only mixes. What's great about mixes is they are designed to provide waves of season-long color, so you don't have to take the time and effort to research this yourself.

Make sure the mix includes lots of clump-forming grasses, which are a major component of most naturally occurring meadows and will crowd out weeds and help prevent soil erosion during the first critical season.

When to Sow

If planting in spring, do so as soon as the ground has thawed to give the seeds time to germinate before sprouting, usually in late spring or early summer, depending on the mix and your climate. Keep watering regularly until the sprouts are 4 to 6 inches tall.

Fall is an even better time because it means the seeds are already in the ground for spring germination; check the packet for specific timing, but fall planting is usually done two to four weeks after the last frost date. Keep the ground damp after sowing until the ground freezes and resume watering regularly in the spring, as above.

How to Sow

1. Clear a sunny spot (wildflowers need full sun) of sod and other vegetation, and amend as needed for texture (avoid fertilizing, which will encourage weeds).
2. Scatter the seeds evenly, following the coverage rate on the packet.
3. Compress seeds into the soil with the back of a shovel or by walking over them; never bury wildflower seeds.
4. Water well and continue watering regularly to keep the soil just damp.
5. Most mixes recommend thinning and also removing weeds, though it can be hard to tell the difference between a weed and a wildflower shoot, so you may want to focus on the weeds you know—or consult a plant identification app for guidance.
6. Allow the flowers to self-seed if you like before mowing the meadow at the end of fall.

How to Make a Seed "Bomb"

Wildflower seed "bombs" are easy to sow, saving you the usual time and effort of direct-sowing individual seeds—just toss and wait! As such, they also fit into a no-till garden since you don't need to loosen the soil before planting. The result is more naturalistic, too. Need more reasons to make them? They're a fun project for kids and a great gift for gardeners.

You can use this same method for edible and single-flower seeds.

1. Gather compost, natural air-drying clay (from a crafts store), seeds, and a tray. Mix five parts clay with one part compost and one part seeds (4 ounces will cover up to 500 feet) and roll into 1-inch balls. Spread more seeds on the tray and roll each ball in seeds.
2. Let dry in a dry egg carton or on waxed paper for a few days. Toss the seed bombs in an area that's free of grass or weeds after the last frost date and water regularly.

Growing from cuttings

With just a single cutting from a favorite plant, you can grow a brand-new identical plant to add to your collection. And unlike when propagating from seeds, the new plant will be identical to the parent plant, allowing you to keep unique characteristics, such as variegated foliage.

WHAT TO PROPAGATE

Plants grown from cuttings also tend to mature faster and flower sooner than when grown from seed. This method is effective for almost any plant that produces stems, including annuals, perennials, climbers, shrubs, and even trees.

WHEN TO PROPAGATE

Cut from healthy, established plants with no signs of distress or disease. Take cuttings early in the day when temperatures are cool and the stems are swollen with moisture.

- ***Herbaceous cuttings*** from non-woody plants can be taken anytime during their growing season and have a high success rate.

  These include tender herbs like verbena and mint; geraniums, coleus, begonias, petunias, and other annuals; and perennials such as salvia, catmint (*Nepeta*), and Agastache, as well as dahlias.

- ***Softwood cuttings*** are taken in late spring or early summer from tender new growth when the stems are soft enough to cut almost effortlessly but still crisp enough to snap when bent.

  These are the easiest and fastest to root and can be taken from deciduous shrubs—rosebushes, hydrangea, hibiscus (rose of Sharon), weigela, and ninebark—as well as evergreen shrubs like azaleas, and certain trees, such as willow, maple, ginkgo, elm, crab apple, linden, birch, sweet gum, and redbud.

- ***Semi-hardwood cuttings*** are usually taken from midsummer to early fall from partially mature wood, so the cutting includes both old and new growth. The wood should be firm and the leaves full size.

  This technique works well on broadleaf evergreens such as holly, boxwood, and rhododendrons; deciduous shrubs such as lilac; woody herbs such as lavender, rosemary, and thyme; and even some conifers.

- ***Hardwood cuttings*** are taken in late fall, winter, or early spring from fully dormant plants. The wood is firm and does not bend easily.

  Most often, this method is used for deciduous shrubs such as forsythia, dogwood, viburnum, spirea, and privet; it can be used as well for many evergreens.

SUPPLIES

It's important to root cuttings as soon as possible after they are clipped, so make sure you have all the necessary materials before you begin.

- ***Small pots*** or other containers; sterilize anything that you are reusing.
- ***A sterile soilless potting mix*** made from about two parts coconut coir to one part each composed pine bark, vermiculite, and perlite (the same medium as for propagating seeds; see page 117).
- ***A pencil or dowel*** for making a hole in the potting mix.
- ***Bypass secateurs*** (hand pruners) are the best tools for harvesting stems, though finer floral shears are better for cutting especially delicate stems. Start by thoroughly cleaning and sharpening the tool—clean cuts expose plants to less damage from disease, pests, and weather extremes.
- ***Rooting hormone powder***, found at garden supply stores and online, increases the chance of cuttings taking root and developing quickly with stronger roots. Decant a little pile into a shallow vessel for dipping, and discard any remaining rather than adding it back to the original container.
- ***Plant markers*** for keeping track of what's planted where.
- ***Large plastic bags***, clear plastic tubs or bins, or glass vessels for creating a greenhouse environment.

HOW TO ROOT FROM CUTTINGS

The methods used for propagating softwood, semi-hardwood, and hardwood cuttings differ slightly but follow the same basic steps outlined below. It's a good idea to take several cuttings at once, since it's likely that not all cuttings will yield growth.

1. Use sharp pruning shears to clip a 4- to 6-inch piece of stem that's growing near but not at the top of the plant (never cut the tip of the plant, since that is where it is still growing). Snip below a node, the area where new leaves form, leaving approximately three nodes on the top half of the stem.
2. Remove the lower leaves, but leave the top leaves for your plant to receive nutrients once it's replanted in soil. Remove any flowers or buds.
3. Moisten the bottom of each stem in water and then roll it around in the rooting hormone and tap the cutting lightly to remove any excess.
4. Use the pencil or dowel to make a hole in the potting mix; the hole should be larger than the cutting, so the rooting powder is not rubbed off.
5. Stick the cutting into the potting mix, and gently tamp the soil around it. You can root multiple cuttings in one pot, leaving 2 or 3 inches between them. (You will transfer them to larger pots as they grow.) Add a labeled plant marker.
   - If you are making a lot of hardwood cuttings, stick them 4 to 6 inches apart in a raised bed outside and cover with a floating row cover.
   - If using pots, place them in a protected location (like a cold frame or shed) where they get some light. Water sparingly during the winter and more frequently as the temperature rises. After the last frost date, move the pot to a shady spot.
6. Add just enough water to moisten the potting mix.
7. To maintain humidity and moisture, place the entire pot inside a plastic bag.
   - Inflate the bag to keep the sides away from the cuttings as much as possible. Leaves touching the bag are more prone to develop mold. Seal the top with a twist tie.
   - Alternatively, you can rest an upturned plastic bin or glass bell jar (or other clear container) over the plant.
8. Place the pot near a window with filtered sunlight.
   - Open the bag (or lift the container) weekly to add fresh air and to check the plants for mold and rooting.
   - The cuttings have rooted when you see sprouts and leaves. Once you notice new growth, open the bag (or remove the container) to reduce the humidity.
9. When rooting has taken place (about three weeks for herbaceous and softwood cuttings, up to six months for semi-hardwood and hardwood cuttings), separate the cuttings and transplant them to individual pots using a quality potting mix.
10. Plant the rooted cuttings outdoors as you would a young plant, watering them regularly.

Easy Propagating Method

Besides taking a softwood cutting and rooting it as described at left, you can try this streamlined method, called layering. Layering works well for azaleas and other woody shrubs.

1. Bend a long branch toward the base of the plant to the ground and then weight it down with a heavy rock or metal clip.
2. Continue to care for the plant as you normally would.
3. After several months, give the branch a tug to see if it has rooted into the ground. If it has, clip the stem connecting the branch to the main plant.
4. Allow the branch to grow in the soil for a bit to establish roots.
5. Carefully dig up the roots with some soil and transplant.

Dividing

This form of propagation offers instant gratification: In a matter of minutes, one plant becomes two or even more, depending on the size of the original. It is also often the best way to rejuvenate a mature perennial. And some plants require dividing every so often to thrive.

WHAT CAN BE DIVIDED

Generally speaking, all clump-forming herbaceous perennials can be divided, though knowing the kind of root system they have can help you determine how and when to divide the plants.

Here are some popular examples of each:

- ***Spreading root systems:*** bee balm (monarda), aster, purple coneflower (echinacea), tickweed (coreopsis)
- ***Climbing root systems:*** astilbe, hosta, daylily, and many grasses
- ***Rhizomes:*** iris (shown opposite), bugleweed, canna lily, and some ferns
- ***Tuberous roots:*** dahlias, daffodils (and other true bulbs), and gladioli (and other corms)

You can also divide shrubs such as spirea and Siberian dogwood that sucker, sending new shoots up from the ground around their periphery.

WHAT CAN'T BE DIVIDED

It's easier to list plants that resist dividing than those that do.

Common examples include:

- lavender, Russian sage, and other shrub-like perennials with single woody bases
- single-taproot plants like butterfly weed
- false indigo, baby's breath, lupine, clematis, and columbine

If you're unsure, ask someone at a trusted nursery or call your nearest cooperative extension for guidance.

WHEN TO DIVIDE

No matter why you're dividing, when you do it is critical and depends on the plant. In general, divide plants when they are dormant.

- For hardy perennials, grasses, and shrubs, this means early spring or in the fall.
- Perennials with fleshy roots such as peonies, Oriental poppy, and Siberian iris are best divided in the fall; cut back their foliage to better see what you are doing.
- In northern climates, spring division gives plants several months to reestablish themselves before facing the stress of winter. If you are dividing in the fall, be sure to do so four to six weeks before the ground freezes.
- In the South, where winters are mild and summer heat and drought are the greater threat, fall division is safer.
- Divide hardy bulbs in summer, after the foliage has yellowed and died back to the ground.

HOW TO DIVIDE

For best results, choose an overcast day to divide plants to shield them from direct sunlight. Avoid dividing on rainy days, when you risk compacting the soil. Scheduling division for when showers are forecasted in the coming days will help transplants settle into their new environment.

1. If the soil around the plant is dry, water it thoroughly the day before dividing, giving it 24 hours to absorb the moisture.
2. Using a spade or shovel, dig a circle outside the plant's drip line (the widest part of the foliage), then remove the soil with a shovel until you see the roots. Gently slide the shovel or a garden fork under the roots, and gently lift the plant out of the ground; shake to remove any loose dirt around the roots.
3. Each division should have healthy roots and three to five shoots. Some plants can be gently teased apart with your hands; otherwise, cut the parent plant through the roots with a sharp hori hori knife or other sturdy blade using a single, smooth motion.
4. Plant the divisions as soon as they're made. If you must wait, wrap them in damp newspaper and keep in a shady, dry spot for no longer than one or two days.

5. When transplanting the divisions, start with well-tended soil; dig a hole that's three times the size of the root ball and about as deep. Place the division in the hole so the top of the root ball is even with the surface, then backfill with soil. Gently tamp down around the plant to ensure the soil and root ball are in contact.
6. Water the plants thoroughly immediately after planting—or time planting before a rain shower—and continue to water regularly to keep the soil damp but not soaking wet.

Nurturing and Maintaining

A beautiful vista and a fresh harvest are justifiably rewarding, but the day-to-day care is also a joyful task. Ask any seasoned pro and their eyes will likely light up when touting the instant and ongoing gratification that comes with tending to and nurturing their plants, of being outside, connecting with the natural world, and enjoying some physical activity.

Maintenance works best when it is based on prevention. Fertilization is most effective at the beginning of a plant's season of active growth—often spring—as opposed to when it shows signs of malnutrition. And weeding is far easier when you keep up instead of catch up.

Carve out time on your calendar to devote to gardening tasks so you're less likely to overlook anything. Spread them out over the course of a week so you can enjoy the process rather than feel overwhelmed by it. And should you have to skip a day, you can more readily make up for lost time on the next.

Plus, the daily rounds you make in the garden can help nip a potential problem in the bud—before it becomes a more labor-intensive issue. Paying attention is a big part of having a green thumb.

Watering

▶ **Clearly, plants need water** to live. Understanding precisely the role water plays in a plant's life, and how plants take in and distribute water, will help you better appreciate how to do it right. For starters, water is absorbed by the roots and travels up through the stems to the leaves, carrying precious nutrients. The leaves need water, nutrients, and sunlight. Water also helps modulate the plant's temperature, keeping it cool in hotter months and regions.

Watering in new plants is important, but it doesn't stop there. An even more important kind of after-planting care is proper watering, year in and year out.

How much water plants need

While some varieties require more or less watering than others, the majority of plants need an inch of water per week—either from rainfall or by your own doing. Double that amount during dry, hot spells (when temperatures consistently remain above 90°F). Other factors include the following:

THE KIND OF PLANT

Drought-tolerant plants like succulents require less water to establish, grow, and thrive. Other plants described as not liking "wet feet" also get by with less water. For these plants, overwatering can lead to root and crown rot.

Annuals, which race to produce as many blooms as possible in just one season, need more water to help them flourish.

THE TYPE OF SOIL YOU HAVE

Water has a harder time penetrating dense clay soils than loamy soils and won't be retained as much by sandy soils.

THE PLANTING MEDIUM

Soil in containers dries out more quickly than when in the ground. The smaller the container, the more frequently you need to water the plant. Soak the soil in the morning, and, if the thermometer climbs to 90°F or above, soak it again in the afternoon.

Raised beds also retain less water than in-ground soil, so you will need to increase the water accordingly.

THE LOCAL CLIMATE

If you live in the Pacific Northwest or another area with consistent rainfall, you can often rely on the weather and supply water yourself only during the occasional dry spell.

On the other hand, gardeners in the Southwest will need to water more frequently (or stick with drought-tolerant plants).

Measuring—and Capturing—Rainfall

Rain is of course the most sustainable source of water for plant life. How can you tell how much your garden is getting?

It's easy to accurately measure the amount of rainfall by using an inexpensive rain gauge found at garden supply stores. The clear vessel is marked with inches, similar to a liquid measuring cup (which you can also use). An empty jar also works just fine.

- Choose a vessel that's at least 4 inches wide; anything narrower can be misleading.
- Set it out in a garden bed at the beginning of the season. Do not place it directly under the eave of a roof or dense tree canopies.
- Check the gauge after each rainfall (or over the course of a week or month, depending on where you live). Once you record the level, empty the vessel.
- Know that an inch of rainfall typically soaks 6 to 15 inches deep into the soil. However, runoff from short, heavy downpours may not all seep into the ground.
- Keep tabs on the amount of rainfall throughout the season to avoid overwatering. Besides being wasteful, too much water can be as damaging as too little because it can promote disease and compromise soil structure.

You can also collect surplus rainwater to use over time in rain barrels, which have a screen at the top to filter out leaves and other debris—meaning you can park the barrel under a roof to collect runoff. This is especially helpful in areas with higher precipitation, when it would be a shame to let the rainwater go to waste. (It also helps reduce stormwater runoff from carrying contaminants; see page 44.)

Look for a barrel with a spigot on the side that you can hook a hose to or use to fill a watering can; one with a tight-fitting lid can be covered between rainfalls to keep from attracting mosquitoes.

When to water

Watering in the morning when the soil is cool will allow the water to reach the roots before evaporating. It also helps the plant deal with the midday summer heat and allows time for the soil surface to dry out during the day.

Avoid watering at night as wet, cool conditions create a breeding ground for diseases to develop.

Periodic deep watering is much better than light daily dousing in promoting the development of vigorous roots. Avoid the temptation to dampen the soil whenever the surface is dry; with shallow watering, the roots never need to reach very far to slake their thirst. Conversely, by allowing the soil and roots to slightly dry out between waterings, soaking the area 6 to 12 inches deep, the plant's roots will reach into the reservoir of water below.

A good way to monitor the soil's moisture is to brush any mulch away from the surface, then poke your finger down about 2 inches—if it feels dry at that level, it's time to water.

Or you can follow a "cake tester" approach: Insert a wooden dowel or chopstick a few inches into the soil and then pull it out; moist soil will stick to the dowel, but if it comes out clean, it's time to water.

There are always exceptions to the rules:

- Newly planted trees and shrubs should be thoroughly soaked two or three times per week for the first month and then weekly thereafter during their first growing season.
- Established trees and shrubs that are at least two years old need to be watered only once every two weeks during dry spells.

OPPOSITE: At about five feet across, this Soderholtz pot holds a giant agave, a profusion of helichrysum, and some red-flowering echeveria.

Watering methods

Remember: The goal is to deliver water where it's needed most—the roots. Contrary to what you may think, spraying foliage that appears wilted is not going to rehydrate it. Instead, watering the roots is the right path to hydrating the entire plant. Damp foliage can also make the plant more prone to fungal disease. The following irrigation methods work best for garden beds.

DRIP IRRIGATION SYSTEMS

These are widely considered the most efficient in minimizing evaporation. Installing one of these networks of tubing and tiny nozzles ("emitters") takes planning and work, but it allows pinpoint precision in water application.

Originally developed to conserve water, drip irrigation, as the name suggests, drips water directly onto the soil above the plant roots, at a rate slow enough (if the system has been designed correctly) that none is lost as runoff.

It's said to reduce a garden's water use by as much as two-thirds, which makes it a necessity throughout much of the Southwest and other regions where water is scarce.

You can find customizable kits with drip lines that can be cut to the lengths you need. Position the opening near—but not at the base of—individual plants so the plants are watered without getting too wet.

Setting emitters right by the plants also discourages plants from extending their roots and foraging for nutrients.

SOAKER HOSE

It may look like a regular hose, but a soaker hose has hundreds of tiny pores along its length, making it more efficient; it's also (much) less involved than a drip irrigation system. Plus, the flexible hose can be woven between plants, including in raised beds, or wrapped around new trees or shrubs for steady watering.

REGULAR HOSE

You can lay a regular hose, without a nozzle, in a bed and turn it to low water pressure, moving the end of the hose as needed to soak each subsequent area.

Using a hose with the nozzle set to the soaker setting is another way to gently direct water to the base of plants, while the shower setting lets you cover larger spaces, such as when dampening a recently planted flower or vegetable bed (before the foliage emerges).

The mist setting is ideal for tropical plants that require higher humidity. (Reserve the jet setting for cleaning jobs, not the garden.)

WATERING WAND

This long-necked hose attachment is helpful for reaching into hanging baskets and offers more control when watering other container plants.

AUTOMATIC WATERING DEVICE

A spike, bulb, or other drip implement can be inserted in pots and raised beds for steady watering, especially if you are going on vacation.

You can also find self-watering pots with a reservoir that waters the soil from below; these are especially recommended for container gardening in hot, dry climates, or for plants that need consistently moist soil (like tomatoes or other annuals).

Tip

To keep a hose from kinking when it's new, stretch it along a path or the edge of the lawn and then loop the business end back to the tap.

BROADCAST SPRINKLERS

These offer convenience when watering large areas, an exception to the general rule of watering only the roots (do this early in the day when the foliage has ample time to dry in the sun).

For example, a rotating sprinkler attachment waters lots of potted plants on a patio and tripod sprinkler systems are commonly used in expansive orchards.

Never direct hard-spraying sprinklers at trees, as this may mar the bark. Instead, reserve harder sprays for open spaces and wide lawn areas and more gentle sprayers for flower and vegetable gardens.

Improving water retention

Water won't reach your plants if it evaporates or drains through the soil too quickly. Take simple steps to increase the soil's ability to hold water and thereby ensure your plants are always appropriately hydrated.

1. Apply a 2- to 3-inch layer of mulch on the surface of garden beds and around individual trees and shrubs (keeping it 3 to 4 inches from the trunk or base). This prevents water loss from evaporation, and also keeps weeds from setting in and competing with plants for water and the nutrients it carries.
2. Work compost and aged manure into the soil—it boosts the soil's ability to hold water like a sponge.
3. Mound up the soil around the planting hole into a low, circular dike to trap rainfall and irrigation water, holding it until it soaks in rather than just running off. Position it right over the perimeter of the plant's root ball.

Fertilizing

You need food and water to live a healthy, active life—and so do your plants. They require nutrients to flourish, but many native soils lack the proper ratio of essential nutrients optimal for growth. Plant food ensures the proper amount of nutrients and can help plants defend against environmental stresses.

Indeed, the success of most gardens can be attributed to zealous fertilizing and watering. Many gardeners are diligent about the latter but may not appreciate how the former can make the difference between a garden that is merely surviving and one that is absolutely thriving.

Begin by testing your soil as discussed on page 19—preferably by sending samples to your local cooperative extension, which can provide you with a soil-analysis kit, including forms to fill out and submit with samples. (Some nurseries also offer this service.)

This is the most accurate way to pinpoint the pH level and whether any vital nutrients are abundant or lacking. Experts might be able to tell whether, for example, shriveled, brown leaves in a rhododendron are a sign of nitrogen deficiency or alkaline soil; the same symptom in one plant can be indicative of something else in another.

For best results, use a clean trowel to dig several soil samples from the garden area to be tested, put them in a nonreactive (stainless steel or enameled) bowl, mix well with the trowel or a spoon, and place the mixed samples in a plastic bag.

Armed with this information, you can zero in on the proper amendment, saving time, effort, and money that would otherwise be wasted on ineffective fertilizers. Testing the soil each season, or every other year, will also ensure that established plants continue to receive the necessary nutrients.

Picking the right fertilizer

In addition to knowing your soil profile, you'll also want to familiarize yourself with fertilizer terminology.

Fertilizer is primarily made of three elements that are essential for plant growth and most likely to be deficient in soil: nitrogen (N), phosphorus (P), and potassium (K).

- ***Nitrogen*** is responsible for healthy foliage—shoots, stems, and leaves.
- ***Phosphorus*** encourages strong roots and flower or fruit development.
- ***Potassium*** improves disease resistance and overall plant health.

The numbers on a fertilizer package indicate the ratio of these three ingredients, NPK, in that order. A balanced fertilizer with a 10-10-10 ratio indicates an even amount (10 percent) of each chemical.

It's important to consider the ratio when selecting fertilizer because each element has a specific effect. For example, if you fertilize a tomato plant with a formula that encourages leaf and stem growth, you'll have big plants but few tomatoes.

Synthetic vs. Organic Fertilizers

Synthetic (or man-made) fertilizers are manufactured formulas that include the essential NPK chemicals and additional elements. The water-soluble formulas are known for being fast-acting because they can be taken up by plants almost immediately.

However, that quick boost doesn't last; you must reapply synthetic fertilizers regularly to keep the results from fading. What's more, these fertilizers do little to improve soil texture or fertility. The rapid results also come at a cost; apply too much and it may burn your plants. And being highly water soluble means they readily leach from gardens into waterways, causing harm to aquatic wildlife and animals that feed on them.

Organic fertilizers such as compost, aged manure, worm castings, kelp, lobster shells, bone meal, and fish meal are made from plant and animal products and contain a more complex variety of nutrients than the pure elements found in synthetic products. The carbon-based products also break down in a garden or lawn more slowly and don't leach as easily into waterways.

Importantly, even when labeled for specific plants (such as the extensive Espoma product line), organically derived fertilizers target the entire soil and promote a healthy soil ecosystem. They do this by stimulating beneficial soil microorganisms, which play a key role in converting the organic matter into soluble nutrients that can be absorbed by plants at a rate they can use, with much less risk of plant burn.

Mined from deposits, rock powders—greensand, limestone, rock dust, and rock phosphate—are another natural source of essential minerals. Use a rolling lawn spreader to apply them evenly, working them into the soil with a garden fork in spring—or, in fall, letting them be absorbed gradually over the winter.

Organic fertilizers won't produce the instant gratification of synthetic fertilizers, but the reward is sturdier plants that are naturally resistant to pests and diseases and better able to cope with drought. Over time, you will also have more productive fruit and flower production. And they require fewer applications than synthetic fertilizers, making up for their higher cost.

When in doubt, ask the staff at your local nursery (or call your cooperative extension) for recommendations based on your soil tests, which will generally include suggested NPK ratios in the report. Don't worry if you can't find the exact ratio; just select a product with a ratio that most closely matches, paying particular attention to the nitrogen percentage, since too much nitrogen can be detrimental for certain plants.

Some fertilizer formulas contain additional ingredients such as calcium or magnesium for specific plants or soil deficiencies. You'll find fertilizers designed for bulbs, annual flowers, azaleas and rhododendrons, roses, tomatoes, citrus trees, and many others. Or you can stick with an "all-purpose" fertilizer (often called "plant food") or a liquid fish emulsion and avoid having to stockpile multiple products.

When to fertilize

Many plants, including perennials, trees, and shrubs, don't need much fertilizer, especially if you add plenty of compost or other organic material to their soil before planting and as a top dressing around established plants in the spring to help ramp up their growth—and again before winter sets in.

- Follow a twice-yearly schedule: once in the spring or early summer to give your plants a boost to get started and then again in the fall as part of continual soil-building.
- Heavy feeders, including fast-growing and prolific bloomers—flowering and vegetable annuals, roses, dahlias, azaleas, rhododendrons, and hydrangeas—benefit from an additional once-a-month application when they are flowering or fruiting.
- All container plants need monthly fertilizing, too, since more frequent watering causes the plants to quickly deplete the nutrients in the potting mix, and there's less soil for them to feed on to begin with.
- Once plant growth slows in late summer and fall, stop fertilizing to allow the plants to prepare for dormancy. Fertilizing late in the season may encourage unnecessary tender new growth that will be susceptible to damage by autumn cold snaps and to further damage by pests. You can, however, top-dress with compost or rotted manure during winter, followed by a layer of mulch.
- Note that when certain conditions prevent roots from absorbing the necessary nutrients from the soil, foliar applications (applying fertilizer to the leaves) can be an alternative. Those conditions include when the soil has a high or low pH, or is either overly sandy and dry or dense and waterlogged. Approach foliar feeding with care—the practice is not as rooted in science as soil applications.
- Plants with pale-green or yellowish-green leaves or overall poor growth are often in need of nitrogen; poor flowering and a tendency to wilt on hot, sunny days is common in potassium-deficient plants, which can appear withered or drooping.
- While poor flowering can be a sign of potassium deficiency, plants that cease producing new leaves may need more phosphorus.

DIY Fertilizers

While some gardeners opt to feed their plants man-made fertilizers, it's easy to use natural options to make your own at home.

Grass Clippings

Freshly mown lawn clippings contain nutrients that are beneficial to other plants. Spread them in your garden beds. You can then either till them into the soil for faster decomposing, or leave them in a ¼-inch layer on top and allow them to gradually release their nutrients with watering—and act as a mulch layer to lock in moisture and prevent weeds.

Tree Leaves

Like grass clippings, tree leaves are a great way to add organic matter to soil for texture and nutrients; leave them in a layer on top, similar to mulch, and they'll break down over time.

Eggshells

Crushed eggshells are a rich source of calcium, which helps plants build strong cell walls and promotes healthy growth. They also provide trace amounts of other essential nutrients. Before using, let them dry in the sun to kill any pathogens.

Coffee Grounds

Coffee grounds contain several key nutrients needed by plants, particularly nitrogen, so save them after your daily brew. The best way to put them to use is in your compost bin, but you can also apply them directly to your soil in moderation. First, dry the grounds in the sun to make them safe for plants, then gently work them into the soil around the plants. Use the grounds in moderation, as they can form a barrier that prevents water and air from reaching plant roots.

Food Scraps

Banana peels, citrus rinds, and other fruit or vegetable scraps feed the good bacteria in your soil. After drying them out—or boiling them in water—to remove any harmful pathogens, crush the scraps and sprinkle them on the soil surrounding the plants.

Compost Tea

Compost tea is made by steeping compost in clean water to extract its nutrients and microorganisms; these beneficial microorganisms flourish and multiply in the liquid, making compost tea much stronger than regular compost. Plus, you can direct the concentrated liquid at the roots, for a more immediate application—and to encourage the roots to grow bigger and stronger. It's also a natural way to ward off diseases and pests.

To make compost tea: Put 1½ cups of finished compost into a mesh bag and put the bag into a 5-gallon bucket. Fill the bucket with a gallon of unchlorinated water. Place the bucket in a cool, dark place. Stir the mixture every day for one week.

To apply compost tea: Pour the liquid into the soil around the base of a plant to send the nutrients right to the roots, which will help increase plant growth. Or spray onto the leaves as a foliar feed to help suppress diseases and pests.

How to fertilize

Carefully follow the feeding instructions on the package in terms of dosage, application method, and frequency of use. The label should tell you the amount to use per 1,000 square feet of garden area (such as when creating a new bed) as well as for individual plants.

Whenever you are handling fertilizers, wear gardening gloves, and avoid applying granules or spraying a foliar application on a windy day, when the fertilizer can blow back in your eyes (and onto other plants).

If for whatever reason you aren't sure how much fertilizer to use, err on the side of caution—there's little harm that can come from underfertilizing, while overdoing it can make it harder for the plant's roots to soak up water and also cause leaves to turn yellow or brown. Try diluting a liquid or granular fertilizer to about half or even one-quarter of the recommended strength the label recommends. This is a good way to feed container plants—water them regularly with diluted fertilizer rather than giving them the full dosage on a less-frequent basis.

GRANULAR FERTILIZERS

Applying granular fertilizers just before a good rain helps work the fertilizer down into the soil where roots can access it, though a thorough soaking with a hose or watering can is the next best thing.

- When planting flowers, bulbs, or shrubs, sprinkle granulated fertilizer into the bottom of the dug hole and mix that into the soil before placing the plant in the hole.
- In early spring, broadcast the granules as a "starter" fertilizer over the soil of each garden bed, then work it into the top inch or so of soil with your hands or a cultivator. If feeding a large bed, you can use a bedding rake to gently mix it into the soil.
- Over the course of the growing season, side-dress the fertilizer alongside rows or by sprinkling it in a ring around plants at their drip line.

LIQUID FERTILIZERS

These water-soluble fertilizers are intended to be mixed into the water you use for irrigation and then either applied to the soil around the base of plants or sprayed onto the leaves and stems as a foliar feed.

- Never apply liquid fertilizer to the soil in the dug hole when planting, as this risks potentially causing root burn and eventual dieback. You may also want to wait at least a month after planting before fertilizing with liquid fertilizers to allow time for the plants to recover from any root damage. In fact, many gardeners reserve liquid fertilizer for intermittent feeding of heavy feeders during their growing season.
- Applying liquid fertilizer to dry soil can also lead to root burn, so always soak the soil with plain water first. Follow the instructions for proper dilution to avoid burning the leaves.

- Spray foliar applications every two to four weeks until the plant improves—and if it doesn't, stop applying and seek expert guidance.
- As with regular watering, the best time to apply liquid sprays is early morning, when the leaves will have time to absorb the material and dry throughout the day. Avoid spraying before rain, which will merely wash it away, or on extremely hot days when foliage is subject to burning.

Storing fertilizers

Fertilizers can be costly, and because you only need to use small amounts, you often end up with opened bags and excess product. Store them properly so you can use them next season.

STERILIZED POTTING SOIL

Most potting soils contain fertilizer, and generally speaking, potting soil can last for more than two years; however, these bags are typically targeted to specific uses, which dictates how successful they are over an extended period of time. For example, it's best to use a fresh bag when working with annuals.

Store potting soil in a sterilized plastic bin with a tight-fitting lid that will keep it dry and prevent mold or mildew from developing.

You can even reuse potting soil from one year to the next. After removing the plants from the pots, add an appropriate granulated fertilizer according to the amount specified on the package. If the soil feels dense or compacted, you may also want to amend it with a bit of perlite for proper drainage.

GRANULAR FERTILIZER

While fertilizer doesn't technically expire, granular fertilizer will remain at full strength for a year if stored in an airtight bag or in a container in your garage. If a bag isn't open, it will last several years—but check the label for specific product recommendations. Buying new granular fertilizer, however, is ultimately best for you and your garden: The longer the fertilizer sits unused, the more likely it is to become damp and clumpy, which could make it hard to spread.

LIQUID FERTILIZER

Excess liquid fertilizer can be kept in a cool, dry place over the winter. When stored properly, liquid fertilizer has a minimum shelf life of three to four years—but will often last much longer.

If you've had your liquid fertilizer for a few years, though, keep a close eye on your plants: if they are showing signs of nutrient deficiencies or excesses, it might be time for a replacement.

Controlling weeds

➤ **Weeds in the garden** are inevitable—and invasive, growing wherever they can: in garden beds, lawns, gravel pathways, stone patios, and practically any other outdoor location. Left alone, many of them quickly overtake healthy flowers, plants, and vegetables, stealing their sunlight, water, and soil nutrients. Weeds can also invite more pests and dangerous plant diseases into your garden. Eliminate weeds when you spot them to avoid these outcomes.

There are many ways to prevent or remove weeds—including the traditional method of yanking them out by their roots. But keep in mind that some weeds are worth leaving because they are valuable food sources for pollinators and wildlife, in many cases flowering before your cultivated plants have bloomed. Allowing an area of your grass to "go to weed" also serves this purpose and provides a helpful habitat.

Weed killers

Remember, anything you use in your garden seeps into your soil and will affect the groundwater and water running through the storm drains. As with fertilizers, if you are growing your own vegetables, you also want to make sure no harmful chemicals come near them. The same goes for avoiding chemicals that can harm wildlife.

WHITE VINEGAR

Vinegar (like a commercial herbicide) is nonselective and will kill all plants it comes into contact with. Spray only on dry, sunny days when there's no risk of rain carrying the solution. If it's cloudy or the leaves are wet, wait. The sunlight will work with the vinegar to burn the leaves. Never spray when it's windy. You'll risk having the mixture blow onto yourself and other plants.

Vinegar works best on smaller, shallow-rooted weeds rather than those with deep roots like crabgrass. For that, you could try using commercial-grade vinegar with a much higher acidity (at least 20 percent), but that application requires extreme precision and can be even more caustic in terms of irritation to humans and wildlife than chemical herbicides. Use with caution—wear eye and hand protection and avoid the sprayed area for a day after application. It is also harmful if swallowed, so be sure to keep it out of reach of children and pets.

VINEGAR SOLUTION

This tried-and-true formula makes use of household supplies: To a gallon jug of distilled white vinegar, add 1 cup coarse salt and 1 tablespoon dishwashing soap; shake until combined. Pour into a spray bottle and spray directly onto weeds, thoroughly saturating the soil around them. Repeat every few days until weeds die.

BOILING WATER

Drenching weeds with boiling water is among the oldest tricks in the book, and it still works on younger, more tender weeds—especially those growing between pavers or in gravel. Be sure to add enough water so it seeps down into the roots; repeat as needed.

PROPANE TORCH

Long-handled torches made specifically for weeds range in price but work the same: You wave the flame end (which can reach 2,000°F) over exposed weeds until they burn away. Flame weeding can eradicate many annual weeds for good, which is why many farmers rely on this method.

PET-FRIENDLY ORGANIC PRODUCTS

You can buy solutions that are safe for your pets at garden supply stores and online. Brands such as Dr. Earth and Mighty Mint replace the usual glyphosate herbicide with all manner of active organic ingredients, such as citric acid, essential oils, spices, and corn gluten. Some products, such as those by A.D.I.O.S., EcoSMART, and Espoma, offer selective control of common broadleaf weeds (like dandelion and clover) and can be used on lawns.

SUPPRESSION

For weeds that don't respond to any of the above (such as Japanese knotweed and field bindweed), your best bet is to cut them back to the ground, dispose of the cuttings (or burn them), and then cover the roots with flattened cardboard or a tarp to deprive them of sunlight, usually for two or three months. Continually and immediately yank out any shoots that emerge around the covering.

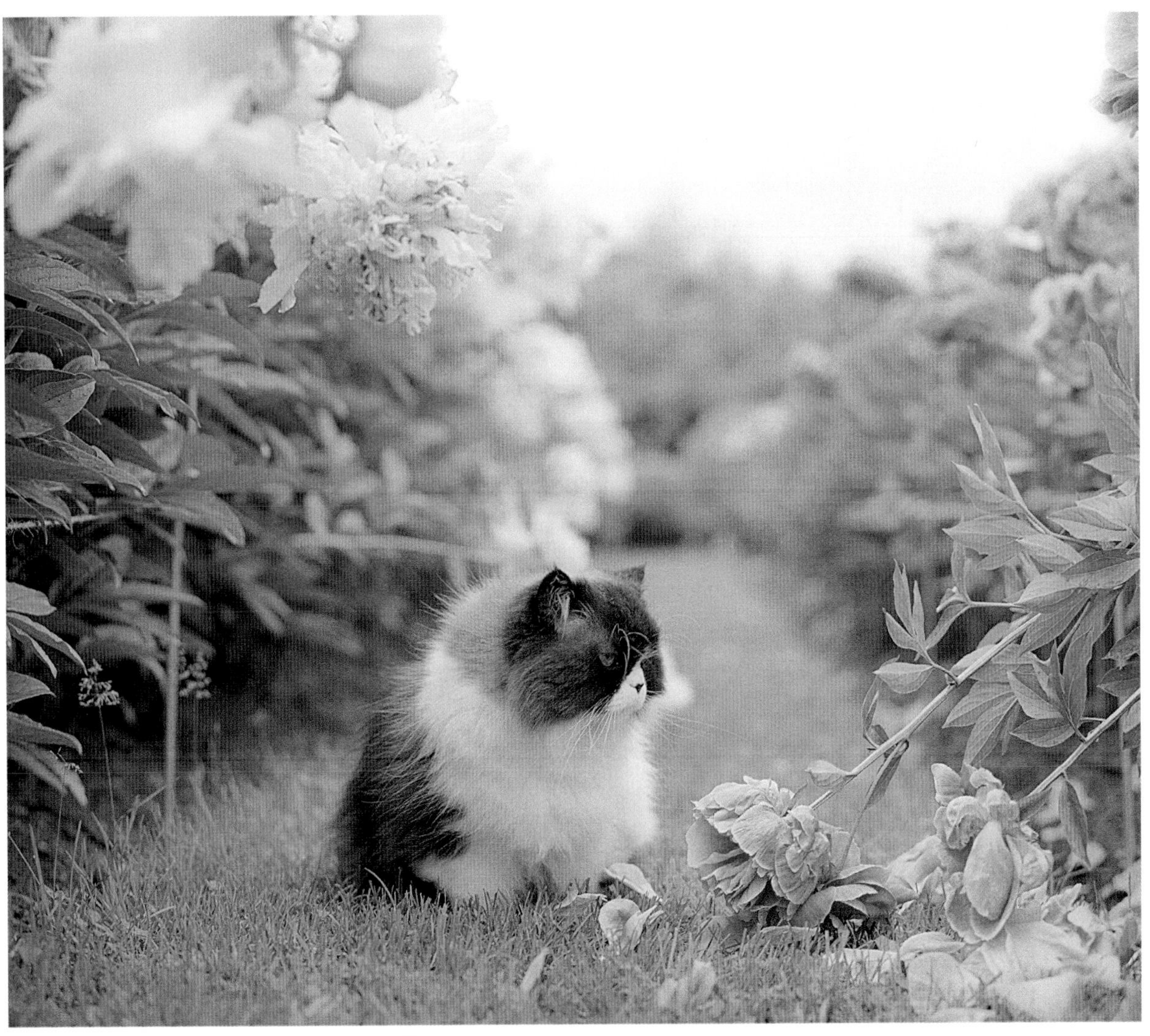

Long-term weed management

Rather than settling on one method, establish a multifaceted weed control system based on a combination of manual pulling, organic herbicides, mulching, and ground covers.

MULCH

Following the "ounce of prevention" philosophy, keeping weeds from setting in is going to save you so much work in the long run. Mulching garden beds and around individual trees and shrubs is the single best method to stop weeds from overtaking your garden year in and year out.

- First, remove any existing weeds (there's just no getting around that), and then apply 2 to 3 inches of mulch to garden beds at the beginning of the growing season and at the end, before winter sets in. You may also want to spread an initial 2-inch layer of compost or aged manure for extra soil conditioning and weed control before topping that with mulch.
- Choose materials that not only suppress weeds but insulate the soil and lend nutrients as the mulch breaks down over time. Dried grass clippings, shredded leaves, pine needles (for acid-loving plants), and wood chips or sawdust are all good options for flower gardens, while straw and buckwheat hulls work well in vegetable gardens. Avoid hay, as it contains countless weed seeds, and commercial wood bark that has been treated with artificial dyes, fungicides, and other chemicals.
- Despite all your best efforts, you may still see weeds poking through at some point, so pull those immediately to keep them from multiplying.

Ground covers

For an attractive alternative to mulch, consider using weed-suppressing plants—aka green mulch. The following options form a thick carpet that prevents harmful weeds from wreaking havoc. Ask your local nursery for other recommendations, especially native ground covers for your area.

1. *Hedera helix* 'Goldchild'
2. *Sedum pallidum* var. *bithynicum*
3. *Viola labradorica*
4. *Sedum oreganum*
5. *Lysimachia nummularia* 'Aurea'
6. *Sedum spathulifolium* 'Carnea'
7. *Soleirolia soleirolii* 'Aurea'
8. *Ajuga reptans* 'Burgundy Glow'
9. *Echeveria* 'Lola'

1
2
3
4
5
6
7
8
9

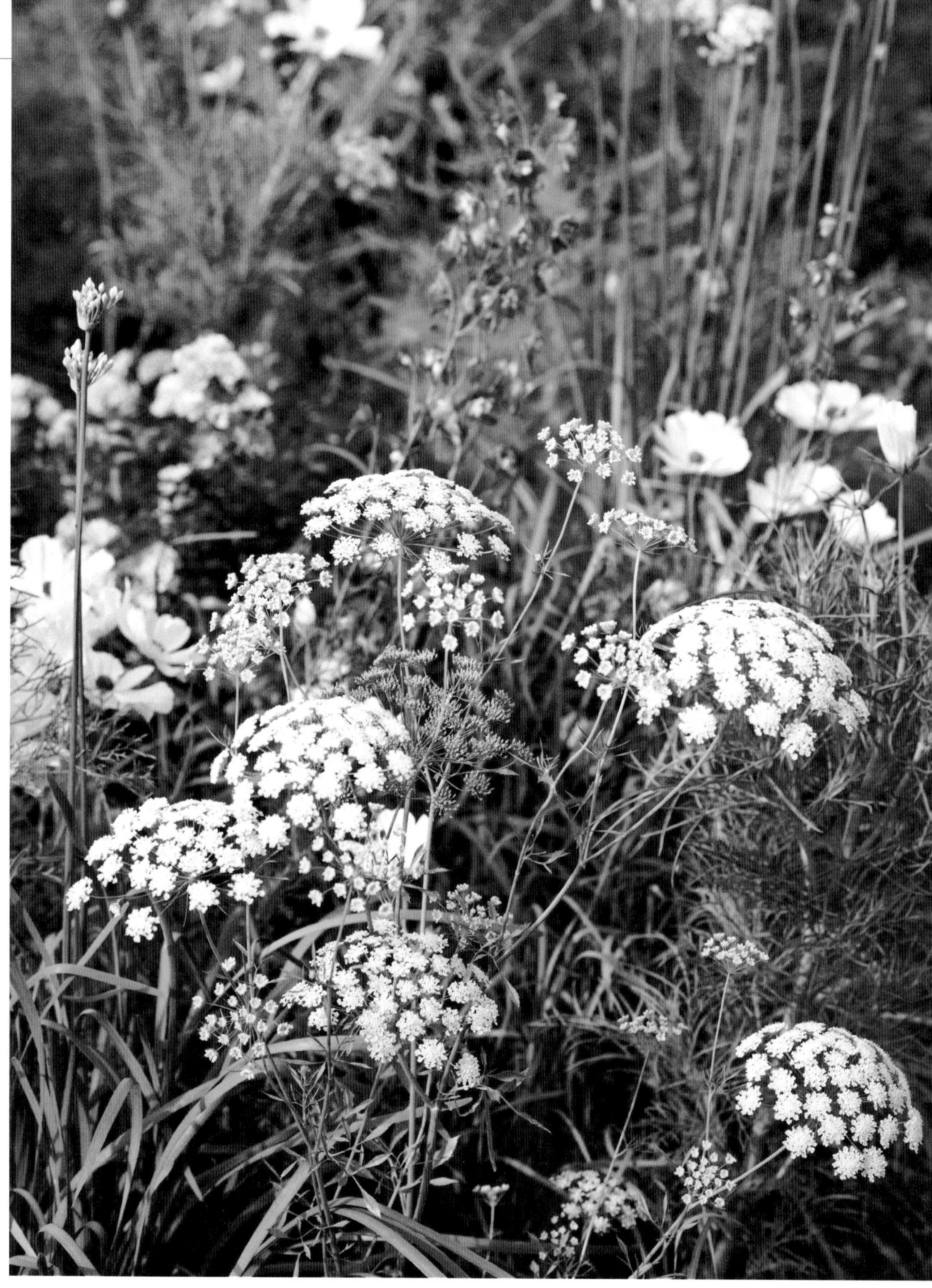

Weeds worth keeping

Weeds can benefit the ecosystem of your yard:

- They are fast growing and quickly cover bare ground to protect it from eroding in the wind or rain.
- They flower frequently and often have dense foliage, which attracts beneficial insects looking for habitat or nectar—and thereby fend off harmful pests.
- Their decaying roots (especially deep taproots) enrich the soil with organic matter and provide channels for air and water as well as worms and beneficial microbes to penetrate.
- Some weeds are even edible or have medicinal properties.

Of course, you don't want weeds to overtake your garden plants, but when quarantined to a corner of your yard—say, where not even grass will grow without chemical fertilizers—or closely monitored, they can be an intentional part of your overall plan.

Here are just a handful of weeds that you may want to leave alone. Allow them to die back on their own or cut (or mow) them after their blooming period, leaving the roots intact—the plant will either regrow, or the roots will decay, enriching the soil.

- ***Dandelion*** is one of the most common and beneficial of all weeds, providing potassium, calcium, and other nutrients to your soil and attracting ladybugs and other beneficial insects. Bees and other pollinators adore dandelion nectar. The leaves, roots, and flowers are all edible and have medicinal properties (such as when enjoyed as dandelion tea). Dandelion will benefit the soil if left to grow and die back on its own.
- ***Chickweed***, which usually shows up in highly tilled soil, has edible, lettuce-like greens. Not only does this weed provide nutrients, such as potassium and phosphorus, to the soil, but it also attracts pollinators in spring and early summer.
- ***White clover*** appears when your soil has low levels of nitrogen, frequently in dry fields and lawns with claylike soil. Besides helping raise the level of nitrogen, it attracts ladybugs and pollinators your lawn may desperately need. Clover is also a great weed to grow if you raise chickens or are feeding wild geese and other birds.
- ***Queen Anne's lace***, typically discovered by the roadside or in meadows and gardens, is a favorite of butterflies. People also find the delicate white blossoms lovely to behold.
- ***Stinging nettle*** does in fact sting if you brush up against it, but it draws insects beneficial to your lawn and ensures your soil is kept moist. Properly cooked, stinging nettle loses its bite and is considered a delicacy. It is also prized for its medicinal qualities in treating a range of issues.

Tip

Not cutting weeds back will make them available to beneficial insects and also pollinators, which is the thinking behind movements such as "No Mow May," in which you are encouraged to let dandelions and other weeds grow in spring, when other food sources for pollinators are in scarce supply.

Preventing disease

Even carefully maintained gardens can become susceptible to plant diseases. Most are nothing too worrisome and can be avoided or mitigated with proper care. Other diseases can be more detrimental; for those, the key is to avoid them altogether.

Knowing what to look for will help you eradicate common plant diseases before they take hold and cause irreparable damage. To do so effectively, you first need to be able to spot the symptoms and then know how to tackle the root causes.

How to protect plants

Observing a few preventive guidelines will help keep your garden disease-free—and spare you the time-consuming (and disheartening) task of tending to struggling plants. This is equally true for a vegetable garden, especially for leafy plants (such as beets) whose foliage is susceptible to disease from being too wet or crowded.

SELECT DISEASE-RESISTANT VARIETIES

While you can't fill your entire garden with these kinds of plants, including them is an easy way to minimize risk. Interspersing disease-resistant plants among plants that are susceptible serves as a protective barrier, too. (See Disease-Resistant Plants, page 156, for more information.)

PLANT AT THE RECOMMENDED SPACING

A plant with crowded roots will struggle to find the nutrients and moisture it needs, and that is likely to stunt the plant and compromise its ability to fend off disease.

ALLOW FOR AIR CIRCULATION

An easy flow of air around a plant offers natural protection against disease by keeping the foliage dry; continuous moisture provides a perfect breeding ground for fungal and bacterial pathogens. Good air circulation also enhances disease resistance by blowing away fungal spores. Improve air circulation by using permeable barriers such as hedges or louvered fencing for enclosure.

DON'T WET THE FOLIAGE WHEN YOU WATER

Wet leaves promote disease. Water disease-prone plants with a soaker hose or a drip irrigation system.

PROVIDE FOR GOOD DRAINAGE

Soil that remains persistently wet encourages root and crown rot in all except wetland plants, and cold penetrates into such soil more deeply in wintertime, increasing the risk of frost damage. Good drainage is crucial to plant health; guarantee it on low-lying sites by constructing raised beds.

PROPERLY CARE FOR DISEASE-PRONE PLANTS

Regularly treat healthy leaves with a homemade fungicide made by combining 1 teaspoon of baking soda and 1 teaspoon of dish soap in a quart of water.

DESTROY DISEASED PLANT MATTER

Do not allow infected foliage or entire plants to remain and possibly infect neighboring plants; remove these as soon as possible and burn or otherwise destroy them. Never add diseased plants to your compost pile. Remember to sterilize your tools—even more important after working with diseased plants.

Disease-Resistant Plants

As a first line of defense, consider incorporating these 10 varieties—each one cultivated to withstand common plant diseases—into your garden.

1. **Largeleaf phlox:** This native plant is resistant to powdery mildew, a fungal disease that affects many flowers. It produces underground runners that slowly spread to form a large mass, with early-summer blooms that last for about six weeks.
   ZONES: 3 TO 8

2. **Garden phlox:** Certain varieties of garden phlox, an herbacious perennial that's native to the eastern US, have been cultivated to be mildew-free. One example is 'Jeana', whose small flowers are prized by butterflies.
   ZONES: 3 TO 8

3. **Wild pansy:** A favorite filler for containers, wild pansy is also commonly used as a winter cover crop. The flowers often have a dark upper petal and two lower petals with spotted or two-toned colors. It is generally resistant to rot and fungal disease, though botrytis can set in when the roots get too wet.
   ZONES: 3 TO 8

4. **Mountain gordlinia:** A fast-growing hybrid tree with large, camellia-like flowers, this is more resistant to phytophthora (root rot) and is also more cold-hardy than its Southeast native parents.
   ZONES: 7 TO 9

5. **Profusion zinnias:** Zinnias are prized for being a summer flowering annual with a long bloom period—and they draw scores of pollinators. When choosing a variety, opt for disease-resistant *Zinnia elegans* 'Profusion', a hybrid with medium-size, self-cleaning, colorful blooms—no deadheading required.
   ZONES: 2 TO 11

6. **'Fuji Waterfall' hydrangea:** A type of lacecap hydrangea, defined by their lacy blossoms, *Hydrangea serrata* 'Fuji Waterfall' is known for being highly resistant to powdery mildew. Its name refers to the way the flower clusters cascade over the dark green foliage.
   ZONES: 5 TO 9

7. **Itoh peony:** When planted correctly, many peonies have minimal problems with disease. The new class of peonies, however, which are a cross between tree peonies and garden peonies, are particularly resistant.
   ZONES: 3 TO 8

8. **Kousa dogwood:** Unlike native flowering dogwoods, *Cornus kousa* is more resistant to powdery mildew and other diseases. It's also smaller and later blooming, with colorful foliage and berries in fall, and attractive mottled bark in winter.
   ZONES: 5 TO 8

9. **'Dandy Man Color Wheel' rhododendron:** With its leathery leaves and ruffled flowers, *Rhododendrum* 'NCRX1' looks like other types of the favorite evergreen but boasts greater resistance to dieback from phytophthora; it is also more heat tolerant.
   ZONES: 5 TO 8

10. **Purple coneflower:** *Echinacea purpurea* (at right) is heat, drought, and disease resistant; it also attracts bees and butterflies. Two especially hardy varieties are 'PowWow Wild Berry' and 'PowWow White', which emerge in spring with brilliant pink or white daisylike flowers.
    ZONES: 3 TO 9

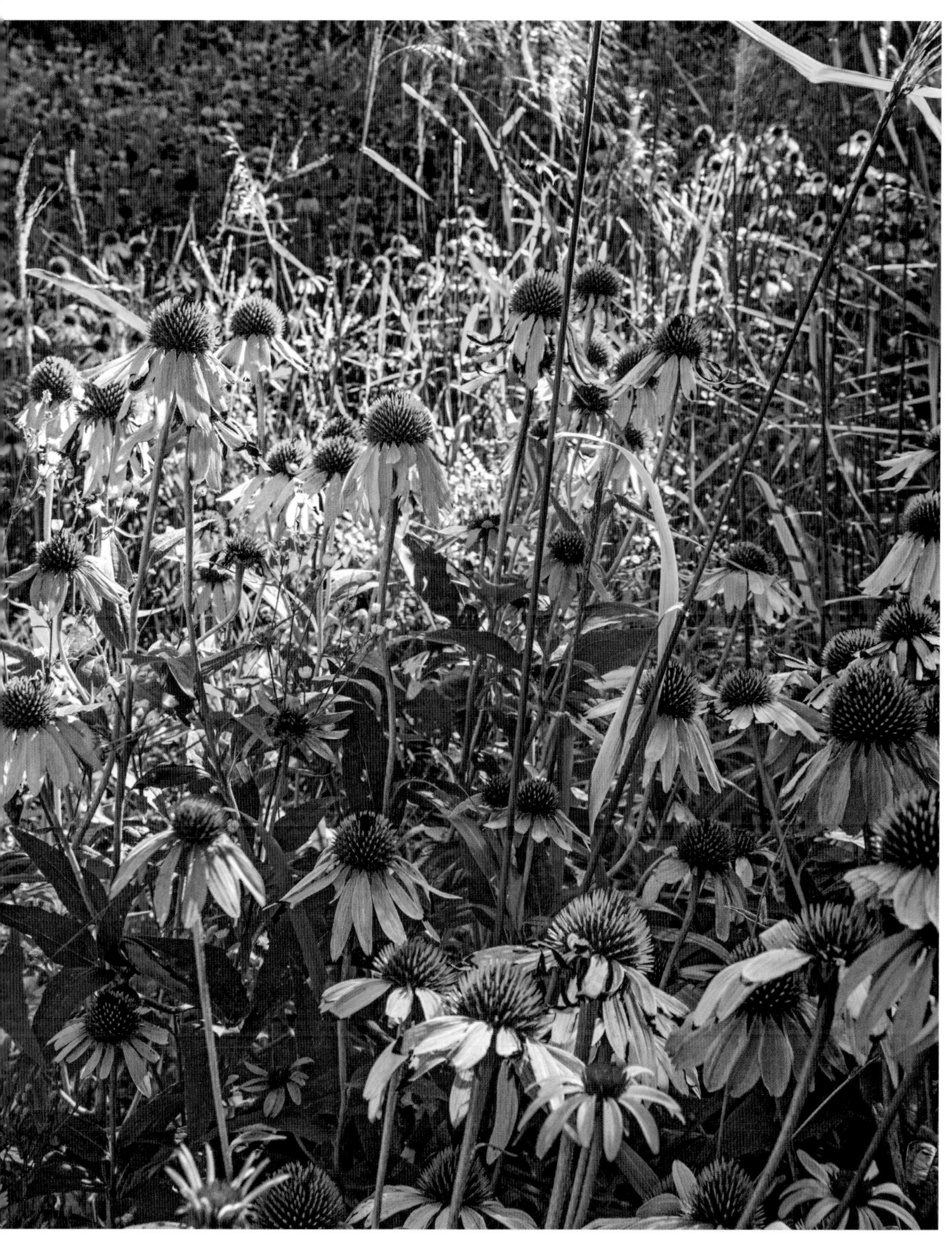

How to spot common diseases

Most plant diseases are caused by bacteria, fungi, or viruses and spread by insects, water, wind, and hands or gardening tools. Generally, for a plant disease to occur, disease-causing bacteria, fungi, or viruses must find a vulnerable host, such as a stressed plant, which is why keeping plants healthy is your first line of defense. Catching problems early is also important. Here's what to look for—and how to treat the culprits.

	SYMPTOMS	SOLUTION
Powdery Mildew	The presence of a white dusty coating on leaves usually signals powdery mildew, a fungal condition that impacts a wide range of plants, including lilacs and roses, phlox and daisies, and edibles such as cucumbers and peas. It usually sets in during hot, humid spells, especially when foliage is not able to dry before evening. Avoid watering after midmorning and give plants good drainage and ample air circulation.	Rake up fallen infected leaves from the ground to reduce the spread of spores. Targeted fungicides are available, but for an organic solution, spray the plant's foliage with a solution of 1 teaspoon baking soda, 1 drop liquid dish soap, and 1 quart water, repeating every morning or so until the mildew is eradicated.
Downy Mildew	When a plant is infected with this disease, the upper portion of leaves will become discolored, while the bottoms develop a fuzzy white or grayish mold. It's caused by fungus-like organisms that attack many flowering and vegetable annuals. Similar to powdery mildew, this condition often occurs during wet weather or in continually moist environments.	No fungicides are available, so your best bet is to remove and destroy infected foliage, or entire plants if the situation is severe. Avoid crowding plants or watering them in the evening, and rotate edibles year to year. Pruning the lower leaves to increase air circulation also helps.
Botrytis Blight	Also known as gray mold, botrytis affects the flowers, leaves, and bulbs of many annuals and perennial flowering plants, notably begonias, dahlias, lilies, peonies, and roses. Infected plants will sport brown spots on their leaves, stems, and flowers; these parts may also be covered with a gray mold after cool, damp periods, which is why botrytis is often confused with powdery mildew or downy mildew.	Instead of using chemical fungicides (although they are available), be diligent about sanitation in controlling the fungi, which overwinter on dead plant debris in the garden; come spring, spores form and spread by wind or water. Clear the garden of decayed matter in the fall and throughout the growing season, since the fungi can invade tissue during all periods of the growing season and multiplies rapidly in declining foliage.
Black Spot	This fungal disease typically arises in cool, damp weather as small black spots on leaves, which then turn yellow and drop off. It's most common on roses, though it can occur on other flowering shrubs and fruiting plants, weakening their immune systems and making them prone to developing other problems.	Black spot fungicides are available, but a better course of action is to remove and destroy infected leaves and canes and keep the foliage dry by watering at the roots. Planting disease-resistant roses, preferably where they receive full morning sun to allow the water to evaporate after watering, is the safest way to avoid the disease.

	SYMPTOMS	SOLUTION
Mosaic Virus	Plants with this disease, which most often strikes in hot, dry periods, have mottled (mosaic) yellow-and-green patterns on the infected leaves, which may also be curled or otherwise distorted. Depending on the strain, mosaic virus infects edibles, particularly tomatoes and other nightshades, and certain fruit trees, such as apple, pear, and cherry. Peonies are also likely victims.	Plants that exhibit signs should be destroyed to prevent spread of the incurable disease, as no chemical treatment exists. Because the fungus can reside in dry soil even after the host plant is removed, you should avoid planting susceptible plants in the same spot for at least two years. Rotating crops is a good way to prevent mosaic virus from taking hold in the first place.
Verticillium Wilt	Verticillium wilt affects hundreds of species of flowers, vegetables, trees, and shrubs, causing branches to wilt suddenly and foliage to turn yellow and fall off prematurely. The fungal disease thrives in hot, dry weather when growing plants need frequent watering.	The pathogens resist any treatment, so proper sanitation is required to prevent their spread. Remove and destroy infected annuals, perennials, and edibles. Prune diseased branches off trees and shrubs. Sterilize cutting tools thoroughly between cuts and after pruning. Improving drainage and weeding regularly helps with prevention.
Rust	Indications of this fungal disease start as reddish-orange or brown spots on leaves that gradually turn black. Each rust fungus attacks a specific host plant, such as roses, daylilies, coral bells, tomato plants, and apple trees—and even grass.	Fungicides are available, though rust is usually just unsightly rather than life-threatening to plants. To limit further spread, remove and destroy any infected plants, especially before putting your garden to bed for the winter.
Root Rot	Root rot can mirror pest infestation in terms of symptoms, making proper diagnosis more difficult. It typically attacks perennials, trees, and shrubs in poorly drained or overwatered soils. Container plants are especially prone to root rot. Short of digging down into the roots (and potentially causing further harm to the plant), you can often identify root rot by noticing what's happening aboveground—namely, stunted growth, small, pale or withered yellow or brown leaves that may fall off, and lack of blooming or fruiting. Evidence of root rot in trees includes leaf discoloration, branch dieback, thinning of the canopy, and possibly cankers in the bark.	If root rot is caught early enough, most plants can be saved. If some healthy, white, firm roots still exist, you can cut out infected roots (cut the healthy root just above the damaged part), and try to restore the plant's health by replanting in fresh, well-drained soil. If the entire root system has already become mushy, however, the infected plant should be removed to control spreading. Always sanitize garden tools after handling diseased plants.

Protecting from wildlife

▶ **Growing a successful garden** that's teeming with flowers and foliage is a bit of a catch-22: All that bounty is appealing to small critters and other animals, too. Obviously, you want to keep them from feasting on your handiwork. However, using chemicals to deter animals from your garden could lead to negative ripple effects elsewhere. Try these seven expert—and harm-free—steps.

1. ***Identify your visitor(s).*** Keep an eye out: You're likely to see deer, rabbits, and birds in action. You can also mount webcams outside near the food source; these are especially helpful for catching nighttime guests. For underground dwellers like moles, you'll need to check for tunnels or mounds of dirt. Nibble marks on leaves and vegetation are sure signs of squirrels and chipmunks; certain birds are known to snack on tender new shoots or to dig up freshly sown seeds. (Lesser goldfinches and house sparrows are notorious for eating the leaves off tender sunflower shoots.)
2. ***Choose unsavory plants.*** Look for plants that are labeled as resistant to deer or rabbits, though nothing is off the table when other food sources are unavailable. Planting pungent herbs (oregano, lavender, rosemary) and garlic around the garden's perimeter can turn off squirrels, chipmunks, and deer.
3. ***Use an organic repellent.*** It's worth experimenting with creature-specific deterrents (especially for deer and rabbits) in spray or granular form, reapplying as directed on the label. Make sure the formula won't harm your plants or the critters.
4. ***Use pantry items.*** If rodents are the culprits, sprinkle the area with cayenne, crushed red pepper, or coffee grounds, making sure to reapply after heavy rains.
5. ***Erect physical barriers.*** Visit your local garden center for helpful supplies, including bird netting and hardware cloth. The netting can be attached to bamboo poles and stretched taut to cover plants, especially younger crops and fruit-bearing trees.

   You can wrap chicken wire or other hardware cloth (with ¼-inch openings) around tree trunks or vulnerable plants. Or use it to build a fence around beds or garden areas, burying it at least 6 feet deep to block out burrowing animals.
6. ***Attract predators.*** Making your yard a welcome home for predators such as owls, which eat mice, can mean fewer rodents over time. Nonprofit organizations—such as the Hungry Owl Project—can help you install nesting boxes for these animals in need.
7. ***Be realistic.*** Though too many visitors can be a nuisance, accepting those who have made your property their home can be a rewarding part of gardening.

Controlling pests

▶ **Skip the harsh chemicals**—there are less extreme ways to banish pests and critters from your yard and keep them from eating the fruits of your hard labor.

Gardens play an important role in your local ecosystem, so using a commercial pesticide isn't the answer. In fact, pesticides can impact unintended targets like birds, bees, and other wildlife that feast on the treated plants and pests.

Remember, too, that certain beneficial pest species are worth keeping around. Aphids, caterpillars, and even slugs, for example, are part of the natural food chain, attracting other beneficial wildlife (like mosquito-eating bats and frogs) to your garden.

The key is to become aware of any pests before a full-blown infestation occurs. Better yet, take measures to keep them from invading your garden in the first place.

How to prevent pests

As when preventing disease, the best plan of action is to avoid conditions that make plants vulnerable and allow problems to take hold.

MAINTAIN SOIL HEALTH

Use organic products (or the DIY solutions on page 144) to keep your soil healthy and fertilized throughout the growing seasons.

ROTATE PLANTINGS

The practice of making sure a certain vegetable or flower doesn't grow in the same spot twice can confuse pests and reduce the amount you attract each season.

USE BENEFICIAL INSECTS

Rather than focusing on particular plants to help repel individual pests, it can be more effective to include a diverse array of plants with different kinds of flowers and bloom times that provide food and habitat for pollinators and other beneficial insects, including some that will be predators of insect pests.

Invasive Jumping Worms

Soil that's teeming with earthworms is generally ideal, but Asian jumping worms (*Amynthas agrestis*), introduced to the US through imported landscaped plants, are threatening to destroy the ecosystems of forests and commercial nurseries throughout the country.

How to Spot Them

True to their name, these worms jump off the ground and thrash when handled, though they aren't harmful to people. They look like regular earthworms but can grow up to 8 inches long and usually have a white or gray band known as clitellum around a dark body.

Why They Are of Concern

They significantly alter soil structure and makeup by feasting on organic matter (including mulch) and depriving nearby plants of vital nutrients. This also increases soil erosion. The worms reproduce rapidly, producing cocoons on the surface of the soil and displacing earthworms. The ultimate concern? Your plants may die and your local ecosystem will suffer.

What You Can Do

The best (and only) way to deal with jumping worms is to keep them from ever entering your property. Buy container plants only from reputable sources, and check the soil before bringing any plant home. Ask the nursery what precautions they are taking to avoid spreading the invasive pest. If you do end up seeing a jumping worm, capture it in a plastic bag, seal tightly, and leave it in the sun for a few hours; dispose of it in the trash once dead.

How to spot common pests

The following garden pests are found across the nation; you may need to do further research to identify regional pests. It is easiest to spot insects in the morning when they're most active. Employ these practices to keep them at bay without resorting to harsh fungicides.

	WHAT TO LOOK FOR	WHAT TO DO
Japanese Beetles	These ruthless leaf-eaters—which have iridescent copper wings and a bright green thorax—are particularly drawn to roses and beans, among countless other plants.	Plucking them off is easy to do, but if you are squeamish, brush them into a jar of soapy water (to keep them from flying away)—or shake a widespread affected area of the plant over a tarp—then dispose of them away from your garden.
Tomato Hornworms	Fortunately, these caterpillars are easy to spot—some grow as large as a finger—because they can ravage tomatoes or other nightshades like peppers and eggplants in a single day.	You can safely pick them up before they nest in your plants (resist the urge to disrupt their cocoons). Pairing tomatoes with companion plants can help fight or prevent infestation. Marigolds exude a strong odor that repels hornworms, and borage is another good option; the plant's star-shaped flowers attract important pollinators.
Cabbage White Butterflies	Before they reach adult form, the fuzzy green caterpillars feed on all brassicas but prefer broccoli, cabbage, and cauliflower the most, leaving holes in the outer leaves and boring into the center.	There's not much you can do about a current infestation other than dispose of the plants. Next time, keep the butterflies from laying eggs on your plants with a mesh overlay from the get-go. Thyme, dill, and lavender planted nearby are other good deterrents.
Potato Beetles	Don't let their striking looks fool you: The half-inch-long beetles, which have orange heads with black spots and yellow wings striped in black, are one of the most destructive pests—and can chew their way through an entire potato plant in less than a few hours. They also feast on fellow nightshades tomatoes, eggplants, and peppers. The prolific egg layers are capable of producing hundreds of offspring each season, too.	Try picking them off, placing them in soapy water as you go. And be sure to rotate the location of the crops the next year—the beetles overwinter in the garden and emerge from the soil in early spring, ready to feed and breed.
Spotted Lanternflies	Spotted along the eastern seaboard and across the Midwest, this invasive planthopper's preferred hosts are grapes and tree of heaven *(Ailanthus altissima)*, but it will feed on a wide range of plants including other crops and trees. There are three stages to be aware of: Egg masses have a pale gray, putty-like coating. Wingless juveniles are beetle-like, with white-spotted black bodies that turn red as they mature. Inch-long adults have grayish-brown folded wings with black spots that open to yellow, black, and red.	Once you positively identify them, the only recourse is to kill them: Spotted lanternfly populations can increase quickly and overtake an area. Pluck the juveniles and adults off plants, and squish or stomp on them. Be sure to scrape egg masses off surfaces with a plastic knife into a plastic bag containing rubbing alcohol and discard (or smash them, too). Also, report the infestation to your local agricultural department to prevent further spread.

	WHAT TO LOOK FOR	WHAT TO DO
Flea Beetles	A wide range of ornamentals and edibles are susceptible to these ubiquitous beetles, which jump (literally) from seedling to seedling, creating leaf pinholes in their wake. A serious infestation can quickly decimate an entire mature plant and its vegetables—beans, corn, lettuce, and nightshades among them.	Catching them is impossible; instead, install row covers and apply organic pest repellent to affected crops.
Aphids	There are several ways to identify aphids from other pests: They move slowly when disturbed, often lack wings, and come in several colors—metallic green, yellow, red, or black. Signs of aphid problems include wrinkled, curled, or puckered leaves and stunted growth; they also excrete a black, sooty "honeydew" that, in turn, attracts ants. Each aphid species usually targets members of a single plant family—from edibles to roses—but multiple species can be at work in one garden. More bad news: They reproduce without mating, so their numbers can soar in a matter of days; they also feed in dense masses and can transmit viruses between plants.	If your vegetable garden is home to one too many aphids, planting dill can help attract a different kind of bug: ladybugs, which love to feast on aphids. Marigolds are also known to deter aphids. For roses, hose aphids off with a gentle stream of water; if the infestation is severe, mix a solution of ½ teaspoon mild dishwashing soap and 1 quart water and apply it with a spray bottle. Repeat applications as needed.
Slugs and Snails	Wet, rainy conditions beckon these common "pests," which are actually mollusks; snails are differentiated from slugs by their protective shell. Because they come out at night, you may only see the voracious eaters' calling cards: irregular holes in young, tender foliage and trails of mucus (yuck). They also devour fruits like strawberries and tomatoes.	Picking them off diligently will keep their numbers from exploding, as will employing one of the following organic methods: • **Use a beer trap:** Fill an empty jar one-third with beer and partially bury the trap; slugs will drown and can be added to your compost heap. • **Apply repellent:** Sprinkle a calcium chloride formula (such as Sluggo) around plants to deter slugs and snails without harming other wildlife. Reapply after rain and watering. • **Use a copper barrier:** To prevent emerging shoots from being eaten, place a copper ring or copper tape (sold at garden centers) around them. • **Plant garlic:** Snails detest the smell of garlic, so plant it around the perimeter of your vegetable garden —and harvest the garlic when it has matured.

Supporting plants

▶ **On a practical level,** supports add height to the garden, allowing climbers and long-stemmed flowers to reach their full potential. They also let you stretch a small (or overcrowded) space vertically—and needn't be complicated or costly.

Types of supports

Generally, supports fall into two categories: decorative arbors, tuteurs, and trellises that are meant to become part of the display and more pedestrian structures that ideally support sight unseen (like peony rings).

Be sure to choose a support that is sturdy enough for the plant. This is particularly important for wisteria and climbing roses, as these vigorous climbers will pull down anything other than heavyweight wooden or metal structures.

- ***Individual stakes*** support tall perennials and annuals that grow in singles—delphinium, foxgloves, hollyhocks, lilies, and sunflowers (to name a few). Bamboo canes are easier to cut and less prone to rotting than untreated wooden stakes. It's also worth repurposing fallen branches and sturdy twigs.
- ***Grow-through supports*** are tailor-made for annuals and perennials that tend to grow in clusters, such as aster, false indigo, garden phlox, goldenrod, peonies, and Russian sage.

  Peony rings are adjustable supports that surround the plant—peonies but also other top-heavy flowers—and are secured to the ground with three (or more) legs.

  Tomato cages are not just for tomatoes (in fact, they really don't work for tomatoes); they can also support dahlias, marigolds, and other flowers (in lieu of a peony ring) as well as other climbing edibles, including sweet peas, runner (pole) beans, cucumbers, sweet peppers, melons, and strawberries.
- ***Linking stakes*** are ideal for flowers that tend to lean after blooming or when pelted by heavy rain. They're also good for flowers that don't grow in neat clumps or that form just too many blossoms to support with individual rings. Japanese anemones, crocosmia, lady bells, and Shasta daisies are common examples.
- ***Tuteurs and obelisks*** were traditionally crafted with branches and twigs tied together with twine—a practice that's easy to implement today. Both work equally well in containers, raised beds, and in-ground areas.

  Tall, four-sided wooden supports called tuteurs ("trainers" in French) are meant for climbers. They are usually shaped like a narrow pyramid that's slightly wider at the bottom and tapers to a pointed top.

  Obelisks tend to have a rectangular form that ends with a pyramid-shaped top, though the names are used interchangeably, and they serve the same purpose of providing height and visual interest in gardens—often on their own, without any plants scrambling up the posts.
- ***Trellises*** are latticed supports that come in many shapes and sizes and models—some are rightsized for containers; others are large enough for a raised bed or in-ground location. Wall-mounted trellises (right) can be attached to an exterior wall, fence, or other structure; freestanding ones have legs that you pound into the ground.

- ***Arbors and pergolas*** are easily confused, but the main difference between the two classic structures is in their placement: arbors usually line pathways and mark entrances to a garden, while pergolas are used to create outdoor rooms—such as on a patio with a dining table underneath. You'll want to ground these supports to withstand heavy winds and rain, as well as the weight of vigorous climbing plants.
- ***Other plants***—namely tall hedges, shrubs, and trees, as well as sturdy perennials—make natural supports for climbing plants, which can entwine themselves up trunks and branches with abandon.
- ***Annual vines*** can be grown on purpose-built structures or among shrubs or even up stair railings or porch posts—anywhere you want a splash of vertical color.

Using the supports

No matter the type of support, the process is basically the same—it must be secure but allow the plant to follow its natural growth pattern. For tying, jute twine and soft plant ties (or drugstore pantyhose cut into strips) won't damage delicate stems. Installing the support early in the season is also important, even if utilitarian versions look temporarily unsightly. As the plants mature, their foliage will hide the scaffolding—and the stems will stand tall and proud.

Homemade Supports

Building structures for climbers can be as simple as tying together a bamboo tripod in a large pot to support the scramble of a morning glory or climbing nasturtium.

For a lightweight vine, a rustic tepee-shaped affair can be made from limbs saved after pruning and tied together at the top. At Turkey Hill, a simple trellis was home to a spring-blooming clematis, followed by white morning glories in summer.

Tripod How-To

Push three sturdy 5-foot bamboo poles into a pot with soil mix. Wire the poles together at the top, and plant a seedling beside each; you'll have a movable, blooming tower of vines that can sit next to a fence or mark an entrance to a gate.

Tuteur How-To

Insert five or more bamboo stakes into the ground a few inches deep and a few inches apart in a circle around the climbing plant or within the confines of a pot. Gather them together at the top and tie them with a length of jute twine or waxed twine. Starting from the top, wind the twine around the stakes, pulling tightly as you go. At the bottom of the structure, tie the twine off to one of the stakes.

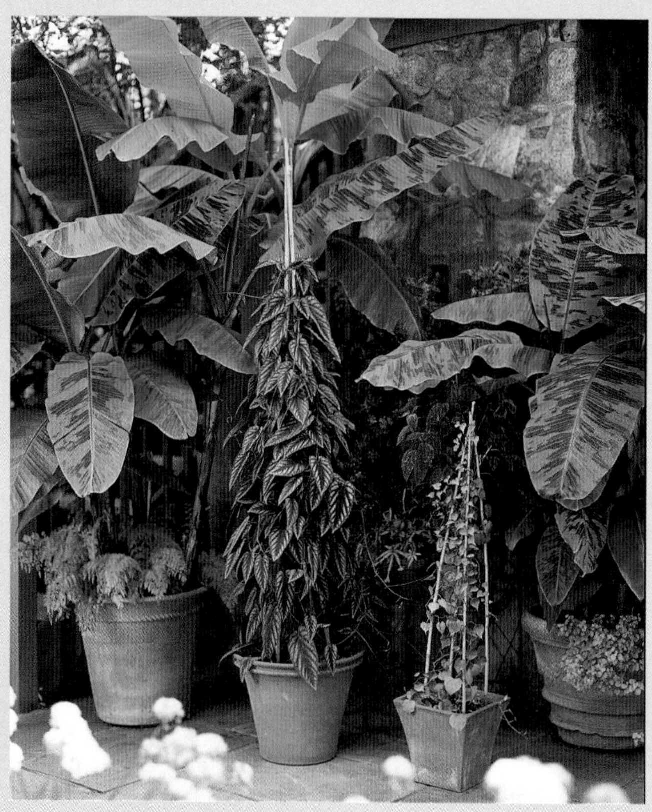

Deadheading

▶ **The act of removing** spent blossoms is not just about beautifying your garden; it also improves the vigor of some flowering plants by signaling them to stop producing seed and to focus on healthy flower and leaf growth. That's especially true for annuals and perennials that bloom repeatedly through the growing season, when deadheading promotes more continuous blooms. For "determinate" perennials and all the spring bulbs that bloom for a set period each season, deadheading greatly improves the plant's chance of surviving the winter and also improves the quality of the next year's floral display.

How to deadhead

The method used depends on the type of flowering plant.

SNAPPING SEEDPODS

Daylilies, Siberian irises, and many other determinate perennials produce prominent seedpods when blooming ceases. At the end of the blooming period, snap the seedpod off each stem as soon as the petals drop, then cut the stem back to the ground.

PINCHING TENDER-STEMMED ANNUALS

Most annuals, including cosmos and marigolds, have stems too tender for cutting with pruners or shears—and torn or ragged edges encourage disease. To deadhead, simply pinch the spent flower at its base on the stem.

CUTTING TOUGH-STEMMED ANNUALS

Sunflowers, zinnias, and other annuals with sturdy stems can be cut with pruning shears about ⅛ inch above a leaf to promote new growth and flowering.

DEADHEADING SPRING BULBS

Most of the larger bulbs such as hyacinth, daffodils, and tulips benefit from having their faded blooms snipped off with floral shears or bypass pruners. Not all bulbs require deadheading, however: The smaller ones, such as crocus, scilla, and *Narcissus bulbocodium*, will reflower successfully even when left to their own devices. The stems will continue to store energy, so only cut them back once they turn yellow (you can tie them to keep them tidy in the meantime).

DEADHEADING ROSES

How to deadhead roses depends on the variety. Shrub roses are generally self-cleaning, dropping their spent petals without any assistance. Same for once-blooming "antique" and "species" roses. Modern roses, on the other hand, require deadheading to keep reblooming: Use bypass pruners to cut hybrid tea roses just above a five-leaf node on the stem. Cut individual spent flowers from floribunda rose clusters; deadhead the entire cluster once all flowers have faded. See page 247 for how to prune roses.

SHEARING

Some indeterminate perennials, such as coreopsis and nepeta, can be cut back to force a second bloom. To shear, gather a bunch of stems in one hand and slice them cleanly with sharp pruners, leaving at least one-third of the plant. Come midsummer, shearing can also revive tired, leggy annuals like snapdragons, petunias, pansies, and violas.

Saving Seeds

By saving and sharing seeds from your favorite plants, you help keep more varieties going—a particularly important way to promote native species. You'll have enough to plant in your own garden and to gift to a friend or neighbor.

Pick the right plants

Seeds from annual self-pollinating plants are the easiest to save.

- Beginner crops include beans, peas, peppers, lettuces, and tomatoes; herbs such as dill, basil, and cilantro are other good options, as are cucumbers, melons, and pumpkins.
- Calendulas, celosia, echinacea, marigolds, milkweed, nasturtiums, sunflowers, and zinnias are among the best flowers; poppies are even self-seeding.
- When buying your starter seeds, look for heirloom and "open-pollinated" plants; unlike hybrid varieties, these produce seeds that are "true to type." (See resources on page 15 for where to buy pure seeds.)

Plant and grow properly

Growing under the right conditions ensures the offspring will be true to type.

- Space different self-seeding plants 10 to 20 feet apart to avoid cross-pollination.
- Watch the plants as they grow to identify the most vigorous specimens; do not save seeds from any that show signs of disease.
- Cease deadheading the flowers you plan to harvest seeds from when the flowers fade and the seed heads are forming.

Gather the seeds

Timing is key to reaping the biggest yield: too soon, and the seeds will lack the necessary genetic material; too late, and the seeds will open and spill their contents.

- Allow crops to bolt—this is well past the time you would usually harvest them.
- Flowers are ready when their seed heads begin to dry, typically about a month after their blooms fade.
- In both cases, wait until the seedpods have changed from green to brown and can be easily split.

How to Save Seeds

Some seeds, such as calendula, are large and easy to pull directly from the plant. For plants with smaller seeds, including milkweed and echinacea:

1. Cut off the flower heads, snipping at a junction in the stem to promote more blooming on the mother plant.
2. Separate the seeds from the flower heads and spread them out.
3. Allow the seeds to fully dry, using a fan to expedite the process, before removing the husks and other plant matter.
4. Tuck the seeds into a sleeve or a sterilized jar, label and date, and store in a cool, dark, dry place until next spring.
5. Your state or county extension service will offer additional tips for both flower and vegetable seed saving; and Seed Savers Exchange, a nonprofit organization that preserves heirloom plant varieties, posts crop-specific guides for growing and storing seeds from different fruits and vegetables.

Dividing and transplanting

Besides being a way to multiply your plants, dividing—or splitting plants through the root into smaller sections—is often the best way to rejuvenate a mature though lackluster perennial. Some plants, such as German iris, need to be divided and transplanted periodically in fresh soil with room to spread, thereby returning them to vigorous growth and healthy blooming.

How to tell if a plant needs dividing

Overgrown plants compete for nutrients and water in the soil and are at greater risk of damage from disease or infestation. So even if hardy perennials like peonies, daylilies, and astilbe don't necessarily require dividing, you may wish to do so to ensure they continue to flourish—or if you notice any of the following signs.

- ***A plant has outgrown its space*** and is either crowding out other plants or spilling over the sides of a pot, a bed, or other location such as a border or pathway.
- ***Fewer or smaller blooms (or both)***—though this can also occur when the plant is getting less sunlight due to other plants and trees growing nearby.
- ***Weak stems*** that need to be staked to keep from falling over (such as with Japanese anemones).
- ***A dead spot*** in the middle of the plant with fresh growth around it—in which case you want to dig up and discard that section and then divide and transplant the rest.

How often to divide plants

Most plants are best divided every few years, though some (like peonies) can go for a decade or more before they could use thinning out. Note that you may lose the blooms in the first season after transplanting, though you should see healthy foliage.

When to divide plants

Here's a good way to remember when to do this seasonal chore: Spring-blooming plants should be divided in the fall and fall-blooming plants in the spring. It's always best to divide perennials early in the morning, preferably on a cloudy day to prevent the sun from drying them out and when showers are forecast to water them in.

Tips for dividing plants

Most plants (including peonies) should be cut back almost to the ground before you dig them up and divide them so the roots focus their energy on getting reestablished rather than supporting the foliage. Transplant at least three divisions, so the new plantings don't appear too thin.

See pages 128 to 129 for more guidance on dividing and transplanting.

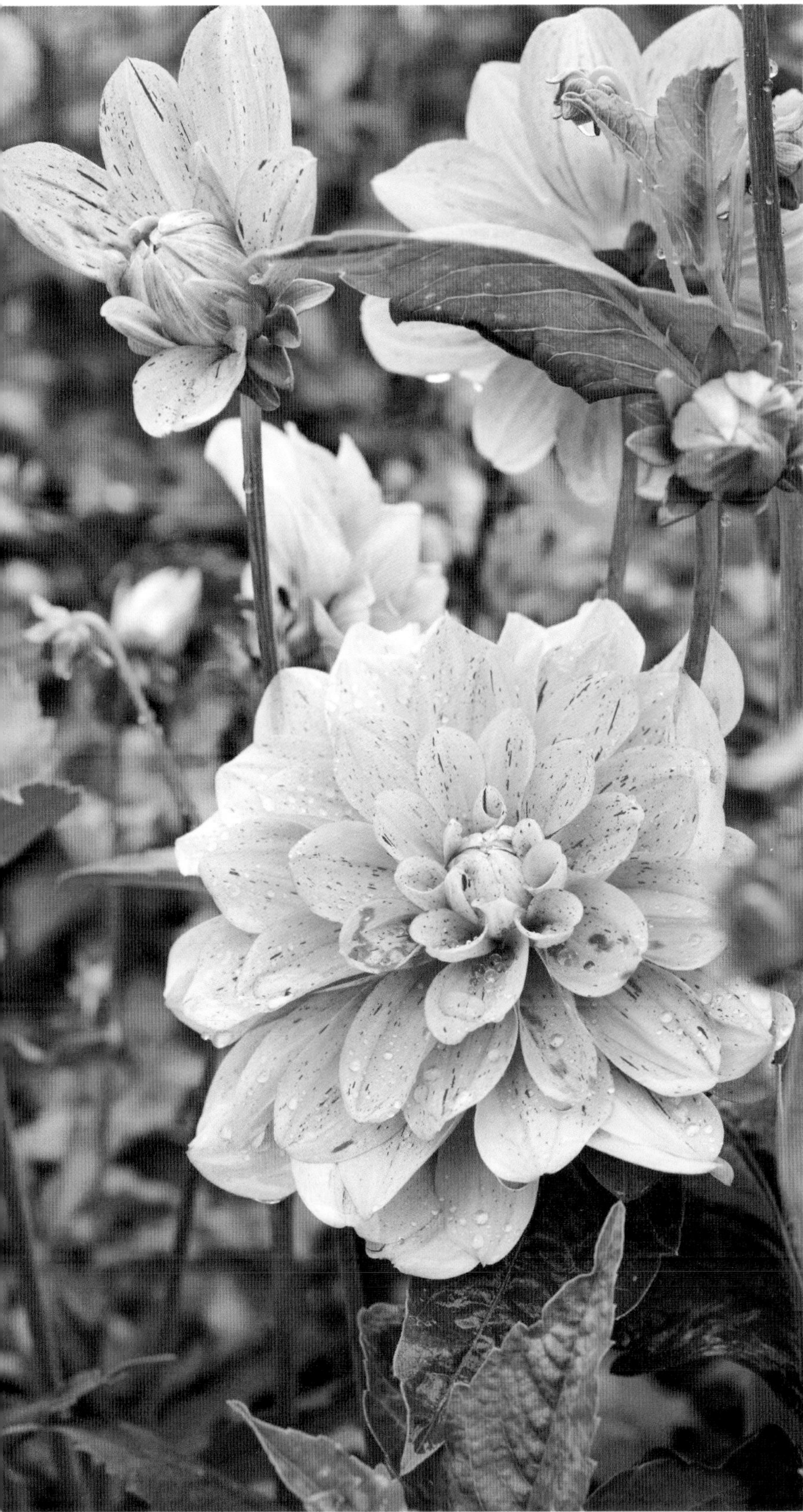

Common Plants That Benefit from Dividing

- Agapanthus
- Anemone
- Aster
- Astilbe
- Bleeding heart
- Dahlia
- Daylily
- Delphinium
- Elephant's ear
- Epimedium
- Euphorbia
- Gentian
- Geranium
- Helianthus
- Hosta
- Iris
- Ornamental grass
- Peony
- Phlox
- Primrose
- Ranunculus
- Salvia
- Sea holly
- Sedum
- Verbena
- Veronica

Winterizing

A critical—and enjoyable—gardening role is paying attention to and syncing with the natural rhythm of the changing seasons. Cooling temperatures can cause heat-seeking plants to decrease nutrient intake, resulting in stunted growth, reduced yield, or dying off (in extreme conditions). What's more, an early fall frost can put newly planted specimens at risk and compromise next spring's flower and fruit production.

But cooler temperatures can also benefit some plants—especially in fall, when they prepare ornamental trees and shrubs for their required dormant period.

Knowing which plants to protect and how to do it ensures your plants survive and thrive in any season. When putting your garden to bed, keep wildlife in mind, too: fallen leaves and flower heads provide shelter and food for birds, pollinators, and beneficial insects.

Frost vs. freeze

These two different weather events pose similar risks to your plants: During a frost, when temperatures are between 33°F and 36°F, ice crystals form on the surface of leaves. This is especially dangerous for crops. A freeze is when temperatures drop below 32°F and water inside plant tissues turns into ice crystals, breaking the cell walls.

The fall frost

Many perennial plants benefit from temperatures that signal the shifting seasons. In fact, they need those changes to help them prepare for the winter by going dormant.

By the time temperatures have cooled enough for a light frost, your annuals are already shutting down for the year. If you want to keep them going past a frost, you can cover them or try bringing them indoors. Otherwise, once annuals get hit by frost, it's time to pull them from the ground.

Vegetables and fruit

Any fall-harvest produce in your vegetable garden can withstand a drop in temperatures. Cool-season vegetables such as beets, carrots, kale, and parsnips can handle light frosts, even becoming sweeter in flavor.

Not so the last of your summer crops; cucumbers, melons, tomatoes, and peppers are easily damaged by freezing temps. Harvest them ahead of time or plan to protect them.

You may want to extend the season by growing cold-hardy herbs, leafy greens, and other vegetables throughout winter in a cold frame (as described on page 313).

Protective materials

Match the following methods depending on your plant's size, location, type, and hardiness.

MULCH

- In your vegetable garden, spread a thick layer of straw or ground-up leaves around cool-season crops, like carrots, radishes, and beets, in the fall to cover the surrounding soil. Do this again to protect peas and other early-season crops planted after the ground thaws.
- Apply a 2- to 3-inch-thick layer of pine or cedar mulch around trees and shrubs, keeping it 3 to 4 inches from the base.
- Adding mulch or raked leaves to perennial beds is also recommended, especially for plants that are not fully cold-hardy in the area.

BURLAP

This natural, breathable fabric can be used to protect trees, shrubs, and many types of young plants, either as a screen against wind or by wrapping for extra insulation. (See page 219 for the technique.)

Container plants

Small plants in containers need to be protected from freezing temperatures, too. If you live in a colder region, the safest method is to move your outdoor potted plants indoors, whether into your home, garage, or heated greenhouse. Come spring, gradually reacclimate them to the outdoors.

For cold-hardy plants, or if you live in a warmer area, you may opt to leave the plants outdoors. Depending on the type of container, you can bury the pot underground, leaving the plant exposed, or pile up mulch to cover the container completely; other options include placing straw bales around it or wrapping it with burlap—which is a good solution for containers that are too large to relocate indoors.

Trees and Shrubs

In their native environments, shrubs grow on the edges of woods and around trees, so it's worth considering how these companions can work together in your garden designs to lend incredible diversity to the landscape.

Yes, these plants represent a greater investment of money and time, but they are worth every ounce of effort, both for their beauty and the role they play in the environment. Plant a hedge for privacy, an allée for elegance, or a grove to replicate nature. Use interesting specimens as focal points. Choose a mix of deciduous and evergreen varieties for year-round structure and color. And be sure to choose trees and shrubs that are hardy for your climate so they can flourish for decades to come.

Trees

Lucky is the gardener who inherits mature trees in their landscape. After all, the best time to plant a tree is 20 years ago. The second-best time? Today. Unlike with annuals and perennials, buying a tree can feel a bit overwhelming. There are countless varieties to choose from, and they tend to be more costly, so there's more at stake.

And here's a worthwhile lesson: If you have an important tree that's approaching its final days, plant a new tree nearby before the declining tree dies.

Selecting

▶ **There's nothing wrong** with buying a tree just because you like it. But different trees serve different functions—for example, deciduous shade trees cool homes in the summer and, once their leaves have fallen, allow the winter sun to heat them; evergreens can provide a windbreak or a privacy screen; fruit trees provide crops for people and wildlife.

You'll also want to make the most of your investment—and your landscape—by planting trees that contribute to year-round interest. Read on for these and other considerations.

Site conditions

Matching the plant to the site is never more important than with long-lasting trees. Take time to know the following factors to ensure you set up your tree for success and reduce its maintenance over the long term.

- Soil conditions
- Drainage
- Exposure to sun and wind
- Space constraints
- Hardiness zone
- Human activity
- Insect and disease susceptibility

Year-round interest

Planting ornamentals and orchard trees rewards you with four-season flare. For example, flowering dogwood (*Cornus florida*) is a lovely understory tree, with white flowers in early spring, foliage that's attractive all summer before turning a dramatic purplish red in fall, and bright-red berries in winter.

Woody plants form the backbone of the garden in every season, but especially in winter, when their majestic profiles or intriguing bark stands out in an otherwise stark landscape.

In particular, the paperbark maple (*Acer griseum*) has exfoliating, cinnamon-colored bark (shown at left), while the coral-bark Japanese maple (*Acer palmatum* 'Sango kaku') maintains its fiery color after its leaves have dropped. Magnolias, beeches, and the Korean mountain ash boast beautiful, smooth gray skin. And white-skinned birch trees are iconic elements of a snowy scene.

Function

Besides good looks, trees serve any number of purposes in the landscape, from providing shade and crops to supplying more structural uses like allées and focal points.

SHADE

Boost your home's curb appeal and lower your energy bill by planting large, thick-canopied varieties. (According to the USDA, a shade tree can lower the temperature underneath by as much as 6°F.)

Pay careful attention to these general rules for placement, too: Plant trees at least 12 to 20 feet from your house and 3 to 4 feet from patios, sidewalks, and driveways, depending on the size of the tree. Another way to avoid damage from roots or falling branches is to divide the mature spread of the tree in half and keep it that far away from structures.

Fast-growing shade trees typically grow 1 to 3 feet each year, gaining considerable height quickly. The chart below includes some options to consider for your own yard.

SCREENS

Trees make great "green" fences to protect your property from passersby, block the views of neighbors, and create a barrier to wind, sun, and street noise.

Use trees with airy canopies such as hornbeams to shield a patio, and plant columnar evergreen trees that can be maintained as a tall, narrow hedge. For example, a row of arborvitae or cypress trees creates a dense boundary that doesn't require as much pruning as a hedge.

For a more formal look, you can prune the trees to give them a uniform shape, most often a straight line across the top, though artful variations on that theme are numerous.

You can also plant trees in rolling waves rather than a straight line, or create setbacks for a pretty container plant or a bench. Some hedges have openings to spotlight a stellar view or sculpture.

Pleached hedges (aka stilted hedges) feature trees that are stripped of their lower branches and then spread out into a hedge higher up. This is often done with maple and oak trees and gives you high screening while leaving the garden visible, such as along a driveway or to partially enclose an outdoor dining or sitting area.

FOCAL POINTS

Also known as "specimen trees," varieties that are planted as focal points include those that perform year-round: ornamental cherry, pear, and crab apple trees, for example, are all covered in delicate blooms in spring, brilliant green leaves in summer, and colorful foliage (and sometimes fruits) in the fall.

Or you can opt for a tree that stands out from the rest due to its striking shape or color—say, planting a Japanese maple, which has red feathery foliage, in a sea of green, or an eye-catching juniper that grows in a tall, columnar shape amid shorter plantings.

Of course, a magnificent elm or an oak tree in the center of a lawn is always impressive, as are trees planted at the end of a walkway (drawing you to their presence), or to highlight a corner or other prominent point in your yard.

Consider the vantage point from inside your home, too, so you can enjoy a specimen tree's beauty from a favorite spot.

Tree	Zones	Mature Size
American Elm	4 to 9	30 to 70 feet tall by 30 to 60 feet wide
Red Maple	3 to 9	60 to 90 feet tall by 30 to 40 feet wide
Sycamore	4 to 9	50 to 100 feet tall by 20 to 40 feet wide
River Birch	4 to 9	40 to 70 feet tall by 25 to 50 feet wide
Bald Cypress	4 to 10	50 to 70 feet tall by 20 to 30 feet wide
Palo Verde	8 to 10	20 to 30 feet tall by 20 to 25 feet wide
Tulip Tree	4 to 9	70 to 90 feet tall by 40 feet wide
Weeping Willow	4 to 10	30 to 40 feet tall by 30 to 40 feet wide
Thuja 'Green Giant'	6 to 8	50 to 60 feet tall by 12 to 20 feet wide
Ficus	7 to 11	50 to 60 feet tall by 30 to 40 feet wide

ALLÉES

For centuries, garden designers have planted trees, tall hedges, or shrubs to flank roadways or walkways, often leading to beautiful structures or views.

WOODLAND SETTINGS

If you have the space, whether it's half an acre or 150, like the farm in Bedford, it's worth dedicating some of it to a natural woodland effect. Pine trees and other conifers—plants that bear cones rather than flowers—are good choices, as are deciduous trees with interesting bark for year-round interest after the leaves fall.

WILDLIFE

Trees provide crucial habitat, from housing nests in spring and summer to shielding creatures from extreme temperatures and weather conditions during winter (especially conifers and other evergreens). Thorny hawthorns and holly trees offer protection from predators.

Fruiting trees, including those with berries not eaten by humans, are a valuable source of food, especially when other food is scarce. Plant varieties that ripen at different times include hawthorn, serviceberry, cotoneaster, mountain ash, mulberry, redbud, elderberry, and cherry. Hazels also produce nuts for overwintering animals.

Flowering trees (ornamentals and fruiting) provide nectar for bees, so include these lovelies in your garden design as well—linden, dogwood, magnolia, cherry crab apple, sourwood, crape myrtle, black tupelo, sycamore, horse chestnut, poplar, and so on. Red maple is prized for its pollen.

"I've been planting the woodlands on my farm with many groves of very, very interesting indigenous trees and plants—including a dawn redwood grove, where many varieties of these prehistoric deciduous conifers are planted, along with hostas, in the understory. You can do the same with just a few well-chosen species in a smaller plot, underplanting them with shade-loving plants such as ferns, which grow prolifically in forests."

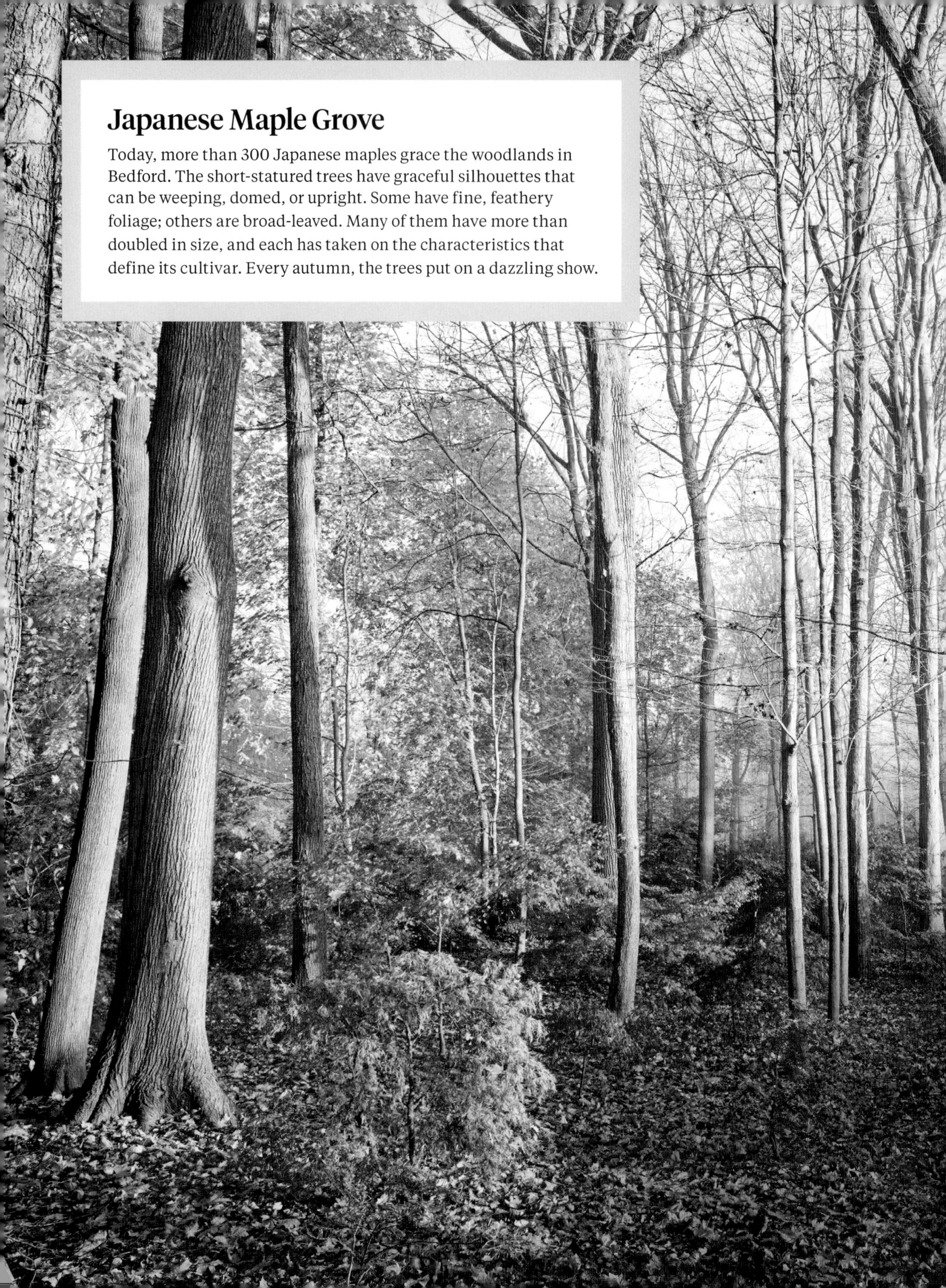

Japanese Maple Grove

Today, more than 300 Japanese maples grace the woodlands in Bedford. The short-statured trees have graceful silhouettes that can be weeping, domed, or upright. Some have fine, feathery foliage; others are broad-leaved. Many of them have more than doubled in size, and each has taken on the characteristics that define its cultivar. Every autumn, the trees put on a dazzling show.

"I became enamored with Japanese maples when I first visited Japan years ago, where I saw many types of this diminutive tree. It was autumn, and their colors ranged from brilliant reds to bright oranges and yellow-golds to the darkest magentas. Entranced, I vowed to plant many different sizes, forms, and colors in my own landscape."

1
2
3
4
5
6
7

Size and shape

After deciding on function, consider the natural shape of the tree and what form would best serve the function. Doing so will mean spending less money in the future to attain and maintain the shape you want.

Always check the plant label for the recommended growing conditions in terms of sunlight and drainage. Also, consider the mature tree size and how it will fit into the space you have chosen. Larger species can cast shade on other plants and compete with them for nutrients and water from the soil. Their spreading roots can also undermine foundations, driveways, and sidewalks.

Japanese Maple Leaf Glossary

There are countless varieties to choose from; these offer different shapes, textures, and colors.

1. ***Acer sieboldianum* 'Seki no Kegon'**
2. ***A. palmatum* 'Hogyoku'**
3. ***A. palmatum* 'Winter Flame'**
4. ***A. palmatum* 'Beni Shichihenge'**
5. ***A. palmatum* 'Inaba Shidare'**
6. ***A. palmatum* 'Osakazuki'**
7. ***A. palmatum* 'Bloodgood'**

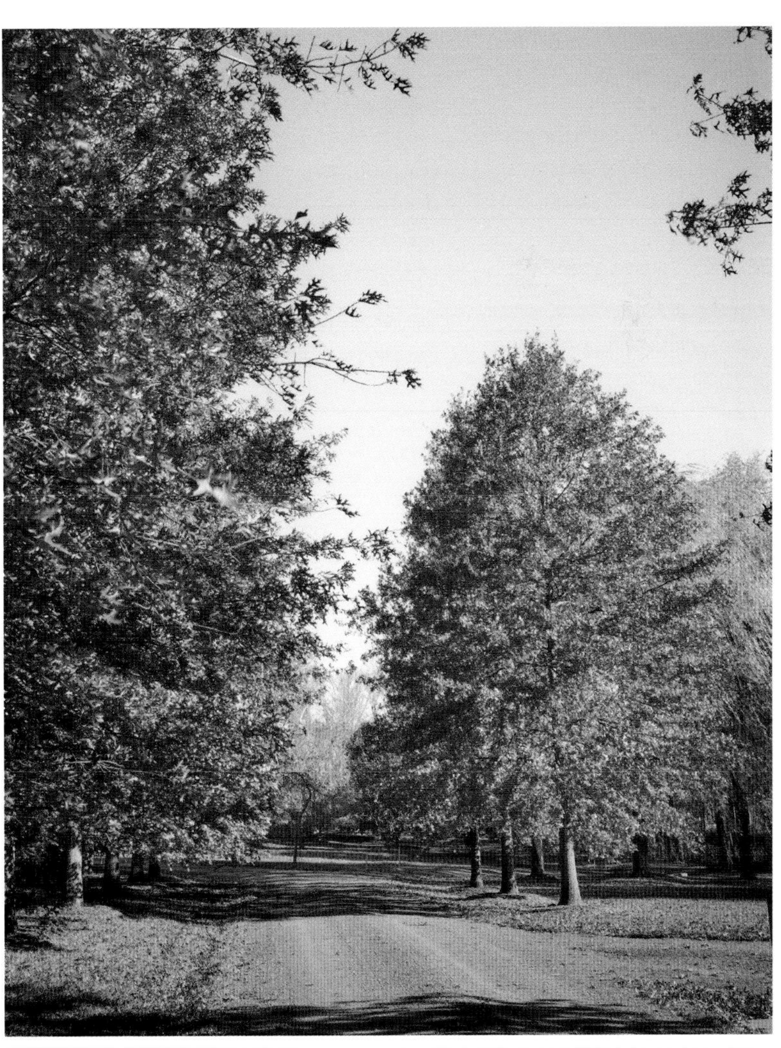

Buying

▶ **Trees are a long-term investment,** so buy them only from reputable nurseries where they are grown in ideal conditions—and which back up their quality with replacements or refunds within a specified time (usually one year from receipt).

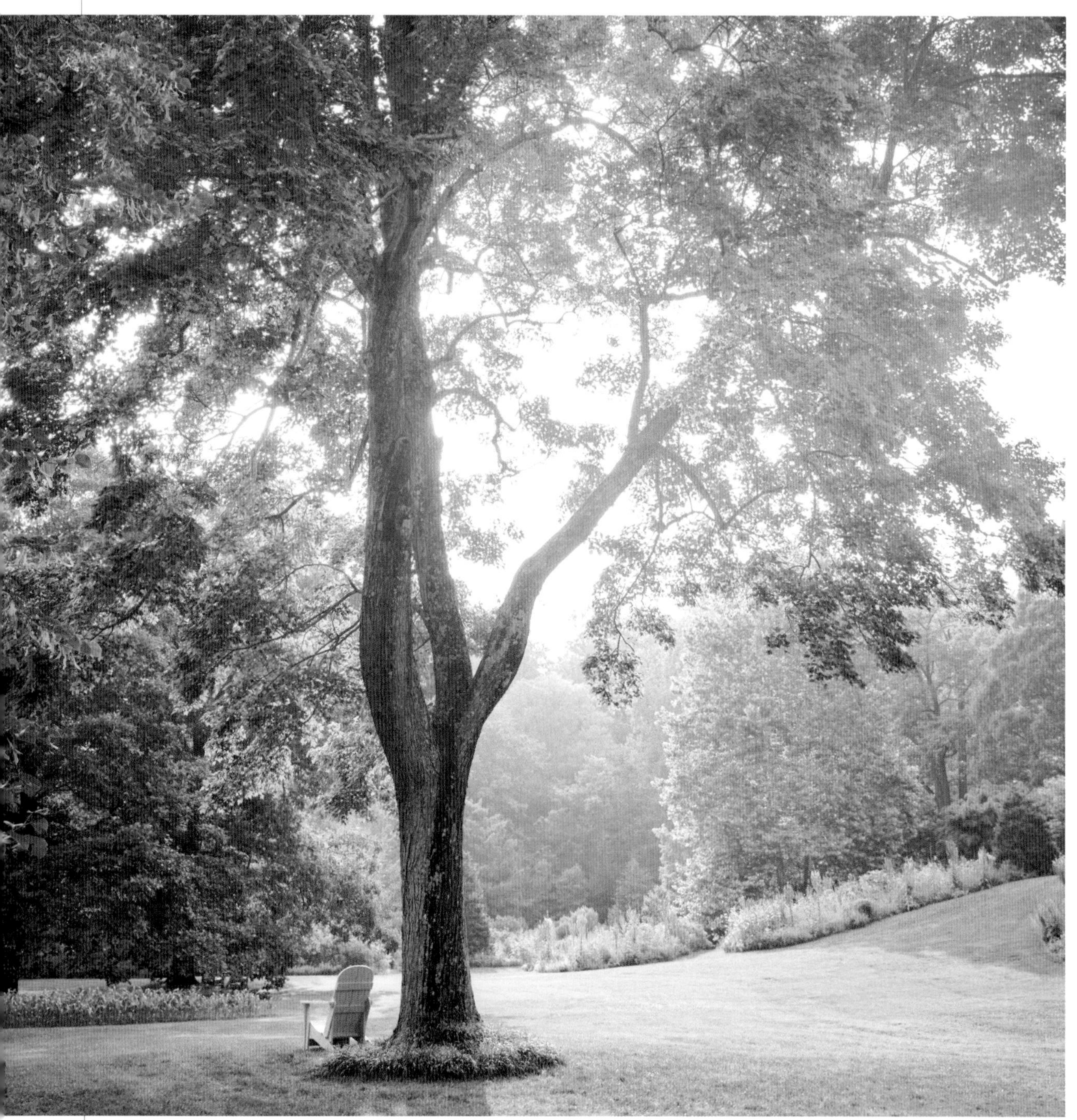

In general, young, freshly dug, well-grown trees with a 2- to 4-inch caliper (or diameter measurement of the trunk) are excellent candidates for landscape planting (rather than mature, large, more expensive specimens).

Select trees that are known to thrive in your area, and buy ones that are grown locally, if possible.

Knowing how trees are grown and sold will help you evaluate your options.

1. ***Balled and burlapped (B&B) trees*** are grown in the field and then removed by cutting their roots with a machine. The remaining root ball is wrapped in burlap and sometimes (but not always) placed in a basket. The size of the root ball depends on the caliper of the tree.

   What to look for: A firm, evenly rounded root ball indicates that the tree has been carefully dug and wrapped for transplanting. Seek out root balls secured with twine made from jute or other natural fibers; avoid nylon cord, which will not decompose in the ground. Check as well to make sure the trunk does not move independently of the root ball; if it does, the root structure is likely compromised.

2. ***Bare-root trees*** are grown in the field for two or three years and then dug up with their roots intact. Rather than being transported in soil-filled containers, they are delivered with their roots covered by a moisture-retaining material such as a large plastic bag. Most often, they are dug in late fall, placed in cold storage, and then sold in early spring.

   What to look for: The number one concern with bare-root trees is their condition when they are delivered. Open the box immediately and inspect the wrapping around the roots to ensure it is still sealed and moist, not dry. The roots should be firm, not mushy. Hold the tree upright by the base of the trunk—it should be straight, without any noticeable curves. Check the trunk, too, for any wounds.

3. ***Container-grown trees*** were developed for the convenience of home gardeners, since they are easily transported and transplanted. They are larger and heavier than bare-root trees but smaller and lighter than B&B trees.

   What to look for: Trees grown in containers are prone to being root-bound (or pot-bound) and can have difficulty establishing deep roots. This in turn compromises the eventual size and stability of the tree. Slide the tree out of its container—the root ball should not have roots wrapping around the entire edge or crossing the top, which could girdle the trunk as the tree grows.

Other ways to tell if a tree is of good quality, no matter how it was grown:

- The trunk should be straight, from top to bottom.
- Avoid trees with wounds or damage from handling, incorrect pruning, or insect injuries.
- The branches should be evenly spaced along the trunk—this is referred to as having strong branch architecture.
- The branches should have firm, sturdy attachments to the trunk; those with narrow angles of attachment may cause problems later.
- Avoid trees with branches that are pressed against the trunk; these areas of contact may become compressed, crack, or die back.

A few broken or torn branches are not cause for grave concern so long as you remove them before planting. And if you notice other problems after planting, corrective pruning is the solution. Start doing this one year after planting and space the pruning over several years.

Tip

If you often plant large numbers at a time, consider ordering bare-root saplings in bulk, which are much less expensive than mature specimens. Rehydrate the roots in water for several hours, then plant each one in a pot, using a mixture of compost and potting soil, and leave them there for a year to 18 months, so their root systems have time to develop before transplanting them into the ground.

OPPOSITE: An 80-year-old red maple (*Acer rubrum*) anchors a hill at the 35-acre public demonstration garden Chanticleer in Philadelphia.

Selecting Trees

Tips for choosing the right tree for you:

- Visit nurseries and pick trees you find appealing, are appropriate to the area, and are necessary for foliage color, impact, and practical functions, such as windbreaks and screening.
- Focus on the more important locations—areas near buildings, along drives, and close to gardens and pastures.
- Pay close regard to landscape designer Humphry Repton's "axis of vision" principle, looking carefully at areas where the eye is regularly drawn and planting larger specimens there to add pleasure and gravitas to the views.

Here are some of the trees that Martha grows:

1. Linden
2. Bald Cypress
3. Sugar Maple
4. Japanese Stewartia
5. Pin Oak
6. Weeping Hornbeam
7. Apple (shown opposite)

1

2

3

4

5

6

7

Planting

▶ **When to plant trees** depends on how they were grown and also where you live, though planting during dormant periods—early spring before bud break or late fall after leaf drop—is ideal. That said, healthy balled and burlapped or container trees can be planted throughout the growing season, whereas bare-root trees are generally planted in the spring. New trees can also be planted at any time of year in tropical and subtropical climates where trees grow year-round.

In general, however, fall is a great time to plant trees. The weather is cool and the plants will have time to establish roots before spring rains and summer heat stimulate new top growth.

Conifer trees (like pine, fir, and juniper), which have needle or scalelike leaves present throughout winter months, prefer warmer soil for transplant and should be planted in late summer to early fall.

Balled and burlapped trees and container-grown trees can suffer transplant shock, meaning the tree will experience a state of slowed growth and loss of vitality.

Proper site preparation, careful handling to prevent further root damage, and good follow-up care reduce transplant shock and promote faster recovery.

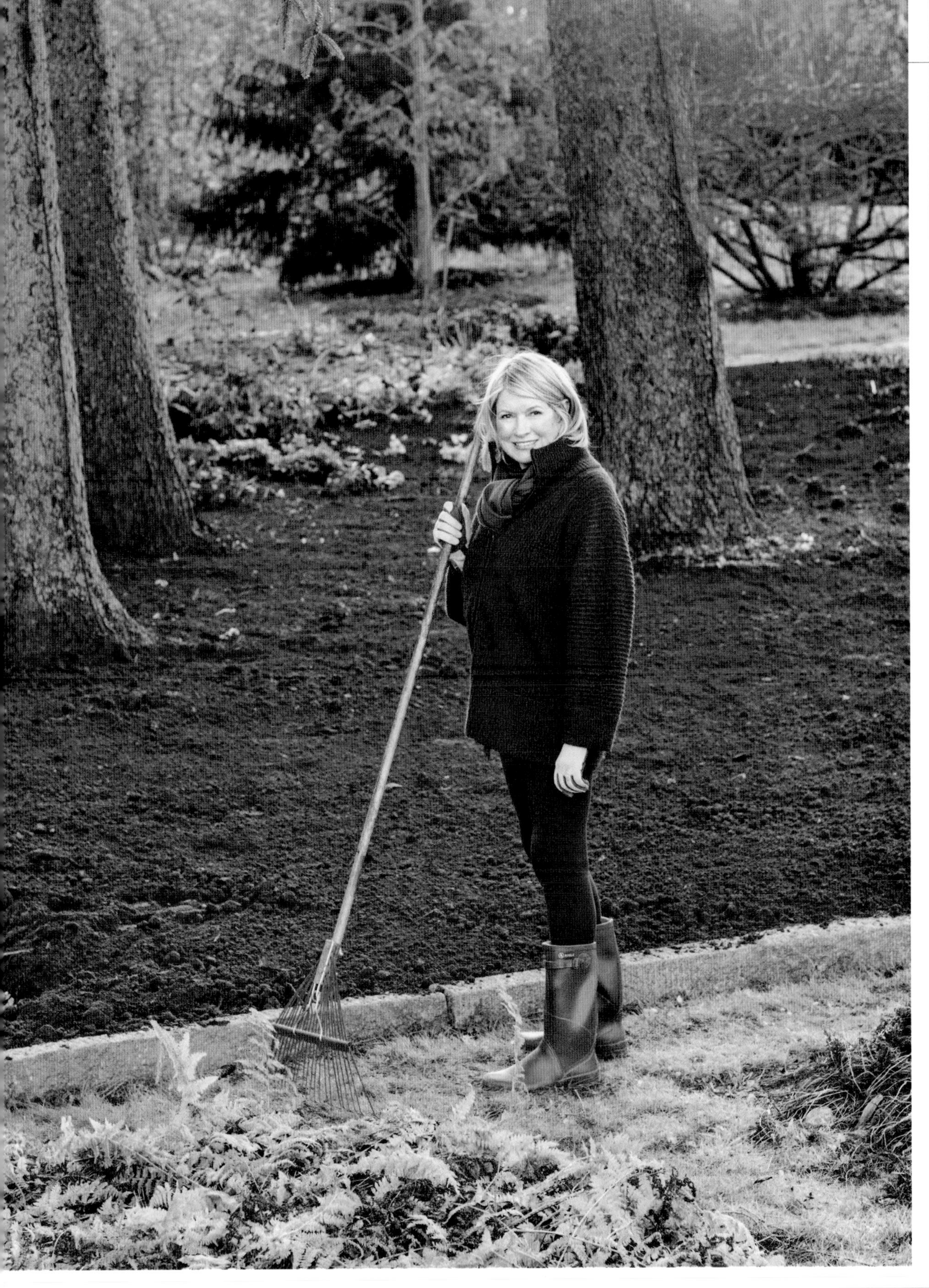

How to Plant a Tree

A bare-root or container-grown tree is easier to plant than a traditional balled and burlapped one, though the process is basically the same.

In all cases, choose the location carefully to meet the plant's requirements (for example, full sun vs. partial shade, dry or moist soil). Also consider the mature size so you don't plant too closely to driveways or structures. And before breaking out your shovel, call 811 to make sure you won't hit any power lines in your chosen spot.

1. Dig the hole

With a sharp spade, dig a hole about three times the diameter and only as deep as the size of the pot or root ball. Loosen the soil surrounding the hole as well as along the sides and bottom of the hole, clearing it of all large rocks.

2. Prepare the tree

For container-grown trees, loosen the edges of the container, and gently slide the tree out, grasping it by the trunk. Break apart the roots with your hands, or slice an X through the root ball with a hori hori knife. For balled and burlapped trees, remove the wire cage (snip off the cage's bottom before placing it in the hole), and cut away as much rope and burlap as possible. Remove bare-root trees from their wrapping.

3. Position the tree

When placing the tree in the hole, lift by the root ball, not the trunk. Follow the guideline "bare to the flare." The root flare, or collar (the place where the roots start to spread out from the trunk), should be flush with the soil line. Mix compost into dug-out soil, then add enough to the hole to reach that height. Then place the tree in the hole, making sure it's straight, and backfill. Lightly tamp down the soil to ensure the roots come in contact with it. Add starter fertilizer to the soil around the edge of the root ball following the package instructions.

4. Prune

Carefully prune dead wood or damaged branches.

5. Hydrate

Water the tree in slowly but deeply. Sculpting a "water well" (as shown) will prevent runoff so water drains directly into the plant.

6. Mulch

Top with 2 to 3 inches of mulch, leaving several inches of the space around the trunk bare, to prevent rot. For the first few months, allow a hose to gently run directly on the spot for about 10 minutes once or twice a week.

Tip

If you need to wrap the trunk, as a barrier to deer and other animals, use biodegradable material and wrap from the bottom to the first branch.

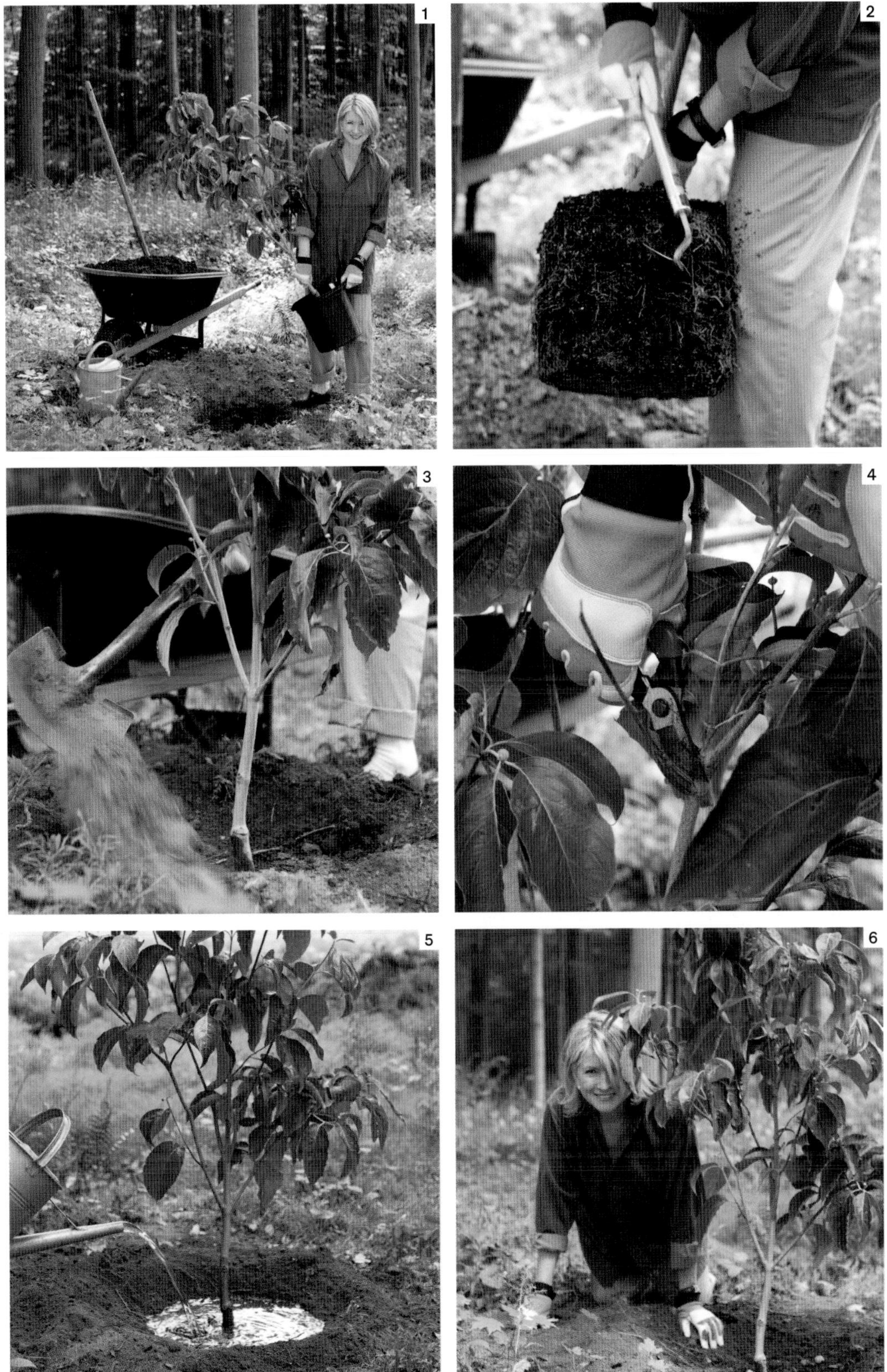
1
2
3
4
5
6

Staking

▶ **Not all trees** require staking—indeed, recent research shows trees can develop stronger roots if they are not staked. However, sometimes this intervention is needed; the key is to do it properly to help, not harm, the tree.

When to stake

Existing trees may benefit from staking at any point in their life cycle if they are leaning due to frequent high winds and/or wet soil. Some new trees may also need staking for the year after planting if they are leaning due to improper structure or heavy winds, or are planted on a steep grade or slope. Recently transplanted mature trees with a large canopy-to-rootball ratio are also at greater risk of shifting or blowing over from high winds until the roots are established.

How to stake

You can buy tree-staking kits or sturdy wooden stakes and other supplies at garden centers.

1. Place the stake on the side of the tree that is exposed to wind. If the site gets wind from more than one prevailing direction, position another stake opposite the first or three stakes in even intervals all around the tree.
2. Drive the stake(s) into the outer edge of the planting hole, safely away from the root system but still within the mulched planting area. A good rule of thumb is for the stake to be about a foot from the trunk.
3. Secure the stem attachment either one-third or two-thirds of the way between the ground and the first set of branches, wrapping it loosely so there's some give at both the tree and stake. Never have the strap touch the branches, as this can cause them to snap in gusty winds.
4. Remove the attachments in the fall for spring-planted trees and for trees planted the previous fall. If the tree's root system still moves in the soil when the trunk is moved or if the trunk still bends, loosely reattach the connections to the stakes and leave them on for one more season.

Pruning

Pruning is about more than just looks; proper techniques improve the health of trees, prevent disease, and encourage better flowering and fruit production. Pruning also helps control the shape, keeps trees fresh and open, and allows for better air circulation through the center of the specimen. Unkept trees can pose safety risks to people and property from falling branches. Pruning to reduce a tree's size is sometimes necessary but can be prevented by choosing the right-size tree for the specific site—another reminder to know the dimensions at full maturity.

When to prune

Remove dead, dying, broken, or severely diseased branches as well as any suckers or competing or downward-bending branches as you discover them, no matter the time of year. When pruning diseased branches, wipe the pruning blade with rubbing alcohol between cuts to avoid spreading the disease. Also, as soon as you discover them, cut any stubs—either left when a branch falls off or is improperly pruned—back to the trunk, as these prevent the tree's ability to heal the wound and allow insects to enter and do their damage.

Call in a professional tree service to handle the removal of large dead or dangling branches, especially near your home or other structures, and to trim branches that are very high or close to power lines. More thorough pruning can be done anytime the tree is dormant and the nutrients are stored in the roots; less sap flows from the wounds of dormant trees, lowering the risk of damage by insects and disease.

- Summer is generally when spring-flowering trees are pruned—do this soon after their blooms have faded, as many varieties carry preformed flower buds through the winter, and if you wait until fall, you risk losing a majority of those blossoms.
- For most deciduous trees, the best time to prune is after the leaves have fallen in October or November, though some experts recommend waiting until winter (January to March).
- Evergreens should be pruned in late winter (February to March), shortly before new growth begins in the spring. (You can of course take clippings for holiday wreaths and garlands in November and December.)
- Avoid pruning trees that are susceptible to certain pests or diseases during peak transmission times. Notably, if oak wilt is present in your region, don't prune your oaks from late spring through midsummer.

Tree-pruning tools

Clean cuts are the key to successful pruning, so you'll want to make sure you have the right tool for each type of cut.

- Secateurs or hand pruners are effective for small twigs and branches.
- Loppers provide more leverage for branches 1½ inches or less in diameter.
- A pruning saw cuts large, woody limbs 6 inches or less in diameter.
- A chainsaw makes quick work of limbs greater than 3 inches in diameter but shouldn't be used on small limbs because of its shredding effect.
- A high-quality pole pruner, which includes a saw and a lopping shear on an extendable shaft, is helpful for cutting branches several feet off the ground.
- Always wear safety goggles and gardening gloves when pruning trees and a hard hat when cutting overhead branches.

What to prune

Step back and look at the tree you are about to prune. Take note of its overall form. Know that many trees are meant to have an irregular, organic shape. Pruning while they are still young is easiest in terms of trimming branches from the trunk or other shaping cuts; you can stop pruning when the tree is about five years old (unless there are dead or diseased branches).

Then examine the branching structure and consider pruning if a branch meets any of the following criteria:

- dead, dying, or diseased branches
- sprouts forming at the base of the trunk
- crossover branches (growing toward or across the tree's center)
- crossed limbs that rub together or may rub in the future
- V-shaped crotches (when possible to prune)
- multiple leaders (upright branches that compete as secondary trunks or may develop into additional trunks)
- nuisance growth (interfering with driveways, walkways, structures)

How to prune

The golden rule to remember is to always cut back to the trunk or to a secondary branch or bud that is pointed in the direction you want the tree to grow. If you're unsure, don't cut. You can always cut it later, but it will never grow back. Never penetrate the branch collar, which is the swollen area around the base of each branch that contains vascular tissues for both the branch and the trunk. Doing so will compromise the tree's ability to fend off disease and insect pests that can damage the trunk. Make your pruning cut outside the collar on the branch side without leaving a stub.

CUTTING SMALL BRANCHES

Cut off the branch beyond the collar; orient the pruners with the blunt jaw pressing on the portion of the branch that will be discarded.

CUTTING LARGE BRANCHES

This requires three cuts to avoid stripping bark from the trunk. Make an initial small notch on the underside of the limb, about one-third of the way into the branch. Make the next cut from above the branch, cutting completely through the limb to remove it; this removes the weight of the branch so you can make your final cut without the branch splitting or falling. Make the final cut just outside the branch collar, parallel to the trunk. See Pruning Damaged Tree Branches for step-by-step (opposite).

Follow the above techniques to prune common structural issues:

SUCKERS

These new shoots are a tree's natural survival instinct, yet they only serve to weaken it over time. Before they are 6 to 12 inches tall, use a lopper to cut the stems back to ground level.

V-SHAPED BRANCHES

Narrow, V-shaped branches are prone to breaking off in wind or ice storms. Some trees that form these junctures (namely maples, ashes, willows, basswoods, hornbeams, flowering pears) benefit from corrective pruning when they are young to strengthen their structure. To train the young tree, remove the least desirable stem, avoiding the branch collar. If you are doing this on a mature tree, follow the steps for cutting large branches.

FORKED TRUNKS

Forked trunks may look attractive but are less stable than a single trunk—the tree may eventually split, or one of the trunks could break off. While the tree is still young, cut off one side of the fork as close to ground level as possible, cutting at a slight angle and being careful not to damage the bark on the remaining trunk.

TOPPING TREES

Follow pruning protocol when cutting branches off the top of trees to reduce their size, such as when they are growing near power lines. Topped trees have shortened life spans, pose safety hazards, and require ongoing maintenance. Instead of indiscriminate lopping, remove small branches to their point of origin, or prune back larger branches to a lateral branch large enough to assume the terminal (or main) role. In some cases, the best solution is replacing a too-tall tree with a more appropriate variety.

Pruning Damaged Tree Branches

1. Wearing gardening gloves and safety goggles (and a hard hat, if necessary), position a sharp saw 1 foot from the trunk. Cut one-third of the way into the branch from underneath, to stop the bark from tearing later.
2. About 1 inch to the right of the first cut, carefully cut off the branch to remove the bulk of the weight, standing back for safety.
3. To the left of the first cut, saw off the remainder of the branch 1 inch from the branch joint, standing clear for safety.

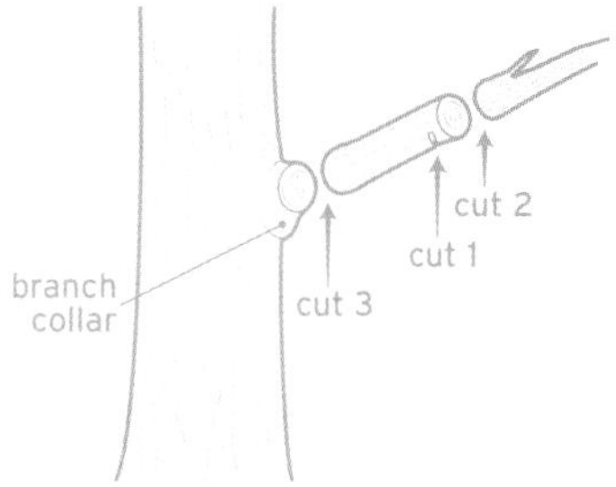

Attracting Backyard Birds

Both migratory and nonmigratory birds benefit from having a habitat in which to rest, nest, and take in nourishment.

Plants are the best source of food for birds, but when they are in short supply—namely winter, but also gaps in the early growing season—birdseed and feeders will help your local and migrating visitors get the sustenance they require. Evergreen trees and shrubs provide year-round shelter. Here are some pointers for creating a haven for these at-risk aviary visitors.

Fruiting Shrubs

Wintering songbirds relish members of the rose family, such as mountain ash, as well as crab apple, hawthorn, serviceberry, and winterberry, a native holly.

Nectar-Bearing Flowers

Tiny hummingbirds fly enormous distances each year, requiring huge quantities of nectar (as in, from a thousand plants daily) to fuel their journey. The perennials and subtropicals shown here are among the best nectar sources to plant at home.

Feeders

You can feed birds year-round, but if you live in an area where the seeds may attract bears, wait until mid-November to put out your feeders and take them down when the weather warms up in spring.

Try to offer a variety of seeds (and matching feeders) to attract a greater number of birds; suet cakes provide the fat and energy needed by insect eaters. Clean feeders regularly.

For hummingbird feeders, avoid commercial nectar with artificial dyes and instead make a simple syrup of one part granulated sugar and four parts tap water (no need to boil it), stirring until the sugar is dissolved. Clean regularly to prevent mold.

6
7
4
5
8
1. Justicia californica
2. J. spicigera
3. Salvia greggii
4. Calliandra californica
5. Lonicera sempervirens
6. Aloe saponaria
7. Penstemon eatonii
8. Bulbine frutescens

Shrubs

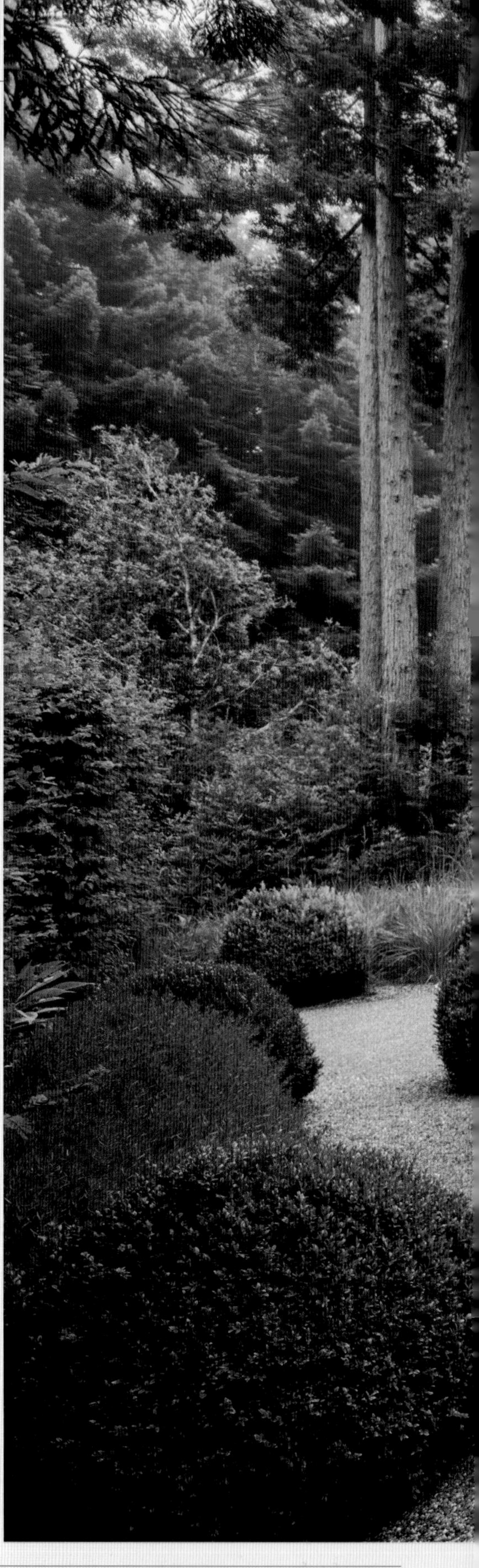

They're known as the workhorses of the garden for the many roles they serve—namely shade, shelter, and screening, as well as cover and food for wildlife. They are wondrously diverse, too, coming in nearly every imaginable size and shape as well as being amenable to all kinds of soil—including acidic environments. These woody plants also offer four-season beauty, flowers for cut arrangements, and an enticing perfume. Beyond their aesthetic appeal, shrubs are a relatively low-maintenance and budget-friendly way to elevate your landscape instantly and for decades to come.

Selecting

▶ **Planting for four-season interest** is easy to do with diverse shrubs. You may also want to pick fast-growing plants to fill in gaps quickly, or focus on those that are low maintenance to ease your efforts. As with any plant, be sure to select a shrub that suits your zone and the specific site in terms of sun or shade, soil type, drainage, and size.

Function

Similar to when selecting trees, you should begin by identifying what purpose a shrub will serve in your design—for example, to form a hedge for privacy, dazzle with showy color or fragrance, or serve as a backdrop for smaller annuals and perennials.

Year-round interest

Give your garden a continual wave of blooms all year long with carefully selected shrubs—most flower only for a short time, but there are options for every month of the year. The blooming time for flowering shrubs will depend on your climate, though the following list is a general guideline. (Note that not all the examples mentioned are hardy across all regions.)

Evergreen varieties, which have needles or green leaves year-round, are the foundation of a beautiful landscape. Deciduous shrubs play an important role in the landscape, too—even though their flowers and foliage fade away come winter, their in-season beauty is breathtaking. Plot a mix of evergreens and deciduous varieties for maximum enjoyment.

And look for four-season shrubs like Persian ironwood, which provides tiny red berries cradled by velvety brown bracts in winter, flossy foliage and spotted bark in spring and summer, and lavish orange-red leaves in fall.

- Popular shrubs that usher in spring include Cornelian cherry dogwood, forsythia, lilac, azalea, fothergilla, camellia, andromeda (*Pieris japonica*), rhododendron, and pearlbush.
- Late-spring and early-summer options include chaste tree, deutzia, Chinese fringeflower, abelia, gardenia, mock orange, sweet shrub, potentilla, viburnum, spirea, and bush rose—some lasting until the first frost or reblooming late in the season.
- Then your garden will explode with hydrangea, hibiscus (rose of Sharon), butterfly bush (look for noninvasive cultivars), summer sweet, and bluebeard (*Caryopteris*).
- Fall is mostly about colorful foliage and sometimes fruit. Consider gold or purple barberry and elderberry, purple smoke bush and ninebark, beautyberry and holly, and one of the variegated dogwoods or weigelas, which offer more than a single moment of appeal.
- Winter-flowering shrubs bloom from January to March. There are dozens of species and cultivars to choose from, including lesser-known members of familiar families—such as winter honeysuckle, whose white blossoms are every bit as fragrant as its seasonal kin. Others, including witch hazel and its relative Persian ironwood, winterberry, sweetbox, paperbark, and Japanese spicebush, are strictly winter bloomers.

Buying

▶ **For starters, local plants** have a higher chance of establishing well in your garden because they don't have to adjust to your specific climate. They are also more likely to be resistant to common pests and diseases in your area. Most shrubs these days are sold in containers, with younger saplings available as bare root. Either way, here's how to spot a healthy plant:

- Avoid plants with leaves that are turning yellow or brown, are wilted or curling under, or appear blistered, sticky, or ridden with holes or black spot—all signs of pests or disease. Check for actual pests on the undersides of the leaves.
- Avoid the temptation to buy plants in full bloom, as they are more likely to suffer transplant shock. Plants with buds are more likely to thrive.
- Also check the roots:

  For container-grown shrubs, look under the pot—you don't want to see roots growing through the openings. Then slide the root ball out of the pot and avoid any plants with girdling, or excessive circling; the roots should be moist but not soggy or falling apart, a sure sign of root rot.

  Bare-root roses should have plump, firm stems, twigs, and buds, and moist (not soggy), well-formed roots with fibrous feeder roots growing from the main root system.

Planting

▶ **Spring and fall** are ideal for planting shrubs. Evergreen shrubs—such as boxwood and rhododendron—are susceptible to winter damage and will benefit from spring planting. Nurseries typically have the best selection during spring, so that may affect your planting schedule.

1. Dig a hole at least two times the width of the container or root ball and the same depth. Remove any big rocks from the hole and the soil.
2. Place the plant (still in the pot) in the hole to ensure the shrub will be at the same level when planted as it was in the container. Like trees, shrubs prefer to be planted high, with their root flare above the surface. Add more soil or compost to the bottom of the hole as needed. Water the potted plant and the surrounding hole.
3. Remove the pot from the hole and carefully slide the plant from the pot. Place it in the hole with the most attractive side facing out or in the desired direction.
4. Enrich the dug-out soil with an organic slow-release granular fertilizer and some compost, then backfill the hole and tamp down the soil to remove air pockets and ensure good contact with the roots, but do not compact it.
5. Add 2 to 3 inches of mulch and water in the plant well. Continue to give the plant 1 to 2 inches of water each week during the first growing season.

Lovely Lilacs

Lilacs are believed to have been introduced into Europe at the end of the sixteenth century from Ottoman gardens, arriving in American colonies a century later. To this day, they remain a popular ornamental plant because of their attractive, sweet-smelling blooms.

Once established, these plants are drought tolerant and low maintenance, and they can thrive in even the coldest regions (they're hardy to -60°F).

Despite their short bloom period, their fragrance, structure, and foliage make lilacs a worthwhile addition to your garden. They also provide some of the earliest forage material for pollinators.

By planting an assortment with staggered bloom times, a lilac show can last for up to two months.

The following are among the most popular options

Common lilac: By far the most popular lilac variety, these shrubs are beloved for their colorful (typically purple but also magenta, pink, or white) and fragrant flowers.

Early lilac: This early bloomer begins flowering as soon as March, offering lovely pale-pink color and fragrance.

Dwarf Korean lilac: Topping out at 6 feet, this is a great option for a lower hedge. It is also tolerant of urban conditions and can thrive in containers.

'Miss Kim' lilac: Manchurian lilacs, including 'Miss Kim', have highly fragrant flowers that range from icy blue and burgundy to lavender-pink.

Persian lilac: Graced with arching branches bearing dark green foliage and bright-pink blooms, the Persian lilac attracts butterflies and hummingbirds.

Chinese lilac: Thanks to its long-lasting, dark-purple blooms and wide, spreading branches, Chinese lilacs (a hybrid of common and Persian lilacs) are great for cut flowers.

'Sensation' lilac: This rare lilac is prized for its bicolor deep-purple petals edged in white on 8- to 12-foot-tall shrubs.

Harvesting Tips

The flowers are a favorite for cutting and using in arrangements.

- Using very sharp, clean pruning shears, cut a ¼-inch slit at the bottom of each stem, or use a hammer or rubber mallet to crush the ends, so water can enter easily. Then plunge the stem in a bucket of cool water.
- Arrange the stems in your desired vessel before filling it with fresh cool water.

Pruning

▶ **Not all shrubs** require pruning, but a good many benefit from a regular once-over to promote overall health, boost the size and number of blooms, and maintain their shape. For example, if you notice lackluster flowering or that the plant is getting "leggy" with long, bare stems topped by a few flower heads, pruning can work wonders. Even those that don't need heavy pruning may suffer dead or damaged branches, which can be removed anytime. If you aren't sure, wait to see if new buds appear. Sometimes looks can be deceiving, especially after a long winter's sleep.

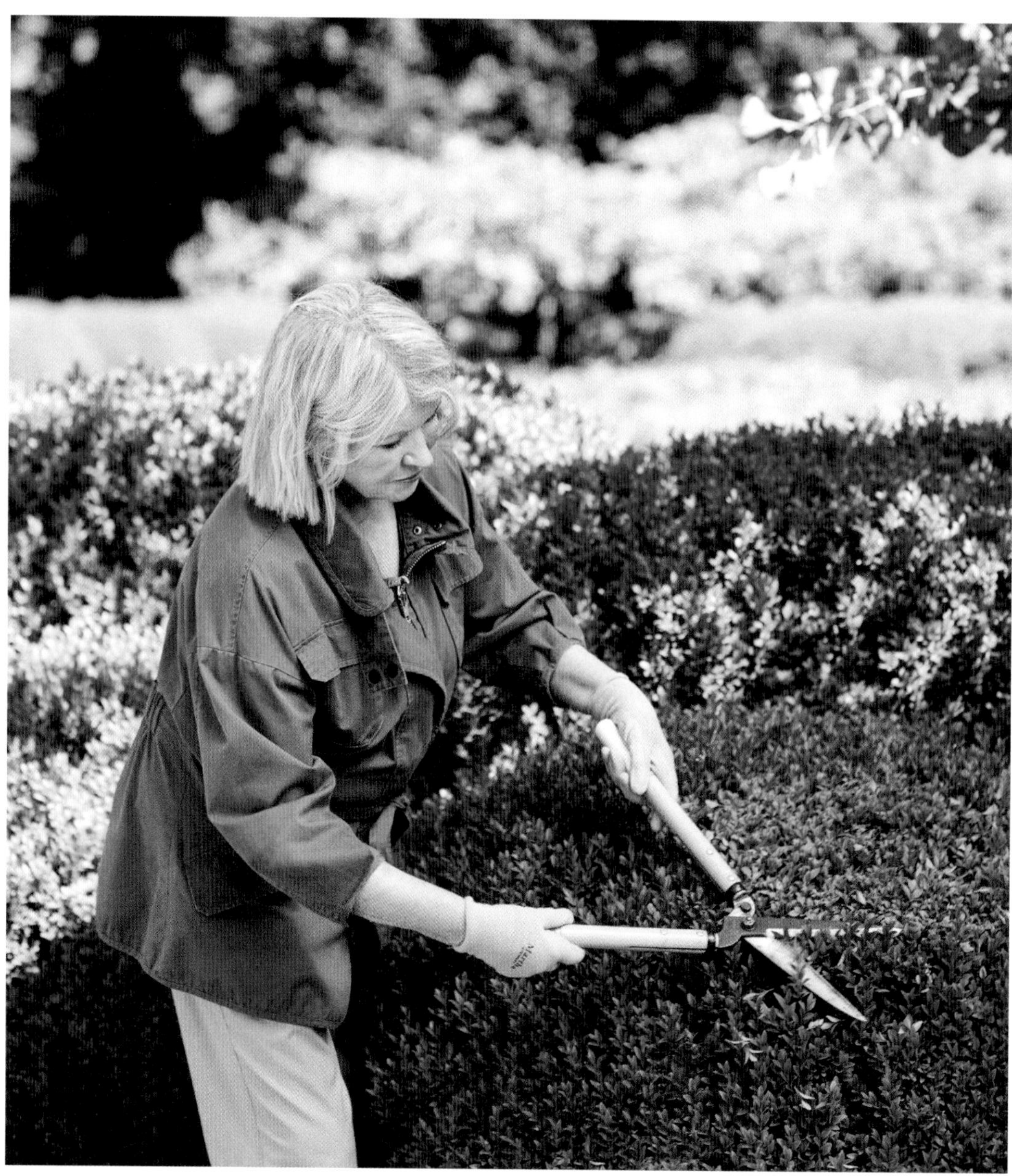

When to prune

Timing is critical and depends on whether the shrub flowers on old wood or new wood.

SHRUBS THAT FLOWER ON OLD WOOD

- These begin forming buds for next year after the current season's blooms fade and carry those buds through winter.
- They typically flower in spring and early summer—forsythia, lilac, deutzia, weigela, rhododendron, mock orange, ninebark, and summer sweet are common examples. Certain types of hydrangea are the exception, blooming in mid to late summer; these include bigleaf, climbing, and oakleaf hydrangeas.
- Prune old-wood shrubs right after they finish flowering to give them time to develop new branches and buds before winter.

SHRUBS THAT FLOWER ON NEW WOOD

- These wait to develop flower buds until growth begins the following spring.
- They generally flower later in the season, such as rose of Sharon, panicle hydrangea, beautyberry, butterfly bush, most types of abelia and spirea, and all rosebushes.
- Prune plants that flower on new wood in early spring; do this after the buds have emerged on the stems and before leafing out so you can easily see where the healthy new growth is located.

How to prune

Successful pruning depends on your goal. Here are the more common issues.

IF THE SHRUB IS WOODY AND TANGLED

Thin out the old wood over the course of three years, removing no more than one-third of the total mass at a time.

- Remove the oldest, centermost branches from the base of the shrub. New growth from the base should follow the next growing season.
- Remove another third of the old wood at the base in each of years two and three.
- After the third year's pruning, the shrub will have only new, vigorous wood and growth.

IF THERE ARE LOTS OF SUCKERS FROM THE BASE

Suckers are new plant shoots that grow (straight up, making them easy to identify) from the base or individual branches; these new shoots compete for nutrients and overcrowd the plant. Those growing on branches make the branches more prone to breakage and disease. Cut suckers back to their point of origin as soon as you see them.

IF THE SHRUB IS LEGGY WITH FLOWERING AT THE TOP

This is especially common with broadleaf evergreens like azalea, rhododendron, Japanese Pieris, and mountain laurel.

- Pinch off the smaller terminal buds of new branches to encourage side branching on the lower part of the shrub. This is also a way to control the shrub's overall size.
- Be careful not to pinch off the larger, plumper flower buds at the ends of established branches.

IF THE SHRUB IS LOPSIDED

Use heading cuts to encourage shorter branches to grow. Yes, you will be cutting the shorter side to stimulate growth.

- Position the pruner on the part of the stem you want to remove, just above a bud that will grow in the direction you want to encourage.
- Never remove more than one-quarter of a stem's length.
- This may take some time and finessing to even out the form, so take a conservative approach to avoid worsening the situation.

Winterizing

▶ **Many trees and shrubs** can survive winter on their own. However, young saplings or prized specimens may warrant a protective barrier to winter's harsh conditions.

Avoid pruning shrubs and trees too close to your first frost date. Doing so can weaken the plant and make it more susceptible to damage.

Cover vulnerable plants—namely broadleaf evergreen shrubs such as boxwood, azalea, rhododendron, and holly as well as short-needled spruces and cypresses—with burlap to protect them from splaying and breaking from the weight of heavy snow, while shielding the foliage from freezing windburn.

Here are two basic methods for protecting shrubs, which can be used in tandem for especially windy locations or as alternative options. In both cases, start by spreading 2 to 3 inches of mulch around the plants and water thoroughly. Spraying an antidesiccant on the plants helps keep the leaves from drying in the wind and cold.

And be sure to remove the coverings once all danger of frost has passed to keep the plants from overheating.

ABOVE: Stone urns are first wrapped in heavy plastic to lock out moisture and then in burlap for an attractive display.

Wrapping

1. Unfurl a large piece of burlap, and with one person holding one end, wrap the other end of the burlap around the plant in a single layer. Be careful that all branches are facing upward.
2. Again, with someone holding the end of a roll of jute twine, wrap the twine around the plant near the bottom of the burlap, then tie it in a knot to secure. Continue winding the twine until you reach the top of the burlap; it should be just tight enough to hold the burlap in place without squeezing the branches. Tie off the end.

Screening

1. Pound hardwood stakes a foot deep in a circle around the shrub (or tree). If you are protecting a row of hedges, place stakes at regular intervals along the windward side.
2. Wrap chicken wire or hardware mesh around the stakes to create a cylinder, pounding fence staples at top, middle, and bottom to secure. This step is optional but provides extra ballast against blustery winds as well as critters.
3. Wrap burlap around the stakes, securing with fence staples at top, middle, and bottom.

"I cannot recall where I first got the idea of tailoring coverings for certain types of plants (and even for garden planters), but we have been wrapping and sewing and protecting woody things like boxwood, tree peonies, clematis, azaleas, and many types of immature plants for a long time now—including the long allées—before the harshest weather arrives. We use eight-foot bamboo stakes to make boxwood tepees, six-foot-wide burlap for the covering, and jute twine for the seams, which are hand-sewn using a carpet needle. The money saved by properly maintaining these cherished gardens is well worth the effort of erecting the protective structures each year."

3

Specialty Gardens

A garden can be anything you want it to be, but having a blueprint upon which to cast your desired design will help you effectively achieve that, so your landscape looks intentional.

The garden types that follow represent the more common examples. Some, like border gardens and cottage gardens, have a rich historical lineage; others, including xeric (water-wise) and habitat gardens, have sprung up in response to environmental concerns. All are open to endless iterations.

Knowing the different garden styles will help you prioritize your budget and efforts. This section also includes plenty of plant-specific insight and glossaries to help you create a landscape you'll love.

Border Garden

It is easy to fall under the spell of border gardens, especially the incredible examples at Sissinghurst, Upton House, and Hidcote in England. Their long, deep beds are packed with plants of varying sizes, colors, and shapes, and are often designed in front of high walls, along allées of trees, or against the foundations of huge, ancient buildings.

One of the most famous examples is the Long Border at Great Dixter House & Gardens, the former British home of influential gardener and gardening writer Christopher Lloyd (1921–2006) in East Sussex (shown opposite).

In Lloyd's description, "The effect should be of a closely woven tapestry. . . . For all the work that goes into it, I want the border to look exuberant and uncontrived."

Another stellar example is at Meadowburn Farm in Vernon, New Jersey (shown on pages 224 to 225), the former home of noted garden writer Helena Rutherfurd Ely (1858–1920).

Planning

Here are some lessons for creating a border garden that's a work of art and a labor of love.

Choose the colors

Given their high-visibility status, border gardens should have a harmonious palette. Select two or three feature colors, then find plants that offer those hues and use them to draw the eye throughout the design. For example, repeating ivory, crimson, and deep-purple flowers stand out amidst pale lavender and golden hues in the Long Border.

Stagger bloom times

Populate the border with plants that have different flowering windows. The Long Border blooms from April to October, with peak interest from mid-June to mid-August.

Create height

Border gardens are typically viewed from one side, so it's important to stairstep the plants from tallest to shortest. Those that are visible from more than one angle should have the tallest plants in the middle. That said, Lloyd wrote, "I do not at all mind bringing some tall plants to the border's front, so long as an open texture allows the eye to see past them. Conversely, channels of low growth can be allowed, at times, to run to the back of the border."

Define the edge

Border gardens look best when they have tidy edges. This will also help prevent weeds and grass from venturing into the bed. You can use bricks, pavers, river rocks, or ornamental edging from a garden center, or something of your own design. A flagstone path runs along the Long Border and is wide enough to allow plants to spill over it while leaving ample room for strolling.

Provide year-round interest

Incorporating evergreen ground covers, shrubs, and small trees into a border ensures it has something to offer long after flowers and deciduous foliage have faded.

Provide a backdrop

Most often, border gardens are planted in front of or alongside a house or other structure, which is the case with the Long Border. There as well, tall sheared hedges provide a contrasting orderly scene for the more organic perennials in front.

Those along streets can be framed by stone walls, split-rail fences, and other boundary enclosures that double as scenic stages for border gardens.

OPPOSITE: The preserved border at Meadowburn Farm features old-fashioned fragrant petunia in white, lavender, and hot pink (in the distance), in combination with white and pink phlox.

FOLLOWING PAGES: Santolina, or lavender cotton, mixes with lavender, to line both sides of a long pathway, offering yellow blooms above its unique silvery gray-green foliage. The drought-tolerant plant is also ideal for xeric gardens (see page 266).

Perennial Garden

Flower gardens have a long and illustrious history, with classic, formal designs gradually giving way to more naturalistic expressions. Modern perennial gardens are as diverse as the flowers they contain—and are best when they have some thoughtful method behind their masses of blooms.

For starters, these gardens should ideally complement rather than compete with the surrounding landscape, such as the meadow-inspired example in the high desert in Santa Fe, New Mexico (shown on pages 230 to 231). There, the bountiful garden offers an inviting transition from the formal courtyards near the house and leads down a southern slope toward the valley, with views of the Sangre de Cristo and Jemez mountain ranges in the distance.

Choosing plants that will thrive in your region is another critical step—especially if you live in an area (like Santa Fe) with extreme weather swings and drought-prone conditions.

FOLLOWING PAGES: This Santa Fe perennial garden overflows with long-season bloomers, like terra-cotta yarrow (*Achillea millefolium* 'Terra Cotta'), Korean feather reed grass (*Calamagrostis brachytricha*), globe thistle (*Echinops ritro*), spires of Agastache 'Blue Fortune', and purple coneflower (*Echinacea purpurea*).

Planning

▶ **A perennial garden** may appear as if it sprung up on its own, but there are some ways to keep it from looking haphazard.

Choose the plants

Start small and expand your perennial garden over time, filling in gaps and experimenting with different hues and specimens as you go.

1. ***Pick a palette:*** As with border gardens, you may want to stick with no more than two or three feature colors. Or follow nature's lead by having a color extravaganza that pleases human eyes and attracts the widest variety of pollinators. The Santa Fe garden, for instance, evolves from the cool purples and pinks of Agastache and coneflower to the warmer hues of blanketflower, coreopsis, and feathery giant sacaton grass.

2. ***Focus on plant combinations:*** Consider having two or three plant pairings serve as focal points that are repeated in the design, with other perennials playing supporting roles. Keep in mind how these plants will look both when flowering and when not.

   The Santa Fe garden's distinct waves of color were created by digging in one- to five-gallon pots of hardy perennials, around which were scattered native grasses and wildflower seeds.

3. ***Provide nonstop color:*** Many perennials bloom for a short time, so choose plants that flower in sequence throughout the growing season—or follow the Sante Fe garden's lead by prioritizing long-season bloomers, such as yarrow (*Achillea millefolium* 'Terra Cotta'), Korean feather reed grass (*Calamagrostis brachytricha*), globe thistle (*Echinops ritro*), Agastache 'Blue Fortune', and purple coneflower (*Echinacea purpurea*).

   Also, consider how the plants look once the blooms have faded, leaving their foliage on display.

4. ***Extend the season:*** Incorporate perennials with seedheads that look sculptural through winter, such as black-eyed Susans and coneflowers (resist the temptation to deadhead them). Besides visual interest, the seedheads provide food for wintering birds and other wildlife. Incorporating grasses and evergreen shrubs ensures they have shelter.

5. ***Match the location:*** Choose plants that thrive in the same growing conditions, including soil type, acidity, drainage, and sun exposure. Prioritize those hardy for your zone, particularly those native to your region, incorporating keystone plants for wildlife—the driving tenet for the Santa Fe garden, which thrums with pollinators.

Prepare for planting

The more variety you intend to include, the more planning is needed in the design phase.

1. ***Cluster similar plants:*** For visual diversity and continuity in the garden, plant in repeating groupings of six or seven similar varieties that combine well, rather than in large masses of a single type of plant.

2. ***Divide a large bed into sections:*** To keep an expansive garden from looking (and being) unwieldy, create subsections, each with its own palette and personality.

3. ***Pay attention to size and spread:*** Perennials grow year after year, so plant them with their mature girth in mind. Some, like daylilies and bee balm, will gradually spread underground; it's best to keep these creepers in their own areas to keep them from pushing out other plants.

4. ***Space closely:*** Weeds can't flourish without room to grow. Plant perennials 15 inches from center to center and grasses at 15 to 20 inches. Economical 4½-inch pots will quickly catch up with gallon size.

5. ***Layer by height:*** If your garden is viewed from all sides, put the tallest plants in the middle and the shortest ones in front. If it is only viewed from one side, have the tallest plants at the back of the design.

Make it practical

Looks aren't everything; considerations such as how you will tend the plants are also important.

1. ***Create pathways:*** You'll need a way to access all the plants for deadheading and weeding, so be sure to leave openings or you'll end up trampling them. You may also want to design paths for people to enjoy the garden from within, such as the pea-gravel path winding through the Santa Fe garden (as shown).

2. ***Fence it in:*** Depending on where you live, deer, rabbits, and other wildlife may try to feast on your flowers. Same for burrowing animals, in which case you will want to bury the fencing at least a few feet underground.

Clematis: The Queen of Flowering Vines

Clematis is a genus of about 300 species within the buttercup family *Ranunculaceae*. Many varieties are lightly scented. An idyllic climbing perennial, clematis can be implemented in landscapes in a variety of ways—on trellises, up a fence, or around an arbor or pergola, such as at Bedford.

More clematis grow across the carriage road on the trunks of the majestic bald cypress trees. In another location near the blueberry bushes, clematis climbs along the outside of the perennial garden fence, on the posts of the blueberry pergola, and around the persimmon trees just in front of the blueberries.

Here's how to use this vertical stunner in your own garden:

Choose the Plants

Typically, the clematis flower has four to seven petals and can range in color from lavender to dark purple and white to deep red; some even bloom in yellow hues. There are a few "bushy" varieties of clematis (and some that can grow as ground covers), but the climbers are more well known.

Various shades of purple, blue, and lavender were chosen for the pergola in the border garden:

- 'Jackmanii'
- 'Parisienne'
- 'Blue Angel'
- 'Eyres' Gift'
- 'Sapphire Indigo'
- 'Arabella'
- 'Comtesse de Bouchard'
- 'Kilian Donahue'
- 'Piilu'
- 'Boulevard Acropolis'
- 'Duchess of Edinburgh' Double White

Pick the Site

Clematis thrives in full or partial sun but does best when the root system is kept cool and shaded, while the foliage gets at least six hours of sun a day. (Remember this mantra: Feet in the shade, head in the sun.)

Plant

It's important to loosen the soil and amend it with lots of organic matter (like compost).

- Dig a hole about 12 inches away from the climbing support to allow the plant room to grow.
- Plant the root ball on a slight diagonal angle, leaning the attached stake (or a bamboo stake) into the support.
- Plant clematis slightly deeper into the soil to protect the crown.
- Add 2 to 3 inches of mulch around the base for extra insulation, then water in the plant well.

Train

As twiners, clematis use a slender leaf stem to hook onto small, narrow supports, such as the bark of a tree, the branches of woody shrubs, or the struts of a trellis, arbor, or tuteur.

To grow it on a smooth pole or fence, you will need to direct its path by attaching plant wire, microfilament (fishing line), or jute twine, wrapping it in a crisscross fashion up and down the support. At Bedford, the clematis clings to sturdy cable around the granite posts in the pergola.

Maintain

Once established, clematis plants are fairly low maintenance.

- They like to be kept moist—but they don't like having wet feet. Water once or twice weekly during the growing season.
- Fertilize at least two times per year—before the first bloom and again before the second round of blossoms later in the year—with an organic fertilizer designed for flowering plants.

Prune

Cut all clematis back to about 4 or 5 inches from the ground in late winter or early spring the first year after it is planted to promote a bushier, stronger, tighter growth habit. After that, pruning can be tricky—different varieties require different pruning tactics. This information is often provided on the plant's care tag; if not, ask a staff member at your local nursery or cooperative extension. Despite these specific pruning variations, clematis is a hearty climber that will usually rebound, no matter how you choose to do it.

Habitat Garden

Growing native plants in your garden can benefit not only the natural environment but local wildlife, too. An ideal habitat garden provides four essential elements—food, water, shelter, and a sustainable habitat for wildlife to raise their young—with a minimum of 70 percent native plants that provide multi-season bloom. In this way, habitat gardens create an ideal ecosystem, free of pesticides or herbicides.

Unfortunately, native plant populations have been declining due to several factors, including development of land, the spread of non-native invasive species, and the use of pesticides and fungicides. So planting natives will help repopulate these essential plants—and anyone can do this, even on a small patio or balcony.

As with all plants, natives will thrive—and help the local ecosystem the most—when planted in the right growing conditions. Doing this will also lighten your gardening load, especially because native plants as a rule need less watering and are more resistant to pests and disease.

Planning

▶ **The tips and** resources that follow will ensure you create a garden that's attractive to you and your local wildlife population.

Choose the plants

All native plants are worth planting, but here's how to make the biggest impact.

PRIORITIZE KEYSTONE PLANTS

Native plant superstars, keystone plants provide the highest level of resources for the foundational species that support the food web, primarily caterpillars, specialist bees, and other beneficial insects.

Research shows that the keystones support 90 percent of butterfly and moth lepidoptera species. Specifically, the plants' foliage serves as nourishment for the larval stage of these caterpillars, which 96 percent of terrestrial birds rely on for food sources.

You can search for keystone plants by zip code on NWF's Native Plant Finder database (see the resources on page 15). To eliminate the guesswork, the NWF also offers keystone plant kits designed for various regions.

Generally speaking, certain species of sunflowers, goldenrods, asters, black-eyed Susans, lupines, joe-pye weed, milkweed (critical for monarch butterflies), geraniums, and sedges are among the more familiar top-performing perennials. Trees and shrubs can be keystone plants, too—different oak, willow, and cherry (*Prunus*) species appear on many ecoregional lists.

PICK A DIVERSE SELECTION

Once you identify the keystone plants for your area, aim for a variety of plants that produce food—nectar, pollen, berries, or seeds—throughout the year. That includes perennials and shrubs that bloom in succession, from early spring through fall. Different insect species rely on plants for food in all four seasons, and a diverse garden will provide that.

Include native evergreens (shrubs and trees) and grasses that offer shelter during frigid winters and sweltering summers, plus nesting sites for birds and small mammals.

Plot the design

Many natives grow in thick stands or colonies, which makes them more attractive and useful to insects and other pollinators and also easier to find.

When planning your garden's design, replicate this by planting groups of three or more of the same species together in the garden (rather than alternating species across the landscape). Planting densely will also allow the mature plants to naturally crowd out weeds.

Consider including habitat features such as bird baths and structures that serve as avian resting spots; dead trees and branches (and cut-up logs) provide nesting homes for many native bees.

Pick the location

Once you have an idea which native plants you'd like to grow, look for spots where they can receive the appropriate amount of sun and shade. For example, in the Northeast, sun-loving natives such as beardtongue foxglove, orange butterfly weed, and smooth blue aster need at least six hours of sun. On the other hand are shade-loving varieties such as wild geranium, big-leaved aster, and great blue lobelia.

Prep the soil

As with any new garden, preparing the soil is critical. Remove any weeds from the bed before planting (and keep up with it during the season). Add compost or other organic matter to create a nutrient-rich soil without the need for fertilizers—native plants do not need chemicals to thrive.

Plant, water, and wait

Follow the plant's care tag for specific planting instructions, then backfill the holes, add a 2- to 3-inch layer of untreated mulch, and water well. Continue to water once or twice a week for the next few weeks and during hot spells in the first growing season. The plants should soon flourish without any further intervention—and begin drawing bees, butterflies, hummingbirds, and other wildlife to your yard.

Maintain the garden

Once the plants are established, a habitat garden shouldn't need watering (unless you are in a dry, hot climate). Neither will you need additional mulch; a combination of tall, medium, short, and ground cover plants will shade the soil and reduce weeds.

Pollinator Primer

Local flora attract local fauna, so meet the pollinators that might visit your native plants. And unlike yellow jackets and hornets, most of the bees below don't sting.

Pollinator	Traits	Favorite Flowers
Common eastern bumblebee (*Bombus impatiens*)	Large, fuzzy, with yellow or orange and black bands. Females' legs have pollen baskets. Noisy.	Clover, rosemary, sunflower, willow.
Hummingbird moth (*Hemaris* genus)	Hovers in place like its namesake; has a long tongue that collects nectar.	Phlox, bee balm, honeysuckle, verbena.
Native bee (4,000+ species)	Vary by species.	Not picky; they love anise hyssop, blazing star, and fruit crops.
Pollen wasp (*Pseudomasaris* genus)	Clubbed antennae.	Western wildflowers such as beardtongue and scorpionweed.
Karner blue butterfly (*Lycaeides melissa samuelis*)	Males are violet blue; females are gray brown. Both are nickel-size.	Lupine, butterfly weed, leafy spurge, blazing star.
European honeybee (*Apis mellifera*)	Fuzzy, about ½ inch long, smaller than the bumblebee.	Sage, Verbascum, lemon balm.
Monarch butterfly (*Danaus plexippus*)	Orange brown with black veins, lined in black with white spots. (It's the only butterfly that makes a two-way migration.)	Milkweed, for the poison that makes monarchs unpalatable to birds; it is the only food for monarch caterpillars.
Hoverfly (Syrphidae family)	Resembles a yellow jacket. Can hover and dart forward and backward quickly.	Yarrow, coyote brush, buckwheat, feverfew, wild mustard.
Bee fly (Bombyliidae family)	Fuzzy like a bumblebee but with two wings (rather than four) and large, faceted fly eyes.	Desert and alpine flora, such as scrub mint and penstemon.
Drone fly (*Eristalis tenax*)	Like a stingerless honeybee, this kind of hoverfly has only one pair of wings and an hourglass pattern.	Alyssum, cosmos, Queen Anne's lace, statice, lupine.

Cottage Garden

Many people are shying away from manicured landscaping and rediscovering the whimsical-wild beauty of British cottage gardens, made famous by designer Gertrude Jekyll and her contemporary William Robinson. These informal gardens offer a range of textures—stone, wood, and otherwise—and dense plantings of flowers and shrubs that are allowed to self-propagate. Indeed, the defining trait of any cottage garden is a bursting-at-the-seams abundance, which doesn't take acres of land to pull off. It's entirely possible to rely on diminutive planters, trellises and tuteurs, window boxes, and hanging baskets to replicate the effect in a tight outdoor space.

Planning

▶ **No matter the** plot size, heed these cottage-garden principles.

Choose the plants

The defining trait of any cottage garden, big or small, is abundance and an organic, carefree approach. Having a riotous variety is another characteristic.

LEAN INTO NATIVE PLANTS

In addition to old-fashioned favorites such as peonies, roses, and clematis, modern cottage gardens increasingly use native plants, which can be planted densely, are easy to maintain, and attract pollinators, to capture the desired bespoke wildness.

LAYER FOR TEXTURE AND DIMENSION

Try pairing flowers and plants that you may not have necessarily envisioned together before. Here are popular annuals and perennials for mixing and matching:

- Allium
- Bellflower
- Campanula
- Columbine
- Delphinium
- Foxglove
- Hollyhock
- Honeysuckle
- Johnny jump-up
- Larkspur
- Lavender
- Phlox
- Poppy
- Rose
- Sweet pea
- Sweet William

Plot the design

The plants are just the beginning. Cottage gardens are meant to be immersive and inviting, so integrate other elements into the scene to lend visual interest.

CARVE OUT A PATHWAY

Being able to stroll amidst the lush plantings is the point of English-style gardens. Mulch, gravel, and stepping stones are low-cost alternatives to inlaid brick and pavers, and every bit as charming.

ADD VERTICAL INTEREST

Include one or more structures for climbing plants (roses, hydrangeas, wisteria, or clematis), such as a rustic fence that can double as a trellis for flowering vines (shown at left), an arbor along a path, or tuteurs located throughout. Taller shrubs and small trees are other ways to lend height.

CREATE VIGNETTES

The idea is to imbue the space with romance and invite sitting and watching pollinators. Tuck a chair at the end of a path or a bench into a canopied nook next to a birdbath. For whimsy, consider adding a wishing well or small arched bridge.

Rose Garden

No other flower has been more celebrated than the rose, whether in ancient Greek mythology, Elizabethan poetry, or modern-day Valentine's Day cards. The prickly plants have long inspired home gardeners, too. These days, the genus *Rosa* (in the family Rosaceae) encompasses some 150 species of erect, climbing, or trailing perennial shrubs with thousands of varieties stemming from a limited number of roses from Asia that were crossbred over centuries with native European and American wild species. Modern hybrids are disease resistant, making them popular with growers who previously shied away from antique varieties.

And no other flower is as associated with Lily Pond. There, the yard was teeming with a panoply of heirlooms, climbers, and English varieties, which were transplanted to Bedford before the East Hampton property was sold.

More recently, a new rose garden took hold behind the main greenhouse at Bedford, where a 68-by-30-foot "room" for the roses is surrounded by a "wall" of boxwoods that frames the garden and provides a bit of protection. A central 5-foot path is also flanked by larger boxwoods at the entrances and smaller boxwoods across the garden.

Planning

▶ **With careful site** and plant selection, preparation, planting, and nurturing, your rose garden should last for decades to come.

Choose the roses

The terminology can be confusing. Botanically, all roses are shrubs, not just the "shrub rose" variety.

UNDERSTAND THE GENUS

Wrapping your head around all the options can be overwhelming. Roses are classified into three main types:

- ***Species roses*** (aka wild roses)
- ***Old-garden roses*** (introduced before 1867)
- ***Modern roses***—hybrid tea roses, David Austin roses, cluster-flowered floribundas, ramblers and climbers, and repeat-blooming miniature (dwarf) roses

The American Rose Society (rose.org) maintains a classification of roses and their characteristics, including those that bear single flowers over a short period along with modern varieties that offer a range of flower forms and a longer bloom time.

OPPOSITE: Martha brought this David Austen variety, 'Constance Spry', from her Turkey Hill garden.

CONSIDER YOUR GROWING ZONE

Prioritize plants that are hardy to your area, though you may want to experiment with others that you particularly love. Contact your local extension/master gardeners, who, in addition to telling you which roses do well, may be able to tell you which to avoid.

PICK A PALETTE

Roses come in every imaginable hue. Subtle color gradations are best for smaller plots; brighter varieties stand out in larger ones. The roses Martha grows range from light pink to apricot to lavender and even pale yellow, golden, and creamy white (selected using a color wheel).

PLANT A VARIETY

Mix and match roses with different bloom times and flower forms for waves of color. The Bedford rose garden includes three modern species that are particularly good for cutting:

- ***Hybrid tea roses***, also called large-flowered roses, typically have only one flower per stem and flower in three flushes from summer to late autumn.
- ***Floribundas*** have many flowers per stem and tend to repeat-flower continuously from summer to late autumn. You'll get hundreds of blooms from a handful of plants.
- ***Shrub roses*** are aptly named for their graceful growth habit, which allows for growing in a container. They feature many roses per shrub that are easily harvested, thanks to their more delicate stems. This species is usually very fragrant—in particular Princess Charlene de Monaco, which holds a prominent place in the garden.

BE REALISTIC

Looking for a rewarding entrée into roses? Knock Out roses are among the easiest to grow—no heavy pruning or even deadheading is required.

Roses for Cutting

Cultivars from renowned English breeder David Austin, which have the fragrance and form of old garden roses but with repeat-bloom and disease-resistance advantages, predominate the following selection.

1. 'Earth Angel'
2. 'Julia's Rose'
3. 'Carding Mill'
4. 'Connie's Sandstorm'
5. 'Silver Cloud'
6. 'Evelyn'
7. 'Distant Drums'
8. 'Stainless Steel'
9. 'Butterscotch'
10. 'Dainty Bess'
11. 'Francis Meilland'
12. 'Koko Loko'
13. 'Sally Holmes'

1
2
3
4
5
6
7
8
9
10
11
12
13

Select a location

Roses can be planted in raised beds or in-ground with other shrubs or perennials, as thorny hedges to protect wildlife, or scrambling over fences, arbors, trellises, or other structures.

- Certain roses also do well in containers. Just be sure to give the roots, which grow deeply, adequate space.
- In all cases, look for a spot that gets at least six hours of direct sunlight; otherwise the plants may produce fewer blooms and become tall and spindly.
- Roses also need good air circulation to prevent fungal and foliar diseases.
- Make sure the soil has good drainage; a pH of 6.5 is ideal. When preparing the site, amend it with compost, fertilizer (such as Rose-tone), and bone meal (according to the package instructions).

Decide on the design

Take time to figure out how you want to organize the plants and whether you want a formal layout or a more organic flow.

Below are some guidelines Martha follows:

- Begin by sorting the rosebushes into color blocks and placing them in groupings.
- Using landscape twine as a guide, line the bushes up in straight rows according to variety and mature growth pattern, planting the rows 4 feet apart.
- Use tuteurs, obelisks, arbors, and other supports for climbers to lend height and interesting shapes to punctuate the scene.
- Plant taller varieties, including hybrid tea roses, in the center with shorter varieties all around.
- Position fragrant varieties such as David Austin roses near the edges, where their scents can be most appreciated.

Buy healthy plants

The largest selection of roses is sold as bare-root plants, which must be planted right away.

Container-grown (aka grafted) roses can be kept in their pots, in a semisunny spot, until you are ready to plant them. These also tend to be easier for beginner gardeners to grow.

When buying bare-root roses, open the package right away; the plants should feel a little heavy for their size.

- There should be at least three sturdy canes, each with several plump, bright-colored, pinkish raised oval areas (buds) and no leaves or visible new growth.
- The roots should be light-colored and evenly dispersed around the central trunk to give it a firm, even anchor.
- Remove any broken or diseased roots as well as any shriveled or dry canes. (See pruning tips opposite.)

When shopping for container-grown roses, inspect the roots: They should be well established and offer resistance when you gently tug on the main stem. (Skip any plants where the stem comes right out.)

Plant for success

If planting bare-root roses, soak the roots in water and a root-stimulating solution (following package instructions) overnight. If planting grafted (container-grown) roses, trim off any blooms and save them for indoor arrangements.

Then follow these steps to plant either type:

1. Dig a hole that is slightly wider than and about two times as deep as the root system.
2. Remove the rose from its pot, tease the roots to stimulate growth, and place it into the hole.
3. Make sure the graft (or the top of the root ball) is about an inch above the soil surface.
4. Backfill, then dig a shallow trench around the drip line.
5. Water thoroughly when planting, then press with the heel of your shoe to compact the soil around the trench.
6. Continue to water deeply and slowly for the next 7 to 10 days, pressing on the soil around the trench each time.
7. Spread a 2- to 3-inch layer of mulch around the plant to retain moisture.

Tend the garden

These divas demand (and deserve) careful and consistent attention.

- Roses are heavy feeders. Keep them well fed with a springtime application of fertilizer designed for your specific variety.
- Every spring and fall, sprinkle 1 cup of Epsom salts (magnesium sulfate) around the perimeter of each established rosebush to add important nutrients, then work it into the soil using a hand cultivator.
- Deadhead stems after blooms fade: Cut toward the center of the bush at a 45-degree angle, just below the first pair of leaves and directly above an outward-facing stem.
- Roses are prone to numerous diseases and pests, including black spot, Cercospora leaf spot, aphids, and sawflies. Problems are easier to manage if detected and addressed early. A preventive spray can help with leaf spot during the plant's growing season, from April through August, and a jar of soapy water placed near the plant can trap summertime pests.

- Throughout the season, inspect leaves, buds, and stems for spotting, blackening, sticky residue, holes in leaves, and leaf yellowing or distortion. Mostly these issues are cosmetic and can be pruned to prevent spreading (clean the blade with rubbing alcohol after each cut).
- Give roses 1 to 2 inches of water every week. Overwatered roses are more susceptible to disease, particularly powdery mildew. Water at the base of the plant to keep the foliage dry, preferably in the morning before daytime temperatures climb.

Prune diligently

Begin by inspecting plants carefully in springtime.

PRUNE DEAD CANES AND BRANCHES

New growth reveals which canes and branches made it through the winter. Cut any dead canes off at the base. Branches partially killed by winter weather should be cut back to a spot just above a vigorously growing bud.

PRUNE ANY BROKEN CANES OR BRANCHES

Canes should be cut back to a healthy side branch or, in the case of a heavily damaged cane, cut off right at the base. Also, prune any that have been injured by grazing rabbits or deer.

CHECK THE REMAINING BRANCHES CLOSELY

If you see brown blotches spreading over the greenish bark, these cankers are the result of a fungal disease. Prune off all such diseased wood, making your cuts well below the lowermost cankers. Dispose of infected debris, but do not add it to your compost bin.

PRUNE INGROWN AND SPINDLY CANES OR BRANCHES

Air cannot circulate through a bush congested with branches that grow toward the center, so cut them off at the base along with any weak branches. Use a lopper to cut through thick canes.

PRUNE THE OVERALL PLANT FOR SIZE

All bush-type roses should have their remaining canes shortened by a half to a third to promote compact, sturdy growth; the best time for this varies with the type of rose. Cut especially thick or hard old wood with a pruning saw.

- Because repeat-flowering "everblooming" roses, such as hybrid teas and floribundas, bloom most heavily on new shoots, cane shortening should be carried out in early spring when deadwood is removed.
- Old-garden roses that bloom once a year bear flowers only on branches at least a year old. Shortening their canes in early spring removes many of the branches that would bear flowers in succeeding months. So wait until right after they bloom to shorten canes of once-bloomers.
- Climbing roses, even reblooming modern types such as climbing hybrid teas, also bear the bulk of their flowers in an early-summer flush. Wait until this subsides before shortening all horizontal side branches by a half to a third. Leave the main skeleton of upright canes intact, unless renewing a neglected specimen.

Shade Garden

If growing perennial gardens is akin to painting with flowers, shade gardens are like sculpting with foliage. The key is to use plants with contrasting colors, shapes, and textures as well as variegation to create an arresting display.

Some gardeners who lack sunlit spaces have no other option than to plant shade-loving plants, but those with stretches of open yard may opt to create shade-garden opportunities for maximum diversity visually and in plant selection.

Plenty of perennials prefer full or partial shade—the sheer variety is intriguing. Take the canopy collage of smaller trees, shrubs, and herbaceous plants in the shade garden at Brandywine Cottage outside Philadelphia (shown opposite), which lies on a one-acre slope under the canopy of native deciduous trees.

Planning

▶ **Learn how to make** the most of dimly lit areas in your own yard with favorite specimens and planting tips.

Choose the plants

Browse the "shade plant" section at nurseries and online, and keep the following considerations in mind when picking specific specimens.

- Plants that thrive in shade have larger leaves for taking in as much light as possible. Those that can tolerate full shade (as noted on the plant tag) can be planted in the deepest, darkest nooks and crannies.
- Foliage may reign supreme, but it's worth including flowering species that tolerate shady conditions, such as Spanish bluebells, bleeding hearts, Hosta 'Francee', and Hosta 'Fire and Ice'.
- Because it is easy for shade gardens to be awash in green, look for opportunities to throw in rich, dark purples, such as wild violets or Virginia bluebells, or glowing white blooms, like woodland phlox or foamflower.
- As always, choose plants with different flowering windows, from late-winter/early-spring ephemerals and spring ornamental trees through late-summer/fall perennials and shrubs.

At Brandywine, spring bloomers include red *Helleborus* 'Brandywine' and *Narcissus* 'Ice Follies'. In summer, the terrain features the camellia-like white petals of the *Stewartia koreana* tree, the variegated foliage of *Hakonechloa macra* 'Aureola', a dark patch of heuchera, the vivid hues of *Hydrangea quercifolia* and *serrata*, and yellow *Corydalis lutea*, which covers the wall. Come fall, the colorful landscape includes reddish *Rhus* sumac, magenta *Cornus florida*, yellow *Magnolia macrophylla*, and white ghost bramble (*Rubus cockburnianus*). See page 252 for more shade plants by season.

- Hostas (see Hosta Hues on page 254) and ferns are quintessential, easy-care shade options. Both come in a dazzling array of forms and shades, including the painted Japanese fern, which sports silvery fronds with purple down the center; ostrich ferns, whose plumelike, arching fronds are reminiscent of tail feathers; and 'Francee' hosta, with dark-green, heart-shaped leaves with white margins and midsummer blooms. Two hosta hybrids—'Blue Umbrellas' and 'Blue Angel'—are drought-tolerant summer stars.
- Choose plants with contrasting appearances—even (or especially) when using just one species. For example, the starry white flower of *Allium ursinum*, also known as bear's garlic, looks lovely with purple heuchera (*Heuchera* 'Plum Pudding') and twinleaf (*Jeffersonia diphylla*, a native perennial named for Thomas Jefferson). Golden hakone grass (*Hakonechloa macra* 'Aureola') combines beautifully with hostas and Solomon's seal.
- Layer the plants by height and also by color—brighter varieties can pop in the darkest depths.

Pick the site

Look for areas with dappled shade, which can accommodate a greater plant selection and allow you to create a woodland effect. Deeper shade will require more careful selection but can be even more dramatic and moody in a good way.

- Natural locations for shade gardens include under the canopies of deciduous trees and in the shadow of thick evergreens.
- No trees? Try the north-facing side of a house or other building and beneath pergolas or arbors covered with climbing plants.

Plot the design

No matter the size, shade gardens typically follow a few general style principles.

- Because they are usually inspired by nature, consider incorporating mass plantings of the same varietal to replicate how many understory plants grow in colonies or stands.
- You can even create a "stream" of different painted ferns along with colorful flowers like Epimediums in a woodland garden.
- Stone walls are another common feature—such as the 300-foot-long rubble wall (built with stones collected from the landscape) containing Brandywine's shade garden. Choice plants grow along this wall and beside paths that wend throughout the hillside.
- Pathways are the backbone of larger-scale shade gardens, inviting contemplative strolling, like the mossy brick walkway below, flanked by tall hornbeam hedges and low-growing pale-hued ferns and bright hostas.

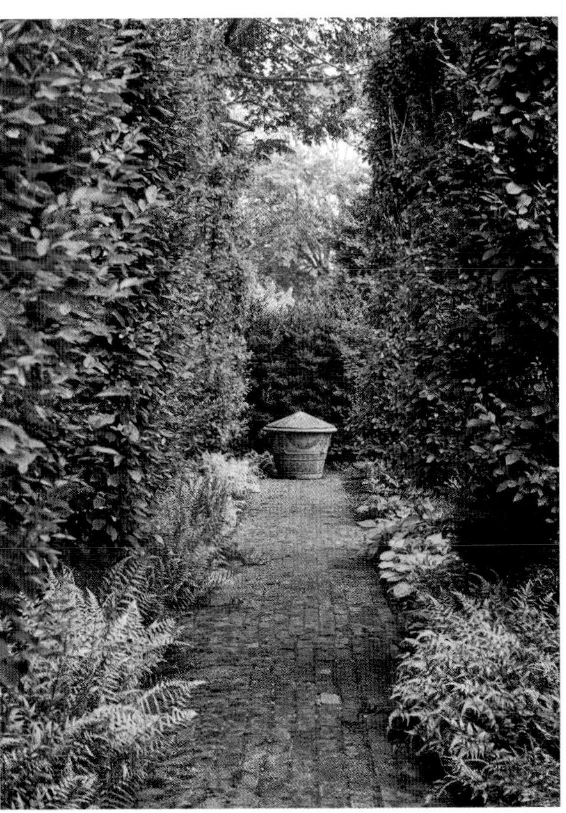

Shade Plants by Season

The following specimens are just some of those to incorporate into your own landscape, including those shown here.

Spring

- Lady's Slipper orchid (*Cypripedium* 'Gisele')
- Rue anemone (*Anemonella thalictroides*)
- Spanish bluebells (*Hyacinthoides hispanica*)
- Bleeding heart (*Lamprocapnos spectabilis*)
- Barrenwort (*Epidemium*)
- Eastern redbud (*Cercus canadensis*)
- Hellebore (*Helleborus*)
- Snowdrop (*Galanthus*)
- Yellow trillium (*Trillium luteum*)

Summer

- Black mondo grass (*Ophiopogon planiscapus* 'Nigrescens')
- Hosta such as 'Francee' and 'Fire and Ice'; also see those on pages 254–255
- Japanese forest grass (*Hakonechloa macra* 'Aureola')
- Japanese painted fern (*Athyrium niponicum* 'Pictum')
- Oakleaf hydrangea (*Hydrangea quercifolia*)

Fall

- American euonymus (*Euonymus americanus*)
- Aromatic aster (*Aster oblongifolius*)
- Bowman's root (*Gillenia trifoliata*)
- White wood aster (*Aster diaricatus*)

Hosta Hues

With so many different colors, textures, and sizes, these shade-loving plants offer nearly infinite combinations that create interest in the garden. Their leaves can be smooth, veined, or puckered, and matte, shiny, or waxy. The color ranges from golden to deep blue-green and two-tone or variegated options.

Golden Varieties

Yellow-green and creamy or white markings bring warmth to the garden.

1. 'Summer Music'
2. 'Gold Standard'
3. 'Cherry Berry'
4. 'Masquerade'
5. 'On Stage'
6. *H. kikutii*
7. 'Patriot'

Blue-Leaf Varieties

These cool-hued hostas (opposite) are prized even by gardeners who find other hostas "common."

8. 'Love Pat'
9. 'David L. Reath'
10. 'Dorset Blue'
11. 'Hadspen Blue'
12. 'Great Expectations'
13. 'Blue Cadet'
14. 'June'

8
11
10
5
9
13
12
14

White Garden

White gardens are a century-old trend popularized by renowned British writer and gardener Vita Sackville-West at Sissinghurst Castle, in the UK (shown opposite). These monochromatic displays look especially stunning at night, when the white blossoms glow in the twilight.

All-white gardens are hardly monotonous. Just as every ray of white light contains a rainbow, "white" flowers present a vast spectrum of pale tones. Then there's the foliage, which also comes in various hues. In fact, Sackville-West, who strolled through her white plot before and after dinner, actually described it as "my grey, green, and white garden."

That statement sums up the ingredients of any successful white-themed display—silvery-gray leaves, deep-green foliage, and shimmery white blossoms.

Planning

▶ **Here's how to adopt** a white-themed garden into your landscape so it shines morning, noon, and night.

Choose the plants

You may be surprised at just how many species fit into a white garden. As with any palette, consider foliage as well as blossoms. Follow Vita's example and create interest with different shapes, textures, and form.

1. THINK BEYOND TRUE WHITE

Taking inspiration from the white-blooming plants at Sissinghurst and other well-known gardens, expand beyond "white" to include bulbs, annuals, perennials, shrubs, and flowering trees in a range of shades. What's more, white blossoms reflect and highlight adjacent hues—and contain touches of other shades, such as blush pink or buttery yellow—and take on a golden glow as they age. Consider, too, plants with variegated foliage for glimpses of white or pale green.

2. EXTEND THE SEASON

Choose plants with different bloom times, referring to the glossaries on pages 260 to 263 for plants that blossom in early spring, late summer, and in between—some featured in the garden at High Meadow Farm, north of New York City.

Although lovely year-round, this garden reaches its apex in late summer, just when most other gardens are beginning their decline. As shown on pages 258 to 259, the billowy grasses have reached full size and the dwarf fountain grass is in bloom, joined by peegee hydrangea, buddleia, white echinacea, variegated sedum, gaura (in foreground, center), and the low-growing rose 'Carpet White'. Not shown are annuals that bloom all season long, along with perennials such as Japanese anemone, joe-pye weed, and echinacea that open in July and continue through September.

Pick the location

Minimalists may opt to devote their entire landscape to a white palette, while others prefer to embrace a white garden as a standout section of a multifaceted landscape, placing it in a strategic spot for maximum enjoyment—such as where it is visible in the glow of moonlight, whether viewed through a window or from a dining patio. The High Meadow Farm garden at left, for instance, holds a prominent spot along an expansive stone terrace overlooking the rolling hills.

Equally entrancing is the sweet fragrance that many white blooms exude at night, an added attraction for nocturnal insect pollinators—and for people congregating or strolling nearby.

Plot the design

As with any garden, you'll want to create visual interest with a variety of plants, including non-flowering specimens—such as the grasses at High Meadow Farm, which soften edges, capture light, and form diaphanous "hedges" in a curved, sweeping pattern. Boxwoods—including white buddleia, a cloud-pruned boxwood—and other evergreen shrubs are other options.

Varying the height is equally essential: Consider ground covers around the edges, rising to *Echinacea* 'White Swan', cleome, white cosmos, *Verbena bonariensis*, and five-foot-tall boltonia, with flowering shrubs like rose of Sharon and climbers such as clematis or roses lending further structure.

Early-Spring Bloomers
1. *Cornus florida* (flowering dogwood)
2. *Helleborus* 'Brandywine' (lenten rose)
3. *Epimedium × youngianum* 'Niveum' (barrenwort, bishop's hat)
4. *Leucojum aestivum* (snowflake)
5. *Narcissus* 'Actaea' (poeticus daffodil)
6. *Dicentra spectabilis* 'Alba' (white bleeding heart)
7. *Fothergilla gardenii* (fothergilla)
1
5
4
3
7
2
6

Mid- to Late-Spring Bloomers

1. *Syringa vulgaris* 'Jan van Tol' (common lilac)
2. *Pulmonaria* 'Sissinghurst White' (lungwort)
3. *Allium* 'Mount Everest' (ornamental onion)
4. *Tulipa* 'Purissima' syn. 'White Emperor' (tulip)
5. *Aquilegia flabellata* 'Alba' (fan columbine)
6. *Iris germanica* 'Alba' (dwarf bearded iris)
7. *Pieris japonica* (Japanese Pieris)
8. *Rhododendron* 'Cunningham's White' (white rhododendron)

1
2
3
4
5
6
7
Summer Bloomers
1. Boltonia asteroides (false aster)
2. Dahlia 'White Alva's' (dahlia)
3. Cosmos bipinnatus 'Sonata White' (Mexican aster)
4. Lysimachia clethroides (gooseneck loosestrife)
5. Phlox paniculata 'Mother of Pearl' (garden phlox)
6. Echinacea purpurea 'White Swan' (white swan coneflower)
7. Nepeta cataria 'Snowflake' (white catnip)

Late-Summer Bloomers

1. *Thunbergia alata* 'Bright Eyes' (black-eyed Susan vine)
2. *Lilium* 'Casa Blanca' (oriental lily)
3. *Platycodon grandiflorus* 'Hakone White' (balloon flower)
4. *Hibiscus syriacus* 'Diana' (rose of Sharon)
5. *Hosta* 'Ginko Craig' (hosta)
6. *Rosa rugosa* 'Alba' (white rugosa rose)
7. *Hydrangea paniculata* (panicle hydrangea)

Climbing Hydrangeas

Native to Asia, climbing hydrangeas (*Hydrangea anomala* subsp. *petiolaris*) love rich soil, thrive in sunny and shady areas, and are hardy to zones 4 to 8.

These strong, sturdy, and ever-so-lovely plants wind their way up the trees, walls, and chimney at Bedford. The vines bloom prolifically over four to eight weeks and are most beautiful during the early summer, with 5-inch white or pink lacecap-like flowers. By autumn, the leaves turn a vibrant yellow, and come winter, the barren, cinnamon-hued, exfoliating bark adds its own kind of beauty.

Their aerial rootlets cling to all surfaces, but be sure to stick to sturdy structures made of stone or brick (first ensuring the mortar is in good condition in brick surfaces); avoid wooden shingles and clapboard, which can be damaged by these hardy "holdfasts."

The first climbing hydrangeas at Bedford were planted to cover the trunks of the large sugar maples and spruce trees growing near the houses. Later, after a hurricane cleared off the tops of six enormous spruces by the entrance to the property, the "stumps" seemed to be ideal climbing stakes, and one vine was planted at the base of each. Today, the stumps resemble huge shrubs all year long. Climbing hydrangea also grows on the chimney, with screw eyes and steel-wire trellising inserted to help guide the strong growers and their long, lateral branches.

Here's the technique

1. Dig a hole about 2 feet away from the base of the support. Loosen the earth 6 inches deeper than the height of the pot. Mix the recommended amount of an organic slow-release granular fertilizer with the loosened soil.
2. Remove the plant from its container, and score the roots with a sharp tool, to help the roots spread out in the ground.
3. Position the plant at a 45- to 60-degree angle, so the tops of the foliage are touching the trunk and the roots are pointing away. Fill in with a blend of the dug-out soil and compost. Tamp down lightly.
4. Water the plant slowly with the hose for several minutes. Continue to water frequently during the first growing season. Once established, water enough to keep the soil moist at all times (about 1 inch in the absence of rain).

Be prepared to prune the vines annually to keep them off windows and frames, and even from spreading like a ground cover in the garden.

Xeric (Water-Wise) Garden

Xeric gardens (aka xeriscaping) have been growing in popularity for their eco-friendly and relatively low-maintenance reputation. With water conservation in mind, these gardens use mulch or gravel for a planting medium in place of soil. A sustainable alternative to some other gardening systems, xeric gardens require about 80 percent less maintenance than the average perennial garden.

And because weeds typically flourish in rich, moist soils, the dry environment of a gravel or mulch garden means weed seeds don't have what they need to germinate, grow, and thrive.

These gardens are practical for people who have a hard time keeping plants alive due to harsh growing conditions, including arid soil, full sun, and high temperatures, or those who live in drought-prone regions. And they support a range of water-wise plants, including bulbs, perennials, ornamental grasses, and certain shrubs. They're an especially excellent solution for converting high-maintenance, water-hogging lawns into a more sustainable homescape—even in areas with ample rainfall and fertile soil.

OPPOSITE: Drought-tolerant pittosporum, silvery lamb's ears, and petite-flowered erigeron line a walkway, while feather reed grass adds texture and movement.

Planning

▶ **No matter your motivation**, the steps to creating a water-wise garden are the same.

Choose the plants

Focus on drought-tolerant plants, notably those native to your region. Also, choose varieties with deep root systems (ask for guidance at the nursery). Seeds won't get the proper sunlight to sprout, so buy only seedlings.

Except where noted, the following plants (some of which may be native to your area) are hardy for zones 3 to 9.

- Prairie dropseed
- Little bluestem
- *Allium* 'Purple Sensation' (zones 3 to 8)
- *Sedum* 'Autumn Joy'
- Pale purple coneflower
- Black-eyed Susan
- Aster 'October Skies' (zones 3 to 8)
- Eastern bee balm (zones 5 to 8)

The following low-growing, water-wise plants are good options when replacing a lawn. When in doubt, go with sedums and other succulents.

- Hen and chickens
- Mullein
- Eryngium
- Thyme
- Gaura
- Nepeta
- Artemisia
- Agastache
- Yarrow
- Veronica

Find the right spot

Choose an area that receives full sun and is not likely to have leaves and other plant debris fall onto the gravel or mulch, as this matter effectively acts like soil (and hence is a breeding ground for weeds).

Also consider the type of soil you're starting with—since you'll be covering it with mulch or gravel, soils that are typically harder to grow in (for example, too rocky, or harder clay) would work well for a xeric garden.

No matter your soil's composition, a successful xeric garden should always drain well, so work in lots of organic matter to help with drainage.

Prepare your yard

As with any garden preparation, you'll need to remove existing grass and other vegetations, either with a sod cutter or using the spade-and-shovel method. Other options include covering turf with black plastic for a year or layering it with flattened cardboard, compost, and mulch until the grass dies. For more information, see page 249.

Either way, begin the xeric garden in the spring and start out small—you don't need to replace your entire yard in one fell swoop. Pick a manageable patch to begin with and then you can learn what works and what doesn't before committing to a larger space.

Provide edging

Installing a border will prevent the mulch or gravel from escaping and weeds from encroaching. You can use rocks, bricks, pavers, cedar planks (avoid treated lumber), or metal, wood, or plastic garden edging—whatever fits your design goals.

Select the medium

Gravel and mulch both work in xeric gardens. It often depends on which material you like best. You may also decide that mulch suits one spot (for a more naturalistic look) and gravel another—such as along the front and sides of your house, where it might be an extension of a gravel driveway or path.

You can use any type of mulch, but the gravel should be small, anywhere from ¼ inch to ³⁄₁₆ inch. Washed gravel, which has been cleaned of any dirt and debris, will be the most attractive, though you can hose off the gravel yourself if necessary. Pea gravel is rounded and looks good in a blend of mixed colors. Sharp gravel made of granite or quartz also works well.

After selecting your material, use it to fill in your border. Spread the mulch or gravel evenly to a depth of about 2 to 3 inches.

Add the plants

Small seedlings work best—those in a 4- or 5-inch pot are the correct depth. Anything too large will require shaving off some of the root base.

1. Lay out your potted plants where you want them to grow, keeping them 12 to 18 inches apart.
2. Remove the plant from the pot and hover it over a bushel basket. Peel off the top inch of soil to remove any weed seeds before planting.
3. Dig about 5 to 6 inches deep, going just past the mulch or gravel into the top inch of soil, and insert the root ball into the hole.
4. Fill the area back in with soil and gravel. Make sure the mulch or gravel encloses the crown of the plant (where the stem meets the roots).

Water the plants

Water thoroughly when planting, then continue watering every day for the first few weeks to encourage the roots to find their way from the mulch or gravel to the soil and allow the plants to get established.

After that, you can water less frequently during the first season, depending on the climate.

Over time, your xeric garden will require less and less water. Eventually, you'll need to water it only when your plants show signs of thirst.

Maintain the garden

Once your plants are established, the most you'll need to do is an annual spring cleanup by cutting the perennials back to about 6 inches. Letting organic matter (such as fallen leaves, spent flowers, and decayed twigs or branches) build up in the gravel will derail the system. Remove those as you see them. The mulch or gravel will also need replenishing over time. Otherwise, no continual weeding and no fertilizing are needed.

FOLLOWING PAGES: Urban neighborhoods, such as this one in Berkeley, California, have been replacing conventional lawns with water-wise plants in what is called "street-edge" gardening.

Container Garden

Just one pot can hold an entire garden in miniature, a world of plants as visually compelling as a mixed bed and yet easier to manage. That's the beauty of container plantings: You don't need a big space to make a big impact.

What you do need, however, are plants that can withstand the quirks of your region, whether that includes the stickiest humidity or the scantiest rainfall. Sunlight requirements are another key factor.

Other than that, potted plants needn't be very compatible; in such a small environment, you can control their care precisely.

Indeed, container gardening is a chance to experiment—for example, by varying the arrangements from year to year. You can place varieties beside each other that might not grow together in the ground, and it's easy to move pots around. You can even display plants on pavement or other areas where you can't do in-ground planting.

At Bedford, planting the pots is an annual task carried out each May, on the terraces, in giant urns along the carriage road, and on the cobblestone courtyard in front of the stable.

And each Memorial Day weekend, a truck loaded with trays of small succulents and large agaves, aloes, and palms propagated and overwintered in the Bedford greenhouses heads north to be potted at Skylands' terrace.

Planning

▶ **These portable gardens** have unique prep, plant, and tending requirements.

Choose the containers

First select the pots, which will outlast the plants they will contain. Buy the highest quality your budget allows.

- Decide where the pots will be displayed, then snap a photo of this area, including some items to indicate scale.
- Stick with a palette, like varying shades of warm terra-cotta or cool, steely grays, then assemble a variety of heights, sizes, and shapes to create a captivating vignette. Keep in mind that most plants will be happier in large pots, where they'll have space to grow; those in smaller pots will need to be watered (and possibly repotted) more often.
- Troughs or other short vessels are ideal for a variety of succulents, which have shallow root systems that require little soil and are generally drought resistant. Mosses are another good option for shallow containers.
- If you live in a cold climate with harsh winters, look for planters that are designated as frostproof, available in Italian terra-cotta, stone, metal, and composite materials. The freeze-and-thaw cycle will cause other pots to heave, so you will need to wrap them (see page 219) or move them inside.

Classic Container Composition

For a showstopping—and foolproof—display, try the "thriller, filler, spiller" formula:

First, cast a "thriller" standout variety as the central focal point, then add a "filler" to fill in the gaps. Finish with a "spiller" plant such as a trailing or vining type that cascades over the rim. View them together in a sunny spot at the nursery to ensure they are truly compatible.

Pick the plants

Opt for varieties that will work with your growing conditions.

- Before you head to the nursery, determine how much sunlight the plants will receive in each location.
- Decide on a color scheme—and consider the hue and texture of the foliage, not just the flowers, which may appear only for a short time.
- Start with a favorite plant or two, or see if anything speaks to you at the nursery; then build the rest of each pot or grouping of pots around its colors and textures as well as growing conditions.
- Make sure to view the plants in sun or shade, depending on where they reside at your home.

Provide a fertile medium

Nutrient-rich soil is the foundation of a thriving plant. You can buy high-quality organic soilless potting mixes at garden centers, or make your own using vermiculite, a naturally occurring mineral. The mineral boosts the health of your container plants and creates a well-draining, nutrient-rich growing medium—whereas standard garden soil can be too dense for container gardens.

To make: Blend 2 gallons of coconut coir with 1 gallon of vermiculite, 1 gallon of perlite, and 1 gallon of compost, then add 1 cup of a complete granular fertilizer.

Before filling your pot, clear out any debris from the drainage hole and loosely cover it with screening material.

Moisten the potting mix and add enough to fill to about 2 inches from the container's rim. Make sure the soil is level but do not compact it.

Pot the plants

Keep in mind that a plant in a too-small container will become root-bound and will eventually dry out; in a too-big pot, the plant may get root rot.

That said, you can grow twice as many plants in a container compared to the same amount of garden space. (So divide the plant tag spacing recommendations by half.)

1. Prep the plants by picking off any spent blooms or yellowing leaves.
2. Loosen the roots, cutting any that are root-bound.
3. Pinch back any plants that are too tall or leggy: To encourage horizontal (instead of vertical) growth, cut directly above the node of leaves that sits at the height you desire.
4. The roots should be covered by soil, with the leaves just above the surface.
5. When grouping plants, start by positioning the tallest in the center of the pot, then add any that will spill over the sides.
6. Use a hand trowel to move the soil to the side when planting, being careful not to compact the soil. Then backfill the soil to keep the plants in place.
7. Finish by filling in gaps with other plants.
8. Sprinkle a handful of slow-release granular fertilizer (such as Osmocote) around the plants.
9. Water in the plants well, adding enough that it drains from the holes.

Maintain

Potted plants need extra—and ongoing—TLC to keep thriving.

- Place the plants in the appropriate sunlight or shade.
- Water thoroughly and regularly, typically when the top 1 to 2 inches of soil are dry. This may be as often as once or twice daily depending on your climate. To promote deep root growth, place a hose on a very slow trickle in the pot, and let the water be slowly absorbed until it starts running out the bottom. Watering at the base rather than wetting the foliage will help prevent fungal disease.
- Since container-grown plants don't get nutrients from the ground, feed them every few weeks with organic fertilizer, like fish emulsion.
- At least once a year, replenish containers with more potting soil and top-dress them with nourishing compost. Clear the drainage holes by tipping the planter and poking through each hole with a sturdy stick or length of bamboo stake.

Prune

Pruning is a must in these mini landscapes.

- For lush and robust plants, pinch back new growth frequently; also pinch or snip off spent blooms from flowering plants.
- To revive plants that begin to wilt in late summer after their blooming period, cut them back to one-third of their size.
- Do this as well if the plants are growing too wild and you want to retain the shape

Troubleshoot

One big bonus of container gardening is that the plants are less susceptible to pests. They are also easier to scrutinize as you go about watering daily and regular feeding. But they are not immune to an infestation, which if allowed to take hold, can quickly ravage your plants.

- The most common container plant pests include aphids, spider mites, whiteflies, fungus gnats, and thrips.
- In general, be on the lookout for these bugs and remove them at first sighting.
- If they are too small for manual picking (such as with aphids and gnats), spray the foliage with a hard stream of water or a solution of 1 tablespoon dish soap per quart of water.

- For heavy infestations, you can try other natural remedies such as hot-pepper spray, garlic repellent spray, horticultural oil, insecticidal soap, or neem oil.

Winterize

Unless you live in a mild climate where the temperature never reaches freezing, you'll need to protect your container plants from winter's harsh elements.

- Those that are too large to budge can be wrapped in burlap (see page 219). This might also be necessary if you lack the space to house them indoors. Make sure the containers are frostproof (see page 272).
- Otherwise, plan to move the pots to a temperate space such as a garage or inside your home, or a heated greenhouse if you have one.
- You can leave the plants in their containers or, to extend the life of these vessels, remove the plants and repot in plastic containers. Then thoroughly clean the emptied vessels, allow them to dry in the sun, and store them carefully until the next spring.

Tip

Window boxes aren't just for windows; they can also latch onto a railing on a sunny porch and be planted with flowering and edible annuals such as herbs for easy harvesting.

Hanging Baskets 101

Classic hanging baskets featuring colorful annuals are admittedly high maintenance. A modern mix of low-maintenance varieties is a smart spin on the tradition.

Gather Your Supplies

It may take a bit of research to discover the very best plants for your area, but succulents—senecios, burro's tails, and echeverias—thrive in hanging baskets with minimal effort. Most of these varieties flourish with moderate feeding and watering, some judicious pruning, and, in the case of staghorn ferns, a good spray bath every now and then.

Choose a sturdy steel basket with strong chains (avoid any made from plastic or flimsy wire, which can break) for your plants, and line it first with beautiful moss, then with coconut coir, which will hold water and won't rot like straw or wicker will.

Arrange the Plants

You can grow just one gorgeous specimen per basket or experiment with different combinations of plants, such as Rhipsalis, staghorn ferns, and the trailing jade shown opposite.

1. **Prep your space:** Place an old towel in the base of a low, wide garden pot. This will help keep the round-bottomed wire basket steady while you're planting.
2. **Line with moss:** Begin by filling the basket with sheet or sphagnum moss, green side facing out. Be careful to cover the space fully, so there are no gaps or holes.
3. **Trim the basket liner:** Using sharp scissors or pruners, cut a coconut-coir liner to fit neatly inside the basket. You don't want to see any of the liner over the top.
4. **Scoop in soil:** Add potting mix, leaving room for the plants (so it's about two-thirds full). Use a blend especially made for containers that includes perlite, coconut coir, vermiculite, and sand.
5. **Place your plants:** Pot up the basket with succulents, like this trailing jade. Fill in with additional soil, as you would when planting a regular container.
6. **Hang and enjoy:** Attach the chain and place the basket in a bright location. Water thoroughly. When the threat of frost is gone, hang it outside in a sunny spot. Continue watering as needed—generally, whenever the soil feels dry 2 inches below the surface or the plants look thirsty.

4

Growing Your Own

Of all the reasons to garden, growing your own food ticks all the right boxes: It's easy to do, economical (especially if you grow from seed), and can be done in small spaces—even in containers. By working the soil organically, you help the environment. Above all, it yields the best-tasting produce—and you'll know where your food comes from. Add some berry bushes and fruit trees for your own U-pick orchard. Unlike annual crops, these plants can produce for decades.

Few people can afford the luxury of buying fresh flowers every week (or day!). But for the cost of one bouquet, you can purchase enough seeds to fill your home with blooms for an entire season. The pollinators will also thank you.

Vegetable Garden

Vegetable gardens can be as pretty as they are productive when you plant colorful crops (rainbow chard, purple runner beans) or tuck in ornamentals here and there. Bright flowers add beauty, attract pollinators and beneficial (pest-eating) insects, and in some cases even repel pests. Take, for example, the expansive vegetable garden at Martha's Turkey Hill that was painstakingly plotted and tended for over four decades. Or the High Garden at Great Dixter in England (at right), where lettuces, curly and flat-leaf parsley, beetroot, fennel, Swiss chard, and parsnips grow in tight rows that get rotated every year. The dense and intensive planting technique discourages weeds and keeps the soil from drying out. Vegetable gardens are a great way for even seasoned gardeners to make new discoveries and learn new things. The key is to provide a solid foundation and heed tried-and-true steps before you start experimenting.

Select the spot

▶ **Where you will grow** is as important as what, so take time to lay the necessary foundation and set your garden up for long-term success.

Choose the method

There are three basic ways to grow edibles: in containers, in raised beds, or in the ground (see the pros and cons of each starting on page 22). Many gardeners choose all three to mine every inch—throwing in hanging baskets, window boxes, and fences or other supports for climbers.

Be realistic: Size up how much space you have or are willing to devote to a vegetable garden, the yield you hope to produce, and the desired maintenance level. The answers could be the difference between a hard-working, high-yield, and high-maintenance kitchen garden packed with many varieties or a few pots of herbs and salad greens on a balcony or near your back door.

Find a location

Most crops—especially fruiting ones like tomatoes, peppers, and summer squash—like at least six to eight hours of direct sunlight daily. Think about whether any tall trees will cast shade after leafing out.

The site should also be level and (for in-ground rows) have well-draining soil. Site the garden where it can be easily watered, such as within a hose length of your outdoor spigot.

Prep your soil

As when creating any new raised or in-ground bed, you'll need to remove all grass and weeds from the area. If growing in the ground, test the soil as discussed on page 18 and amend as needed. In general, vegetables prefer slightly acidic soil (a pH between 6 and 6.8). It should contain plenty of nutrients and organic matter. Prior to planting, also enrich your plot with a layer of compost. If you are using raised beds or containers, get a high-quality organic potting soil mix. Some well-known companies (such as Coast of Maine) sell special blends for raised bed gardening.

Plan for critters

If deer, rabbits, and other wildlife are a concern, you'll want to enclose the garden with fencing, which can include relatively inexpensive hardware mesh or chicken wire. Bury the fence a few feet deep to keep burrowers from gaining access. Covering the area with bird netting is also helpful in keeping birds and squirrels at bay.

Pick the plants

A good rule of thumb is "grow what you eat," and include favorites of family members, friends, and neighbors in your accounting. Here are other factors to keep in mind when deciding on your crops.

Consider your climate

Talk to fellow gardeners, visit your local nursery and farmers' market, and look through seed catalogs to learn what grows well in your zone and the climate in your area. Do you have cool summers and cold winters, warm summers and cold winters, or hot summers and mild winters? Different varieties thrive in each of those conditions.

Plan a steady harvest

Be sure to pick plants that produce at different times, from early spring right on through fall (and winter if you want to extend the season; see page 313). This way, you can transition to a second or third harvest in the same spot—say, from peas to runner beans, cool-season lettuces to summer varieties.

Calculate the space

For a small yard and containers, choose compact, high-yielding crops such as cherry tomatoes, leafy greens, and herbs, and avoid sprawlers such as melons and winter squashes.

Use this chart as a rough guide to figure out what 10 running feet of each vegetable will yield over the growing season. Plus, there'll be a little left over to give your friends and neighbors.

Vegetable	Amount	Yield
Asparagus	7 plants	3 to 4 pounds
Beets	10 to 12 plants	1 to 2 pounds
Broccoli	5 to 7 plants	10 pounds
Carrots (main crop)	10 feet	10 pounds
Corn	10 to 12 plants	11 to 13 ears
Cucumbers	8 plants	10 pounds
Onions	10 feet	10 pounds
Peppers	5 to 7 plants	80 peppers
Pole beans	5 plants	3 to 4 pounds
Potatoes (main crop)	6 plants	30 pounds
Salad greens	10 feet	5 pounds
Summer squashes	2 to 3 plants	60 to 100 squashes
Tomatoes	2 to 5 plants	60 pounds

Expand your palate

Be open to planting heirloom varieties—such as 'Green Zebra' tomatoes, 'Black Knight' runner beans, and 'Little Gem' lettuce, among countless others. Indeed, being able to explore new flavors and savor these hard-to-find foods is one of the main reasons for growing your own.

Decide on seeds vs. seedlings

You'll find a vastly wider selection by buying seeds, which are also incredibly inexpensive, but tomatoes, peppers, and other varieties need to be started indoors. Those that are direct-sown will take longer to harvest.

Seedlings, on the other hand, give you a handy head start, which is especially helpful for new and busy gardeners, though the selection is much more limited and the cost higher.

Buy local

You can buy seed packets from anywhere, but get seedlings at your local garden center or farmers' market. They'll carry the varieties that are best suited to your location.

Plot the design

▶ **Careful planning and preparation** are the foundations of successful vegetable gardens. Consult seed packets and plant tags for guidance.

Start small

Seed catalogs can tempt you to buy one of everything, but seeds don't last forever—and a little goes a very long way. Edit the selection to your top four or five must-haves for the first season, as you can always expand the following year. This will also allow you to figure out what flourishes in your soil and what doesn't. (Keep a journal!)

Sketch it out

Draw your garden design to scale, keeping mature plant sizes and growth habits in mind in terms of spacing as well as height, so taller (or climbing) plants don't block sunlight from shorter ones. Leafy greens, however, can tolerate some shade and even prefer cooler temps.

- In-ground rows should be no wider than 4 feet so all plants are within arm's reach.
- If growing in raised beds, note what will go in each one.

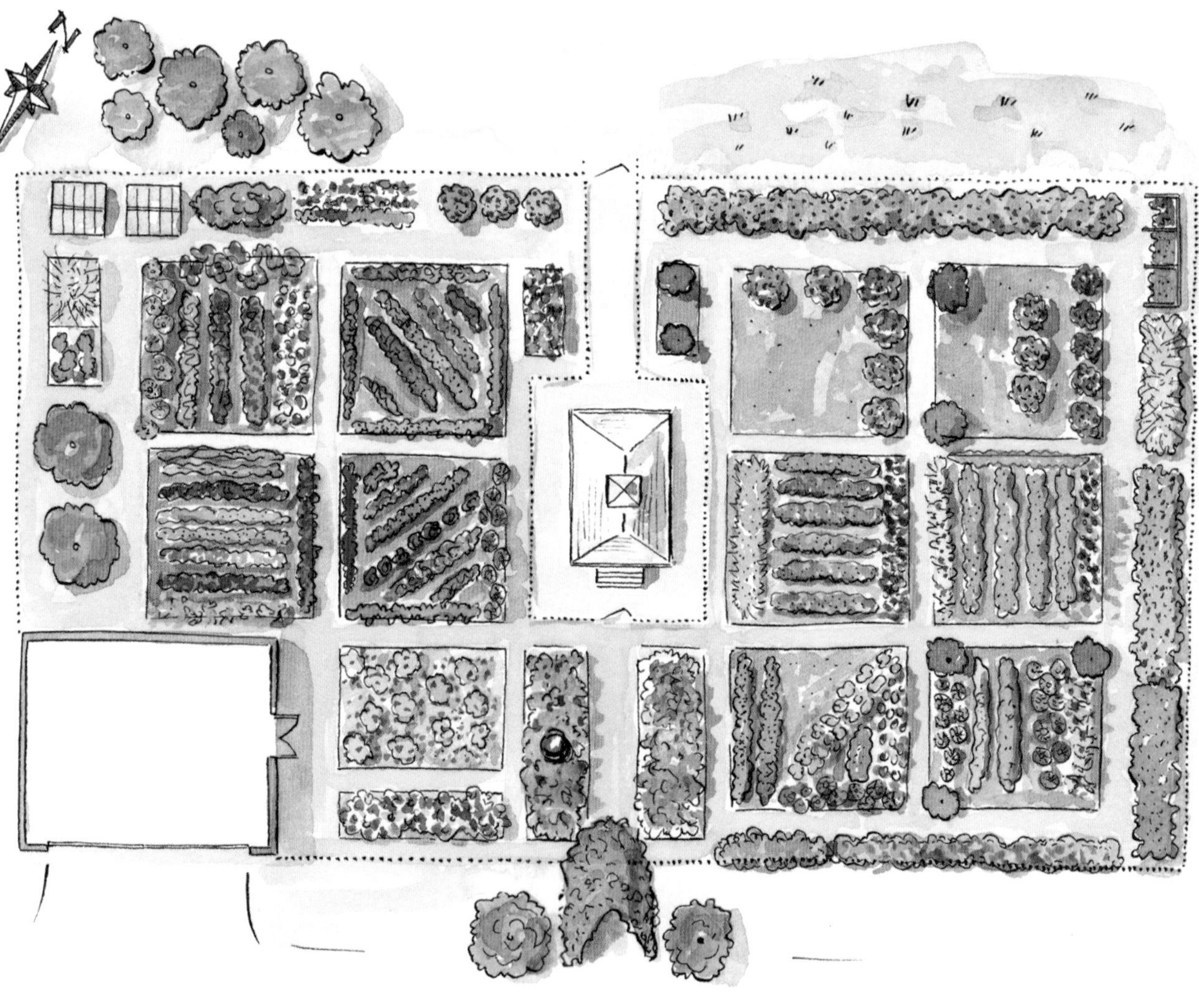

Include succession planting

For maximum yield, you'll want to get at least two or sometimes three different crops in each spot in the garden, usually transitioning from spring growers to summer crops—for example, swapping out peas with cucumbers, which also grow vertically, and cool-season lettuces and leafy greens with heat-seeking eggplant, peppers, and herbs (basil, cilantro, marjoram).

Plant like with like

Make the most of your space and streamline your tasks by grouping plants that require similar amounts of sunlight and water in the same row, raised bed, or pot. Siting plant families together also makes it easier to rotate your crops (especially nightshades) from year to year to prevent problems from diseases and insects that live in the soil.

Practice companion planting

One way to ensure your flora stays healthy is by growing plants that mutually benefit one another together. This is especially important when growing edibles and is a key tenet of permaculture, also known as sustainable or regenerative growing, a method of growing food and other plants in a way that mimics natural cycles and supports the entire ecosystem.

Companion Planting Primer

Followers of this gardening practice can experience a more fruitful bloom and harvest season, while better caring for the earth. A companion plant may repel pests, attract beneficial insects and pollinators, improve the growth or flavor of another plant, build up the soil, and thereby reduce the risk of disease. Having a partner plant that doesn't compete for nutrients also means less space for weeds to grow. One of the most famous examples is the Indigenous farming practice known as "the three sisters": The cornstalks are climbing supports for the beans, whose roots add nitrogen to the soil; the spreading squash acts as a living mulch, keeping the soil moist and weed-free.

See the chart below for more ideas.

Crop	Companion Plants
Asparagus	Basil, marigolds, oregano, parsley, tomatoes
Beans	Corn, tomatoes, eggplants, carrots, cucumbers, pumpkins, radishes
Carrots	Onions, chives, rosemary, radishes, nasturtiums, cilantro
Corn	Beans, marigolds, sunflowers, cucumbers, nasturtiums, squash
Cucumbers	Beans, dill, marigolds, radishes, chives, zucchini, peas
Lettuces	Carrots, garlic, peas, radishes, strawberries, onions, chives
Onions	Beets, carrots, lettuces, tomatoes, watermelon, eggplants
Peas	Apples, carrots, radishes, raspberries, turnips
Peppers	Basil, garlic, onions, radishes, nasturtiums, cilantro, marigolds
Potatoes	Basil, beans, corn, nasturtiums, peas, rosemary
Squashes	Beans, nasturtiums, mint, radishes, dill, basil, sunflowers
Tomatoes	Basil, marigolds, nasturtiums, carrots, garlic, chives

For the Love of Tomatoes

Today, vegetable gardens teem with dozens of tomato varieties—from trusted heirlooms to exciting new cultivars—in shades of red, yellow, orange, and even indigo.

Here are tips for growing, staking, harvesting, and preserving this delectable summer fruit.

Choose

Experiment by having a mix of new hybrids, old standbys (like 'Big Boy'), and many heirlooms.

Plant

Don't plant too soon (or too late): Tomatoes grow best when the daytime temperature is between 65°F and 85°F. They need at least six hours of full sun and well-drained soil.

In addition, while they love hot weather, tomatoes won't set fruit when the temperature rises above 85°F. Regardless of whether you started the seedlings yourself or got them from a nursery, it's important to harden off the plant. Gradually increase the amount of time you leave your tomato plants outside—one hour on the first day, two on the second day, and so on—over the course of one or two weeks.

Plant deeply: A common mistake among beginning gardeners is planting tomatoes only 1 or 2 inches deep. Instead, bury two-thirds of the plant underground so only the two topmost leaf sets are visible. This applies to tomatoes planted in the ground, a raised bed, or a container. If the seedling is already too tall and wobbly, dig a trench instead of a hole and lay the plant on its side with the top leaves aboveground.

Plant in succession: It takes about 50 to 90 days for tomato plants to reach maturity. Stagger the plantings to produce early-, mid-, and late-season harvests. Determinate varieties tend to ripen earlier and set all their fruit at once, while indeterminate have a longer growth period, continuing to produce tomatoes into the frost.

Stake

Proper support lets tomato plants grow sturdier, minimizes pests and rot, and allows sun to reach more fruit, thus ensuring the greatest possible yield. The kind of support your tomatoes need will vary according to the cultivars you choose.

Determinate tomato cultivars such as 'Super Bush' tend to be naturally bushy and will often produce an attractively compact plant that requires no more support than a couple of bamboo stakes slipped into the soil next to the principal stems. The stems can then be tied to the supports with loops of twine.

Indeterminate tomato cultivars are vining, tend to sprawl, and require sturdier support. One traditional method is to make angled tepee-like structures for each bed using sturdy hardwood and bamboo stakes, purchased affordably in bulk, and jute twine.

1. Secure pairs of stakes into the ground at the end of each row and at regular intervals along its length (about 4 feet apart), pushing them 8 to 10 inches into the ground and angling them to cross at the top.

2. Tie the criss-crossed stakes with twine, then cradle stakes (or sturdy twigs) in the top of the tepee structure.

3. Tie a length of twine on the horizontal stakes for each tomato plant and secure it into the ground with anchor stakes.

4. Finally, tie each plant to the vertical twine support where needed with more twine, using a simple figure-eight knot so the stems are not crushed. Continue to tie to the support as it gets taller.

FELCO 2

Prune

Indeterminate vines continue growing throughout the season, producing a lot of new shoots—aka suckers—between a "V" of the main stem and a side branch. If left unpruned, you can end up with a whole plant of just suckers with no fruit. Be sure to remove any suckers beneath the first fruit cluster so they won't slow the development of the fruit. This also keeps the plant open, allowing for good air circulation.

Troubleshoot

Regular pruning also helps prevent soilborne diseases such as bacterial spot and early blight as well as tomato hornworms. Should these pests gain access, you can deter them with an organic, concentrated neem oil. (See more about these pests on page 162.)

Another key to maintaining a healthy vegetable garden is to rotate the tomato bed each successive year between a few spots in the garden.

Harvest

Ripe tomatoes are shiny and glossy—and, given a gentle squeeze, should have a bit of give to them. You can harvest them as soon as they start turning their mature color and allow them to continue ripening in the kitchen; however, the flavor will be best when allowed to fully ripen on the vine.

Picking tomatoes in the morning, before the heat of the day sets in, will help them to stay fresh longer. It's also important to harvest ripe or almost-ripe tomatoes before a heavy rain, especially when it follows a period of dry weather; these conditions are a major cause of cracked and split fruits.

Once they are picked, place tomatoes on a tray, stem side down. The top of the tomato ripens last, so this extends their shelf life.

Preserve

To get the most out of your harvest, preserve tomatoes for use throughout the year. Canning tomatoes is only one option; the following alternatives do not require any special equipment.

1. **Oven-dried tomatoes:** Bake sliced tomatoes, drizzled with olive oil and seasoned with salt and pepper, in a single layer on a parchment-lined baking sheet at 250°F until dry but not crisp, 2 to 3 hours. Let cool, then freeze on another baking sheet until firm; store in an airtight container and use within a year (without thawing) on pizza or in pasta dishes, or (thawed) in salads and sandwiches.

2. **Tomato purée:** This makes a versatile base for soups, stews, and sauces, like simple marinara. Score an X in the bottom of tomatoes and blanch in a pot of boiling water for 10 seconds; plunge into an ice bath until cool, then slip off the skins. Quarter tomatoes, scoop out seeds and juice, and pass flesh through a food mill, removing pulp as you go (reserve seeds, juice, and pulp for tomato water, below). Season tomatoes with salt, then freeze in jars (leaving ½ inch of headspace) for up to a year.

3. **Tomato water:** Strain reserved tomato pulp, seeds, and juice from purée in a cheesecloth-lined sieve over a bowl. Refrigerate for at least 8 hours and up to 1 day. (Tip: For clear liquid, don't stir the pulp.) Transfer tomato water to an airtight container and refrigerate up to 3 days or freeze into ice cubes to use throughout the year. Stir a few spoonfuls into salad dressings, or use ice cubes to enhance a Bloody Mary or gazpacho.

4. **Tomato confit:** Slow-cooking tomatoes in oil, garlic, and herbs intensifies their natural flavor and perfumes them with aromatics. Try varieties like 'Early Girl', 'Noire Russe', and 'Better Boy'. Blanch and peel tomatoes as above, then place whole tomatoes in a baking dish, drizzle with olive oil, season with salt and pepper, and add sliced garlic and basil. Bake at 350°F until tender, about an hour. Transfer tomatoes with their juices to quart-size glass jars, leaving ½ inch of headspace. Freeze until ready to use, up to a year.

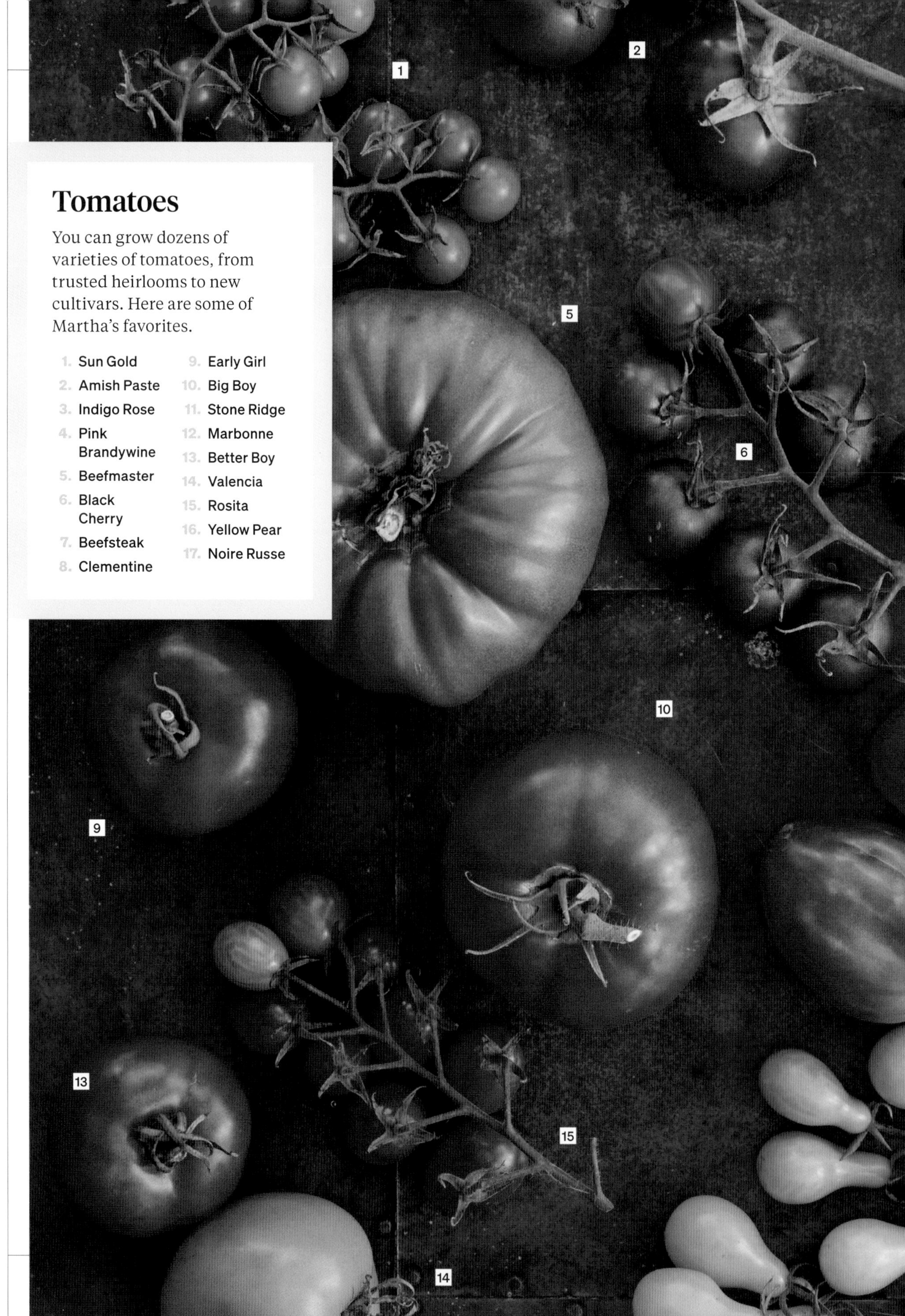

Tomatoes

You can grow dozens of varieties of tomatoes, from trusted heirlooms to new cultivars. Here are some of Martha's favorites.

1. Sun Gold
2. Amish Paste
3. Indigo Rose
4. Pink Brandywine
5. Beefmaster
6. Black Cherry
7. Beefsteak
8. Clementine
9. Early Girl
10. Big Boy
11. Stone Ridge
12. Marbonne
13. Better Boy
14. Valencia
15. Rosita
16. Yellow Pear
17. Noire Russe

3
4
7
8
11
12
16
17

Plant the crops

▶ **Garden design in hand,** seed packets organized, and seedlings ready to go, it's time to get digging. Or is it? Patience is a virtue in gardening, and haste definitely makes waste. Here's how to nail the opportune time and method.

When to plant

This varies greatly depending on the crop—cold-tolerant peas, for example, can be planted as soon as the ground has thawed in early spring, while heat-seeking beans and eggplant need the consistently warm temperatures of summer.

Bracket your growing season with the first and last frost dates in your area and then plan out your plantings accordingly, consulting seed packets and plant tags for ideal growing times. The chart on the opposite page is another helpful resource.

How to plant

There are two key ways to grow a vegetable garden: row or intensive cropping.

ROW CROPPING

This method involves planting vegetables in straight rows with ample spacing between them, making it easy to cultivate and manage the garden, but it can require more space.

INTENSIVE CROPPING

A space-saving option whereby your plants will grow in grids or raised beds that are close together. This way, species are co-selected and can support one another. It takes a bit more patience and planning, but the results can be spectacular when done right.

Follow the steps on pages 120 to 121 for direct-sowing seeds and transplanting seedlings. Always save the seed packet and plant tag so you can reference information on planting and tending (covered below). Label each row or bed with a marker and note where everything is planted in a journal.

What to stake

Vining plants that require staking include peas, runner beans, tomatoes, melons, and cucumbers. Other edibles such as eggplants and bell peppers also benefit from being kept off the ground to prevent the risk of rot. Staking also makes these plants easier to harvest.

Using tepee-like structures in the vegetable garden is an easy way to support these plants and to add eye-catching texture to the garden beds. (See For the Love of Tomatoes on page 294 for how to stake tomato beds.)

Other options include trellises, tuteurs, arbors, and tomato cages—or even a fence. Trellises work well for peas and beans but are not suitable for heavier crops like tomatoes and melons.

Planting Guide

Here are general guidelines to follow to help you make the most of your growing season. In the left column are the vegetables' preferred temperature range, with the range they can tolerate right below.

Temperature range	Vegetable					
70°–85° (65°–90°)	eggplants	okra	sweet/hot peppers	sweet potatoes	tomatoes	watermelons
65°–75° (50°–90°)	beans	black-eyed peas	cucumbers	melons	sweet corn	squashes
60°–65° (40°–75°)	artichokes	beets	broccoli	brussels sprouts	cabbages	carrots
	cauliflower	celery	chard	collards	endives	fava beans
	fennel	kale	kohlrabi	lettuces	parsnips	peas
	potatoes	radishes	rutabagas	spinach	turnips	
55°–75° (45°–85°)	garlic	leeks	onions	shallots		

Tend the garden

Edibles require much more hands-on attention than other types of plants to reach their full potential and taste their best. Plan to check on them daily if possible, toting your basket along to gather any crops that are ready for picking.

Feed

Add about an inch of compost at the start of the season. Then apply an organic fertilizer such as fish emulsion (many a gardener's secret) or another thin layer of compost as the season progresses.

Hydrate

Water according to plants' individual needs. In general, water deeply when needed, about an inch once a week, directing water at the soil around the base rather than spraying from above. Steady, even watering encourages more productive crops. Pay special attention to crops that require less water as they approach harvest, such as potatoes and pumpkins.

Mulch

Aim for a layer 2 to 3 inches thick, as you don't want to obstruct water filtration and drainage and any less will wash away. Look for municipal programs that distribute free untreated chopped bark or leaves. Other good options for vegetable gardens include cocoa hulls, pine needles, leaf mold, fresh grass clippings, straw, and salt hay (but not regular hay used for feed, as it contains weed seeds).

Weed

Do this often, especially early in the growing season—weeds are much easier to manage before they gain a foothold. Once vegetables become tall and vigorous, they'll help shade out invaders. Mulching is your best line of defense, especially if you practice no-till gardening.

Thin

When planting from seed, follow the packet directions for thinning—and don't skip this step. To avoid pulling up clumps of plants in densely seeded rows, thin seedlings with scissors, snipping just below the soil surface.

Resow

Similar to succession planting, resowing fast growers like lettuces and radishes every few weeks ensures you have a steady supply. Stagger the timing, too—so when one crop fades, another one is hitting its peak.

Prune

There are different reasons to prune a plant, but generally, you want to remove any leaves that show signs of pests or disease (such as yellowing) or are simply unsightly.

To promote production in fruiting plants (tomatoes, cucumbers, squashes, melons, peppers), cut off stems that are putting out only leaves, which will direct energy to those with fruit.

Avoid pruning when plants are wet, as this can spread disease, and prune from the bottom to the top.

Troubleshoot

An ounce of prevention definitely applies to maintaining a problem-free vegetable garden. The healthier your soil and plants, the more resistant they will be to disease and harmful pests.

DISEASES

See the chart on page 158 for symptoms and solutions for common plant diseases. If all else fails, your best bet is to pull up and destroy affected plants before they infect the rest of your garden.

- ***Fungi:*** Fungal diseases love wet, cool conditions. If that describes your climate, ask about disease-resistant hybrids at your local nursery. Left untreated, fungi such as blight or powdery mildew can quickly destroy an entire crop. Watering only the roots and not the foliage can help prevent destructive fungi from getting a foothold, as can spacing plants to allow for plenty of airflow. Remove affected leaves at the first sign—or you may end up having to rip out the whole plant.
- ***Bacteria:*** Pathogens can be introduced to the garden from plants, tools, footwear, and previously contaminated soil. Reduce the risk by sanitizing pruners after each use, maintaining plant and soil vigor by fertilizing with organic products or compost, removing weeds that compete with nutrients, and watering in the morning so the plants can dry in the sun (bacteria thrive in humidity).
- ***Viruses:*** As with bacterial and fungal organisms, viruses can live in soil, plants, crop residues, tools, and hands. They are often transmitted by sucking insects, so prevent the spread by getting any infestation under control. Sap transfer is another common vehicle; disinfect your tools with rubbing alcohol and wash your hands regularly. Use mulch to add a barrier between the soil and plants, too.

PESTS

Insects—good and bad—come with the territory. The goal is to attract the good (praying mantises, lacewings, and ladybugs) and deter the bad by promoting healthy soil and strong plants.

See page 162 for how to spot—and banish—the most common interlopers, including slugs and snails, cabbage white butterflies, tomato hornworms, and three kinds of beetles (flea, potato, and Japanese). For an all-purpose approach, use horticultural oils and soaps rather than chemical fungicides.

In addition, check carefully and often for insects, their eggs, and telltale damage such as nibbled foliage, leaf loss, and browned edges as you weed and water.

Harvest

▶ **Timing is everything** when it comes to peak-of-season flavor, so monitor closely. After all, there's nothing better than eating a ripe tomato right off the vine. (Bring a little salt into the garden to do just that.)

You'll know when your vegetables are ready by their size, shape, and vibrant color. Most crops taste best when fully ripe, though some plants, like beans and turnips, are extra-delicious and tender when picked young. Always consult the seed packets for the best time to harvest that specific variety.

Keep up with your harvest to encourage new growth: Some plants slow their production when not picked, while others—notably basil and leafy greens—turn bitter once they bolt, meaning you'll want to harvest them frequently during the long, hot days of summer.

BEETS, CARROTS, AND RADISHES

These (and other root vegetables such as turnips, parsnips, and rutabagas) can be gently pulled or dug as soon as the tops are large enough to handle.

BROCCOLI AND CAULIFLOWER

The "florets" of these brassicas are so named because they are unopened flower buds, so the plants must be cut before those buds sprout tiny yellow flowers—and the flavor turns bitter.

CANTALOUPES

When a cantaloupe (or other vining melon like honeydew and watermelon) is ripe, it will slip easily from the vine, and its surface "netting" will turn beige.

CORN

Harvest the stalks when the silks turn brown and the ears feel full through the husk from end to end.

CUCUMBERS

Cut these from the vines when they are young, small, and softly spined—before they develop unwanted seeds.

EGGPLANTS

Pick them when their skin is deep purple and glossy and they feel slightly firm to the touch; overripe eggplant is dull, brown, and spongy.

KALE, CHARD, AND SPINACH

If you want to harvest baby greens for a salad, pick the leaves when about 3 inches tall. Or wait to harvest until the plant is fully grown.

For continual growth, harvest a handful of outer leaves at a time; twist them off with your hands or cut at the growth point, where the main stem meets the base.

Or you can pull up the entire plant and sow another in its place—especially if it is bolting (the bottom 2 inches of the base are no longer growing leaves and flowers are beginning to sprout from the top).

LETTUCES

There are two ways to harvest lettuces: You can clip individual outer leaves as needed, or harvest the full head once it has reached its mature size. Make sure to leave the base intact, so you can harvest it again in the coming weeks when it regrows.

PEPPERS

Depending on the variety (and whether sweet or hot), peppers can be picked when they reach their mature size and color. Their flavor is best during periods of high heat.

POLE BEANS AND SNOW PEAS

Pick when the seeds feel small in their pods to ensure they will be tender and stringless.

POTATOES

Harvest new potatoes two to three weeks after they have finished flowering. Larger, mature potatoes can be harvested two to three weeks after their plants' foliage has died back. Use a fork to dig the potatoes up and, to make them last longer in storage, remove any soil or dust with a brush instead of washing them.

SUMMER SQUASHES

For the best flavor and texture, pick when still small—they become tough and stringy when large.

TOMATOES

These fruits continue to ripen after picking, but they develop the best flavor when left to reach their full color on the vine. They'll easily release with a gentle tug.

3
2
1
6
12
11
8
10
9

Roots and Tubers

These delicious, earthy vegetables store nutrients in their roots or underground stems (tubers).

1. Potato (*Solanum tuberosum*)
2. Celeriac (*Apium graveolens*)
3. Sweet potato (*Ipomoea batatas*)
4. Jicama (*Pachyrhizus erosus*)
5. Beet (*Beta vulgaris*)
6. Turnip (*Brassica rapa*)
7. Rutabaga (*Brassica napus*)
8. Jerusalem artichoke (*Helianthus tuberosus*)
9. White yam (*Dioscorea alata*)
10. Parsnip (*Pastinaca sativa*)
11. Yuca/Cassava/Manioc (*Manihot esculenta*)
12. Carrot (*Daucus carota*)

Preserving Produce

Enjoying crops at their peak is the best reason to grow them, and you can capture that sun-kissed, just-picked flavor to savor long after summer fades. It's part of a sustainability ethos where nothing is allowed to go to waste. Start with these easy ideas, then improvise to come up with your own preservation profiles.

Drying Herbs

This method works best for woody herbs (oregano, thyme, rosemary, sage, and bay leaves) and tender herbs that you may want to steep and enjoy as tea (mint, lemon verbena, chamomile, and lemon balm).

Hang small bunches upside down and out of direct sunlight or spread them out on a paper towel–lined wire rack in a cool, dry spot. It will take a week or two for herbs to dry completely, depending on your kitchen's environment. (A dehydrator that dries at a very low temperature is another option.) Once dried, strip leaves from the stems and store in an airtight container in a cool, dark place (their flavor will diminish after six months). To use, rub the herbs between your fingers to release their flavorful oils.

Freezing Herbs

Freezing preserves the bright flavor of tender herbs like basil, cilantro, chives, dill, parsley, and tarragon. Spread stripped leaves on a parchment-lined baking sheet and freeze for a few hours, until hard. Transfer to an airtight freezer container, labeled with the herb and date. Use as you would fresh herbs, adding them at the end of cooking or sprinkling them into salads (they thaw quickly).

Alternatively, roughly mince or slice the leaves, put them in ice cube trays, and cover with olive oil. (For bigger quantities, use a food processor to pulse the leaves with your cooking oil.) Once frozen, transfer the herb cubes to a (labeled and dated) airtight freezer container and use within six months. Drop into soups or sauces or use to make pesto.

You can also make ice cubes with chopped mint to add flavor to cocktails, smoothies, lemonade, or even water.

Quick Pickles

You can pickle all kinds of produce—not just the classic cukes. Layer these sweet or sour (your pick) "refrigerator" pickles onto sandwiches, cheese boards, and salads—or just nibble them right out of the jar. Some make great cocktail garnishes, too.

SWEET PICKLE BASIC BRINE

Makes 2 pints

1. Combine 1½ cups distilled white vinegar or apple cider vinegar, 1¼ cups sugar, ½ teaspoon mustard seeds, ½ teaspoon whole black peppercorns, ¼ teaspoon celery seeds, ¼ teaspoon turmeric, and 2 tablespoons coarse salt in a saucepan.
2. Bring to a boil, stirring until sugar is dissolved.
3. Fill clean containers tightly with desired vegetables or fruit (see below for suggestions). Add boiling brine to cover completely. Let cool, then cover, label, and refrigerate for at least 1 week before serving, or up to 3 months.

Cucumber chips: 16 ounces Kirby cucumbers, trimmed and cut into 1-inch rounds, and ½ small white onion, cut into ¼-inch wedges

Shaved golden beets: 12 ounces peeled and very thinly sliced golden beets

Peaches (from your fruit tree; see page 326): 6 small peaches, preferably freestone, peeled (see Preserving the Harvest on page 333), halved, and pitted; replace spices with 2 small dried bay leaves, 1 whole clove, ¼ teaspoon whole peppercorns, and ½ medium cinnamon stick

SOUR PICKLE BASIC BRINE

Makes 2 pints

1. Combine 1½ cups distilled white vinegar or apple cider vinegar with 2 teaspoons sugar, ½ teaspoon whole black peppercorns, ½ teaspoon coriander seeds, 3 whole allspice berries, 2 dried bay leaves (omit for tarragon beans), and 2 tablespoons coarse salt in a saucepan.
2. Bring to a boil, stirring until sugar is dissolved.
3. Fill clean containers tightly with desired vegetables or fruit (see below for suggestions). Add boiling brine to cover completely. Let cool, then cover, label, and refrigerate for at least 1 week before serving, or up to 3 months.

Cherry tomatoes: 4 cups very small cherry or grape tomatoes, plus 2 small sprigs rosemary

Chile cauliflower: 4 cups small cauliflower florets, plus 4 sprigs thyme and 2 small fresh chiles

Dill cucumbers: 1 pound Kirby cucumbers, trimmed and cut into ½-inch wedges, plus 8 sprigs dill and 4 cloves (peeled) garlic

Green tomatoes: 1 pound small green tomatoes, cut into ¼-inch slices, plus 6 thin slices white onion

Onions and peppers: 8 ounces each small red onions and baby bell peppers, plus 1 small jalapeño, all cut into rings

Radishes: 32 very small radishes, trimmed, halved if large

Dill beets: 12 ounces baby beets, peeled and cut into ½-inch wedges, plus 8 sprigs dill and 4 cloves (peeled) garlic; add beets to the brine with the spices in step 1

Spicy carrots: 10 ounces baby carrots, peeled and cut into ⅛-inch slices, plus 2 thin slices habanero chile

Tarragon beans: 12 ounces green or wax beans, plus 2 sprigs tarragon (omit bay leaves)

Put the garden to bed

Practicing fall cleanup is the first step toward next spring's planting. Besides making the garden look neat and tidy, the following steps will help improve soil health—allowing no diseases or pests to overwinter in your garden. When to do this, and what plants need winterizing, depends on where you live.

Harvest crops

Pick end-of-season bunches of kale and other greens, tomatoes (let ripen indoors), peppers, corn, melons, squashes and pumpkins, and herbs. Dig up any root vegetables, as well as potatoes (for cold storage).

Protect overwintering vegetables (such as garlic) with row covers, layers of straw, or other mulch.

Prune perennials

Prune back any perennial flowers or ornamentals in your vegetable garden to the ground in the fall (or do this in the spring if you like their seed heads). This also applies to perennial herbs like chives, oregano, lovage, sage, and mint.

Remove all crop debris

Be sure to remove and discard all decomposing tomatoes or other fruits—these are the primary source of pathogens that cause soil diseases and viruses. Pests and rodents also love to burrow in leftover plant matter during the winter.

Yank out the entire plant, or for a no-till garden, cut off the stems at the base—the intact roots will break down and feed healthy microorganisms in the soil. Then run a rake over the entire garden to gather any remaining decaying fruit.

Compost or burn

So long as you don't see any signs of disease or pests, you can add crop debris to your compost bin. Otherwise, throw it in the trash bin or burn pile. If you're not sure, do the latter.

Cover the beds

Spread a 2-inch layer of aged compost or manure over each raised bed or row, then top with a 3-inch layer of straw or other mulch. Raked leaves are especially convenient. The organic matter will feed microorganisms in the soil and prevent soil erosion and weed development.

Some gardeners in harsh climates lay a tarp over the mulch for added insulation and protection against erosion.

Alternatively, you can sow cover crops such as winter rye, hairy vetch, clover, or alfalfa, which will also improve your soil and leave it rich in nutrients for spring planting. Do this at least a month before your first frost date to allow the seeds to germinate, covering with straw and watering regularly to keep the soil moist. In spring, you can turn the soil to stop the crop from growing, or (for no-till gardens) either mow it (if in the ground), clip it near the soil surface, or leave it in place and plant right through it.

You could also smother it with a thick layer of cardboard or black garden plastic and leave it in place over the winter.

Extend the season

▶ **If you live** in an area with mild winters, you can likely grow at least cold-tolerant crops all year long. But no matter your region, there are ways to have a 12-month harvest of some varieties.

Cold frames

These simple structures—basically a wood frame with a transparent lid—are built low to the ground and utilize solar energy and insulation to create a microclimate suitable for growing or overwintering plants.

Cold frames are available in multiple sizes as prebuilt options or kits, though they are easy enough to construct if you're a DIY type. For best results, place the cold frame in an east-to-west orientation, as north-facing cold frames may not get enough light.

The setup works best for cool-season crops, such as spinach, kale, lettuces, endive, escarole, purslane, chervil, radicchio, carrots, and radishes, though it's worth experimenting with other plants.

FOLLOWING PAGES: This backyard homestead in Vermont features climbing supports made of tree trimmings from the property. Tomatoes and other crops are rotated each year to prevent soil-borne illnesses; at the end of the season, the produce is either canned, frozen, or stored in the root cellar for winter.

Hoop houses

Hoop houses are a step up from cold frames, and function in much the same way. There are two basic types:

- "Garden bed" hoop houses are designed to be attached to an existing raised bed, making them the most convenient. And you can quickly assemble them in case of an unexpected early frost. Portable versions can be purposed to go above in-ground gardens by building a simple rectangular wood frame on which to attach the hoops.
- A freestanding hoop house functions like a small greenhouse (and is tall enough to stand up in), without the cost. While more expensive to build than a garden bed hoop house, it offers permanency and versatility in what and how much you can grow, especially if you use polyethylene material instead of plastic as the covering.

Greenhouse

One very good reason to have a greenhouse is to grow produce all year long. It's also an ideal location for starting seeds well before the last frost date so they'll be ready for transplanting once the ground thaws and temperatures are reliably above freezing.

You can find greenhouse kits that are relatively easy to assemble—they just snap together and don't require a foundation—and come in a range of sizes, from small ones that fit on a balcony to those that are over 50 feet long. Design plans are also available for purchase for you (or your construction pro) to build from scratch.

In the Greenhouse

The crops shown here are an example of one day's harvest in Martha's greenhouse. Other produce includes root vegetables, brassicas, and strawberries, plus a grapefruit tree in one corner and a carambola (also known as star fruit) in another.

1. Red 'Salad-Bowl' lettuce
2. Tuscan kale
3. Cutting celery
4. Siberian kale
5. 'Royal Oakleaf' lettuce
6. Flat-leaf parsley
7. Curly-leaf parsley
8. 'Red Cross' lettuce

Custom Salad and Herb Mixes

Lettuces and herbs are among the easiest and quickest crops to grow at home, and there's nothing more rewarding than taking your basket and harvesting a little of this and that for each day's salad.

Salad Mix

The possibilities are endless and depend on your flavor preferences. Succession planting will ensure your salad bowl is brimming all season long.

- Sow premixed mesclun seeds or your favorite "cut-and-come-again" lettuces like buttercrunch, romaine, and red or green leaf, all of which you can continually harvest by removing the outer leaves only and leaving the center leaves.
- Add tatsoi, mizuna (mustard greens), endive, radicchio, escarole, and baby greens such as kale, chard, spinach, and arugula.
- Consider building a salad with contrasting colors and textures by growing carrots, radishes, celery, cucumbers, peppers, tomatoes, and more—again sticking with what you actually like to eat.
- Flavorful herbs and edible flowers are other excellent additions.

Herb Mixes

Even if you only have a windowsill or space for a few pots, you can grow a culinarian assortment of herbs in very little space.

- A few herbs like thyme, rosemary, sage, and oregano are stalwarts (and perennials), but you may also want to plant brighter herbs like basil and mint for warm-weather harvesting. Others to try include lovage, lemon balm, marjoram, borage, sorrel, and lemon verbena.
- Vary the selection of herbs to suit your preferred flavor profiles, from Southeast Asian (cilantro, Thai basil, makrut lime leaf, lemongrass) to Mediterranean (chervil, chives, tarragon, lavender) to Latin American (epazote, papalo, Mexican oregano).
- As with all plants, herbs have different growing requirements and habits. For example, if you live in a cold-weather region, you will need to bring the pots indoors during winter. And beware of mint, which will quickly take over a garden and is best planted in a container.

Raising Backyard Chickens

While you may not have the space or wherewithal to care for horses or donkeys, consider raising a small flock of chickens, as the rewards are plentiful. The eggs are rich with golden-yellow yolks and have a far superior taste to standard store-bought varieties. Here is a primer on raising chickens in your own backyard.

Space

Keep in mind that each bird will need at least 2 square feet of space in the coop, and at least 10 square feet each to roam freely outside. As at Bedford, consider providing a variety of natural perches for resting spots.

Choose

Poultry shows and country fairs are an easy way to meet experts, look at different breeds, and select the best ones for your needs.

The breeds at Bedford include Araucanas, Polish, Cochins, Speckled Sussex, Olive Eggers, Jersey Giants, Mille Fleurs, Silkies, Orpingtons, Silver Laced Wyandottes, Minorcas, and heritage Barred Plymouth Rocks, as well as Cream Legbars (prized for their pale blue eggs) and Cuckoo Marans (which lay dark brown ones).

House

Stuff nesting boxes with fresh wood shavings so hens have a comfortable place to lay eggs. Electric heaters keep things comfortable in colder months, too. Clean the coops thoroughly every week.

Protect

Protect the birds from predators—foxes, hawks, and raccoons—with fencing and overhead netting.

Feed

Give the birds easy access to feeders filled with organic pellets fortified with protein and calcium (to help produce flavorful eggs); those at Bedford are hung 6 inches off the ground. There, the birds also eat fruit and vegetable scraps from the kitchen and wheatgrass grown in the greenhouse, and they have winter access to the vegetable garden.

Water

Chickens can get dehydrated quickly, so make sure water troughs and dispensers are refilled several times a day.

OPPOSITE: Martha (c. 2010) holds one of her friendly flock, others of which perch on homemade roosts made from rustic logs.

Backyard Berry Patch

Having an orchard in your backyard may seem out of reach, but a single small berry patch (or one or two fruit trees, covered in the next section, starting on page 326) can provide a wonderful U-pick experience at home, producing enough fruit to fill your baskets from spring through fall.

Generic, store-bought varieties don't hold a candle to fresh, sun-kissed strawberries, blueberries, blackberries, and raspberries. All these plants are easy to grow and care for, too. They can even be grown in containers on a sunny balcony or roof deck.

Planning

All berries benefit from the following gardening know-how.

Choose

Seek out varieties that are well suited to your area and reliably cold-hardy for cooler regions. Some cultivars are bred specifically for container gardens in case that's your goal.

STRAWBERRIES

These are among the easiest berries to grow, with cold-hardy varieties and those that easily adapt to different growing conditions. Unlike other berries, strawberry plants produce for only a few years, so you should implement successive planting to ensure a steady harvest. It's also worth having a mix of June-bearing and everbearing varieties, the latter of which produce a heavy June yield plus lighter harvests in late summer and early fall.

Popular varieties include 'Alpine' (which can be planted from seed), 'Jewel', 'Galletta', 'AC Valley Sunset', 'Earliglow', 'Sparkle', and 'Honeoye'.

BLUEBERRIES

In good years, prepare to be amazed at how many berries a single mature bush yields—plus, in the ideal spot, the plants can produce for decades. Most blueberry bushes are self-pollinating, but you'll get much bigger harvests if you plant two varieties that bloom at the same time and cross-pollinate. Having several varieties that fruit at different times will yield months of berries.

Among the many blueberry varieties are 'Bluegold', 'Chandler', 'Darrow', 'Jersey', and 'Patriot'.

RASPBERRIES

Raspberry plants are unique because their roots and crowns are perennial, while their stems, or canes, are biennial. The canes produce leaves in the first year and bear flowers and fruit in the second before dying off. The mother plant, however, continuously puts out new canes—so once established, it will yield fruit every year for a decade or more. The berries come in different colors, for example, red, golden, and black. Select a mix of summer- and fall-bearing varieties, as well as cultivars that ripen at different times, for an extended harvest.

BLACKBERRIES

These sturdy plants thrive in colder zones—most varieties can be grown in zones 5 to 9, though some have been bred to be hardy in harsher winters, and other hybrids will bear fruit in warmer climates. All blackberry plants must spend at least some of their dormancy below 45°F.

Blackberries are either erect (aka self-supporting) bushes or trailing, which have long canes that require supports, though there are also hybrids. Keep an eye on trailing varieties, which can spread aggressively and put down new roots if the canes curve back toward the ground. (Prune these canes as needed.)

CURRANTS AND GOOSEBERRIES

These smooth-skinned, jewel-toned berries of the *Ribes* genus are well loved in many other countries, and are slowly gaining popularity at local farms and home gardens in the US, too. A federal ban on all plants of the *Ribes* genus was lifted in 1966, but some states still do not allow the growing of currants and gooseberries or require a permit to do so. Check state regulations for restrictions before planting.

Currants and gooseberries are generally hardy for zones 3 to 8. Some cultivars have been bred as cold-hardy to zone 2. Red, white, black, and pink currants and gooseberries are grown for eating out of hand and using in cooking.

Plant

In cooler regions, early spring—after the ground has thawed—is the best time to plant berries, followed by fall, before the first frost. In warmer areas, plant in late fall or early winter. Currants and gooseberries, however, do better planted in fall or early spring while plants are still in dormancy.

- Select a spot with full sun.

  Strawberries like a good 8 to 10 hours of sun, while blackberries can tolerate afternoon shade, especially in the hottest regions.

  Currants and gooseberries can tolerate partial shade (though black currants prefer full sun) and do best in a cool, moist environment with good air circulation to prevent powdery mildew.

- Many berry plants will grow just fine in average, well-drained soil. However, a few have particular soil requirements, as noted below.

  Strawberries and blackberries prefer soil that's slightly acidic, with a pH of 5.5 to 6.8.

  Blueberries require acidic soil (pH 4.5 to 5.5) to grow well.

  Avoid planting raspberries in a bed where nightshades (tomatoes, peppers, potatoes, eggplants) have recently been grown, because diseases such as verticillium wilt can spread from the plants to the raspberries.

  Raspberries and blackberries should be planted far from wild berries, as pests and diseases can quickly spread to your cultivated plants.

- Always follow spacing and depth recommendations on the plant label.

  Strawberries and raspberries: The crown (the part connecting the roots and the stems) should be above the soil surface. If it is buried, the plant could rot. Once planted, cut raspberry canes to 9 inches tall to encourage new growth.

  Blueberries: Plant at the same depth as the nursery pot. Planting closer together encourages cross-pollination.

  Blackberries, currants, and gooseberries: Plant about an inch deeper than in the nursery pot.

Stake

Unless otherwise noted, berries do not require any supports.

- Taller varieties of raspberries require support to hold up the hollow canes. You can grow them in rows along a fence or by staking posts at either end and stretching jute twine or galvanized wire between the posts, starting at 12 inches above the ground and adding more horizontal supports as the plants grow. Individual plants can be supported by a trellis.
- Trailing blackberries can be supported by planting them alongside a fence or a trellis, or using a bamboo tepee-like structure.

How Many Plants to Grow

The following counts, based on average yield of a mature plant, will help you determine the number of plants you need. Exact harvests will depend on the variety, growing environment, and annual weather conditions.

Strawberries	1 pint per plant
Blueberries	3 to 4 quarts per plant
Raspberries	1 to 2 quarts per plant
Blackberries	1 quart per plant
Currants and Gooseberries	3 to 4 quarts per plant

Tend

Follow plant label instructions for fertilizing and watering.

- Dig up any raspberry and blackberry canes that grow away from the rows; compost them or replant elsewhere.
- Keep the soil around blueberry plants covered with an acidic mulch such as pine needles or shredded oak leaves throughout the year to help maintain the pH level.
- Just before the blueberries begin to emerge, you may want to protect the developing fruit from birds with plastic netting, pulling it taut to the ground and securing with sod staples.

Harvest

Pick berries in the cool of the morning or early evening when they are fully ripe, as described below.

- Strawberries should be firm and deep red, without any white or yellow spots.
- Wait until three or four days after blueberries are uniformly deep blue or purple (or red, depending on the variety), including near the stem.
- Pick blackberries when they are plump yet firm, fully black, and release easily from the stem.
- Raspberries are ripe when they are uniformly colored and firm; plan to gather them every day or so, before they turn soft. Avoid picking after a rain or watering.
- Currants should be picked when they reach their final color and before they drop to the ground.
- Gooseberries ripen over a period of four to six weeks; some people prefer to pick them when they are still green, tart, and hard. For a sweeter flavor, allow the fruit to ripen to a pinkish color and softer feel.

Freezing Berries

After harvesting, the shelf life of berries is short—a couple of weeks in the refrigerator, tops. Preserve their flavor, color, and texture by freezing while they are still ripe.

1. Spread the berries in single layers on baking sheets, then place in the freezer until firm. (Leave the stems on the currants; they are easier to pick once the fruit is frozen.)
2. Transfer the frozen berries to resealable freezer bags or airtight containers (such as repurposed take-out soup containers), label and date, and use straight from the freezer in smoothies or let thaw on the counter and add to sweet and savory sauces.

Prune

Annual pruning produces larger berries in greater volumes, ensures good air circulation and light throughout the plants, and helps control diseases that might otherwise spread through the patch.

- To increase fruiting, regularly prune strawberry plants that send out runners to no more than three daughter plants.
- In fall, first cut any dead, diseased, or damaged branches of blueberry bushes all the way back to where they join a thicker branch. Then cut about one-third of the remaining branches (focusing on old wood) all the way down to the ground.
- Prune raspberries after the harvest is finished, cutting all the old, weak, diseased, and damaged canes back to the ground. Then trim new canes back to the last visible node.
- Cut old blackberry canes back to the ground after all fruiting has finished, preferably in late fall or winter. Erect blackberries also benefit from pruning new canes to about 4 inches tall in late summer.
- In winter, remove any dead or diseased wood, as well as any crossing or rubbing branches, from all currant plants. For black currants, cut all old (brown and hollow) canes back to the ground.

Fruit Trees

If you are willing to commit to a long-term, larger-scale, higher-maintenance endeavor, fruit trees will provide an excellent return on your investment. Many gardeners are put off by the extra effort required to nurture them, but once planted, they will delight you with their flowers and fruit—and the avian population they attract to your yard.

Taking lessons from the hundreds of orchard trees that thrive at Bedford, here's how to plant and care for them—and to preserve the fruits' peak-of-season flavor throughout the year.

Planning

Refer to the section on ornamental trees starting on page 200 for guidance on planting and tending, then supplement that information with what follows.

Choose

As with other edibles, keep the focus on growing what you love to eat, whether fresh out of hand, processed into jams and jellies, or baked into pies. Once you've zeroed in on your favorites, here are other important factors to consider when exploring the many cultivars.

Location: Check your local cooperative extension for a list of fruit tree varieties that will flourish in your climate zone and resist local pests and diseases. Consulting with a local certified arborist is another sound option.

If you have your heart set on fruit trees that are not cold-hardy for your region, some varieties can be grown in pots on your patio and brought indoors for winter. For example, at Bedford, citrus trees grow in one of the greenhouses and the hoop houses.

Pollination: Many types of trees come in both cross-pollinating and self-pollinating (self-fertile) varieties—and some trees have multiple varieties grafted on the rootstock to be self-fertile. Cross-pollinating trees need to be planted in pairs to produce fruit, and even self-pollinating trees will yield a bigger harvest with another tree nearby.

Size: These trees need a good amount of room to grow, and the mature size will dictate your spacing requirement and the ideal location in your landscape. Check the plant tags at the nursery or research online. If you have a small yard, look into dwarf varieties.

The Bedford Orchard

At the Bedford farm, an orchard around the pool counts more than 200 different fruit trees. Fruits also grow on espalier trees and in groves—those recently planted, and those that are original to the farm.

The largest orchard is dedicated to hundreds of apple trees, with plum, cherry, peach, apricot, nectarine, pear, medlar, and quince trees rounding out the offerings.

Here are some of the varieties growing in the orchard at Bedford.

Apple: Baldwin, Black Oxford, Cortland, Cox's Orange Pippin, Esopus Spitzenburg, Fuji, Golden Russet, Grimes Golden, Honeycrisp, Liberty, Redfield, Roxbury Russet, and Windham Russet

Pear: Bartlett, Columbia, D'Amalis, Ginnybrook, McLaughlin, Nova, Patten, Seckel, Stacyville, and Washington State, plus many Asian varieties, such as Hosui, Niitaka, and Shinko

Plum: 'Green Gage', 'Mount Royal', 'NY9', and 'Stanley', plus plum hybrids, such as 'Black Ice', 'Grenville', 'Kaga', 'Pipestone', 'Toka', and 'Waneta'

Peach: 'Garnet Beauty', 'Lars Anderson', 'Polly', 'Redhaven', and 'Reliance'

Ease: Apple trees are vigorous growers and producers, though they do require careful pruning—and unless you want two trees, you'll need to find a self-pollinating variety.

Lower-maintenance options include peach trees, which can produce fruit after the first year, and plum trees.

In general, look for a sunny spot where the tree can have plenty of room to grow and won't overshadow existing sunseekers. Here are a few more specific guidelines:

Sun: Fruit trees produce best when they receive at least six to eight hours of direct sunlight. Make sure the fruit tree will not be shaded by existing trees.

Soil: Fruit trees prefer loamy, well-draining soil with a pH of 6.0 to 7.5. As always, it pays to conduct a soil test to determine what, if any, amendments are needed. Doing a drainage test is important for fruit trees, too—most varieties will not survive in boggy conditions.

Space: Depending on the variety, fruit trees can grow to as tall and wide as 25 feet. You may also need to plant a pair for cross-pollinating varieties (these should be at least 15 feet apart). Avoid planting too close to a driveway or a structure so the growing root system doesn't do damage.

Buy

Many of the Bedford trees were bare-root cuttings that were nurtured in pots before planting. You can find bare-root trees, balled and burlapped trees, or container trees (as discussed on page 197). Follow the planting steps for each type of tree starting on page 200.

Fruit Trees by Zone

Planting a tree that's not hardy to your zone is risky, so start here. Then find a specific variety that is suitable for your area.

Apple	zones 3 to 10
Cherry	zones 4 to 10
Citrus	zones 8 to 10
Fig	zones 7 to 11
Olive	zones 8 to 11
Peach	zones 5 to 9
Pear	zones 3 to 9
Pomegranate	zones 7 to 11

How to Espalier a Fruit Tree

If you've ever marveled at a wall adorned with a beautifully shaped plant, you may be interested in learning how to replicate the art of espalier in your own landscape.

Espalier refers to the process of training trees, shrubs, and woody vines to grow in a desired pattern against a flat surface, such as a wall, fence, or trellis. Depending on the plant, this can take at least one or two years to establish, with hands-on care until that happens. After that, espaliers need light pruning to maintain their shape.

1. **Choose a pattern:** Classic shapes include what looks like a menorah, with consecutively smaller U-shaped branches growing from a central stem, or a wider U-shape with branches extending upward from the horizontal section. Another traditional option, and one employed at Bedford, is to plant multiple trees in close intervals and train the branches into a crosshatch pattern (known as a Belgian fence).
2. **Select the location:** Practically any vertical surface—including a freestanding fence or trellis—works so long as it is sturdy and allows ample sunlight. You can even plant in containers (choosing those that can withstand any winter freezes).
3. **Pick the plant:** Most fruit trees can be espaliered, though apple, pear, and quince are the most reliable options.
4. **Plot the supports:** As with climbing plants, you'll need to provide heavy-gauge wire for the branches to grab on to, running it in the desired pattern and using nails, hooks, or other mounts appropriate for the surface.
5. **Plant the tree:** Position it about a foot away from the structure with at least two of the strongest branches running in the direction of the wires.
6. **Train the branches:** Attach a shoot from each branch to the wires with soft ties (prune any additional shoots). As the central trunk grows, continue to attach new side shoots to the wires and remove the rest.

Prune

Initial pruning is an important part of planting—it will help train the tree into the ideal shape for bearing fruit. There are two general pruning techniques depending on the type of fruit tree.

CENTRAL LEADER

This shape is great for apple and pear trees.

- Choose a vertical leader with about four evenly spaced scaffold branches around it.
- Prune back the central leader to 18 inches above the highest scaffold branch.
- Cut scaffold branches that aren't 45 to 60 degrees or are too close to one another.
- Prune the scaffold branches so that they are 12 inches long.

OPEN CENTER

Also called a vase shape, this is great for apricot, cherry, fig, nectarine, olive, peach, pear, and pomegranate trees.

- Remove lower branches growing less than 18 inches aboveground.
- Prune any branches growing upward in the center.
- Choose three to five evenly spaced 45-degree main branches and cut the rest.
- Prune back scaffold branches by one-fourth of their length.

Maintenance

This is equally fundamental to fruit trees' success—and where many home growers get stymied. Yet of all the tree types, fruiting trees need pruning the most: More branches does not equal more fruit—rather it equals smaller yields and poor fruiting performance. Aim for your tree to have six to eight main branches.

- Remove dead, damaged, and diseased wood as needed to improve airflow, disease resistance, and fruiting.
- Once a year, thin the remaining (healthy) branches to allow sunlight and air to reach the middle branches, improving your fruit yield from both inner and outer branches.
- For both height and width, prune back the youngest branches to keep the desired shape and size (according to the initial pruning guidelines). Otherwise, those new branches will take all the growth, and those aren't the branches that make fruit.

Harvest

Patience is key to successful harvesting—timing is important, so don't rush to gather your much-anticipated crops. Keep these tips in mind before you get started.

- Young fruit trees can be slow to launch—it takes a lot of energy to put out fruit, so give them time to muster that strength. Some may produce in the second year; others more like the fifth.
- Certain fruit trees are biennials, with alternating heavy and light harvests. Fertilizing and pruning can help boost the yield for more year-after-year consistency.
- Don't expect all the fruit to ripen at once (and that's a good thing). Gather the choicest examples as they reach their picking point.
- Speaking of: Some fruits continue to ripen off the tree, while others don't. See page 332 for examples of each type.
- Fruit trees are subject to climate conditions—such as a late-spring frost that kills some flowers, or a late-season drought that saps the tree's resources. Consistent care is your best recourse in helping them survive and rebound.
- On the other hand, have a plan for storing or preserving a generous yield so nothing goes to waste. It's fine to leave some fruit on the tree for your wildlife visitors. You may also want to see if you can donate extra fruit to a local food bank.

SUPPLIES

Knowing which tool to use and how to do so will greatly ease your efforts and ensure you don't inadvertently cause harm to your fruit tree.

Secateurs: Besides pruning, these handy shears can get fruit that refuses to budge by pulling. Use telescoping pole pruners for high-up fruit. Be sure to disinfect the blades and make a clean cut when harvesting.

Fruit-picker basket: This handy tool has an extension handle so you can reach fruits that can be pulled off easily; wrap the hooks around the fruit's stem, give it a tug, and the fruit falls right in.

Tarp: Apple and other fruit trees will drop their fruit at the slightest shake, so laying a tarp (or an old sheet) on the ground will make them easier to gather. Better yet, have two people hold the tarp with a little slack to provide a softer landing spot.

Ladder: When a telescoping pruner or basket won't do, you may need to use a sturdy ladder to gather hard-to-reach fruit. Make sure it is on level ground (and doesn't sink into soft earth), preferably with someone steadying it while you gather fruit.

Harvesting basket: Keep bushels or totes for hauling your harvest inside. If you are picking on a ladder or on multiple trees, a hands-free harvest bag that you can sling across your body is a convenient option.

Garden gloves: Protect your hands from prickly thorns (on citrus trees) and sharp branches and twigs by wearing gloves. If you have a lot of trees, you may want to invest in special arm guards or long gloves.

TIMING

Think of harvesting as shopping for the choicest fruit at the farmers' market or grocery store. It should have the fruit's characteristic color, feel heavy for its size, and have a pleasant fragrance.

Don't be put off by misshapen fruit or a few bruises—homegrown crops aren't built for perfection. And add any spoiled fruit to the compost bin.

Some fruits should ripen fully on the tree; others are best allowed to ripen after harvesting.

Pick before ripe: These fruits should be picked while still firm but with a little give, using pruners if necessary. The color will mostly be set. They should give off a subtle fragrance. Store at room temperature until ripe, then prolong their freshness by storing in the refrigerator.

- Avocados
- Mangoes
- Pears
- Persimmons
- Quince

Pick when ripe: Fruits that should be picked when fully ripe will often be easy to pull or twist off the branch. These can be refrigerated to extend their shelf life.

- Apples
- Cherries
- Citrus
- Figs
- Olives
- Pomegranates

Pick before or when ripe: The following stone fruits can ripen fully on the tree, though they will continue to ripen after harvesting, too; keep them on the counter until ripe, then refrigerate. These are the easiest to gauge, as they should be softer toward the stem and give off their distinctive aromas.

- Apricots
- Nectarines
- Peaches
- Plums

Preserving the Harvest

If you are a canning aficionado, by all means put those supplies and skills to excellent use in putting up your go-to recipes. For everyone else, or if you are only making a small batch, follow this no-can (can-do) method for making delicious jams.

Note: The skins from stone fruit will contribute color and flavor to the jam. But for a smoother mixture, you can start by peeling peaches or nectarines: Carve an X in the bottom of each and plunge them into boiling water for 30 seconds, then transfer them to an ice-water bath to stop the cooking; the skins will slip off. For plums, just lift the skins out of the cooked jam with a fork.

1. Stir together 3 pounds fruit (cut into chunks if large, pits removed), 3⅓ cups sugar, and ¼ teaspoon coarse salt in a large heavy-bottomed pot. Bring to a boil, stirring until sugar is dissolved and mashing fruit with a potato masher. Add 2 tablespoons fresh lemon juice; continue to boil, stirring frequently, until bubbles slow, chunks of fruit show at top, and the mixture clings to a spoon but falls off in clumps, 10 to 12 minutes. Skim foam from the top.
2. Ladle jam into clean containers, leaving ¾ inch of headspace. Let cool completely. Cover, label, and refrigerate for up to 1 month, or freeze for up to 1 year.

Mixed berry: 1 pound each raspberries, blackberries, and strawberries

Nectarine-raspberry: 2¼ pounds nectarines plus 12 ounces raspberries

Peach: 3 pounds white or yellow peaches, peeled (optional)

Peach-plum: 1½ pounds peaches, peeled (optional) plus 1½ pounds plums

Plum: 3 pounds plums

Raspberry: 3 pounds raspberries

Apple Cidering

Every autumn, after all the wonderful apples around the Bedford farm are picked, out comes the cider press—everyone at the farm loves to help.

The same American Harvester model from Happy Valley Ranch in Dothan, Alabama, has been used for over a decade. The manual press is designed to grind and squeeze at the same time.

The apples used don't have to look pristine, but they need to be free from spoilage, which would cause the juice to ferment too rapidly. They should also be well washed, so they're ready to go through the press.

Cider-Press Method

For a gallon of cider, you'll need between 30 and 40 apples. Then follow these simple steps.

1. Set up the press, and add a mesh bag to the bucket. Rinse the apples, and place several at a time in the rotating cylinder equipped with sharp teeth.
2. Start turning the wheel on the cylinder to grind the apples. As the apples are pulverized, the pulp will fall into the tub, which is also known as the hopper. Continue the process, adding more apples and turning the grinder.
3. Once the hopper is full of pulp, put the pressing plate down directly on top. Place a clean bucket beneath the downspout, and turn the handle clockwise to lower the screw onto the tub. This part can require some strength, so take turns!
4. Keep turning until every last drop is squeezed out. Compost the pulp (or feed it to your chickens!). Skim off any froth that forms on top. You can strain the cider through a double layer of cheesecloth for a clearer cider, though that is optional. Pour the cider into clean bottles, and refrigerate for up to 1 week.
5. For longer storage, cider needs to be pasteurized: Heat the cider to between 160°F and 185°F for at least 10 seconds. Let cool completely before transferring to jars, leaving an inch of headspace. Refrigerate for up to 1 month or freeze for as long as a year.

Easy No-Press Method

A food processor is an easy stand-in for a traditional cider press.

1. Wash, core, and cut 7 pounds unpeeled apples into wedges. Working in batches (don't fill more than halfway), grind apples to the consistency of thick applesauce, scraping down the sides as needed. Transfer each batch to a large colander lined with a triple layer of cheesecloth (leave an overhang of a few inches) placed over a large pot.
2. Once all batches have been added, gather the cheesecloth overhang and enclose the applesauce, twisting to close. Weight it down with a heavy pot. Refrigerate for at least 4 hours and up to overnight.
3. Remove the cheesecloth bundle and compost the applesauce (or feed it to your chickens!). The cider can be refrigerated in an airtight container for up to 1 week or frozen for up to 3 months.

Cutting-Flower Garden

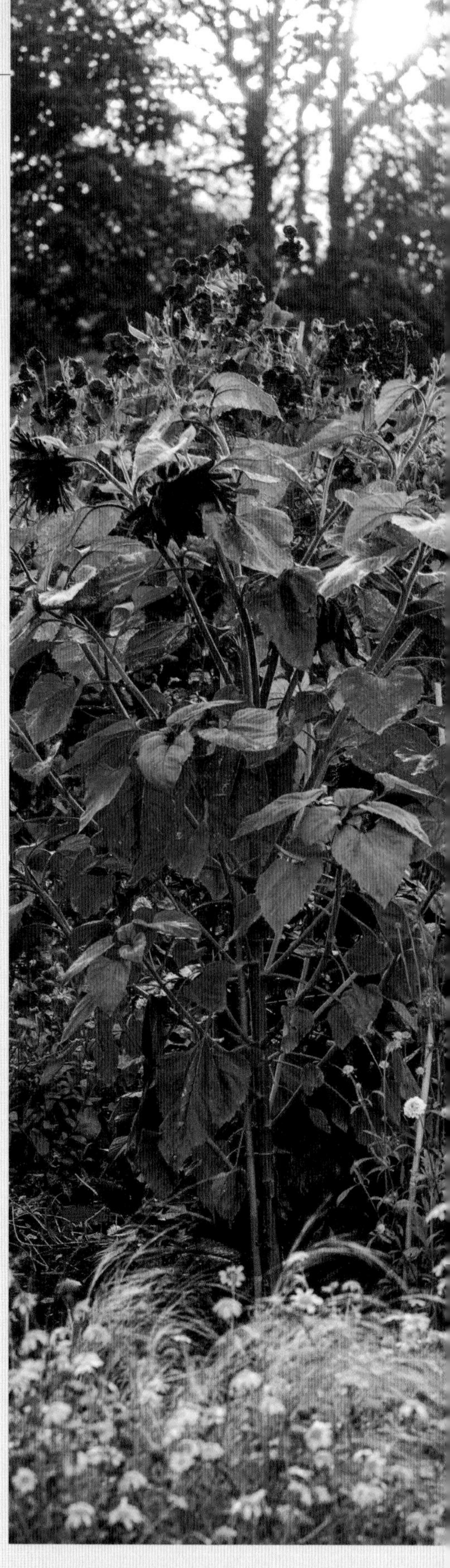

Strolling into an exuberant garden (like the one shown here) in the early morning, bucket in hand, and snipping stems is a wonderful way to start any day—and then you get to continue to enjoy the beautiful blooms indoors or share them with others. Being able to pick flowers at different stages—tight new buds, partially opened blooms, fully open flowers—as well as foliage accents for a single arrangement allows you to replicate nature in a vase.

When you grow a cutting flower garden from seed (or bulb), you will open the door to a staggering variety and rare species that you just can't find at a florist. It's also much more affordable than buying arrangements, which can seem like a luxury, and you'll be supporting your local pollinator population.

Planning

▶ **The steps to success** here will help you grow your own patch of paradise.

Choose the plants

A cutting garden starts with the plants, which run the gamut—from annuals, perennials, bulbs, and biennials to shrubs and ornamental grasses. With "grow what you love" as your guiding mantra, there are ways to ensure your garden delivers all season long—providing beauty indoors and out.

- Annuals are inexpensive, easy to grow, bloom for a long time, and respond well to cutting. Perennials—including bulbs—provide steadfast, year-after-year additions. Aim to have a mix, prioritizing those hardy for your zone and also natives.
- Diversity is important if you want to have interesting arrangements, so choose plants with a variety of colors, textures, sizes, and scents. Foliage counts, too.
- You can choose a palette that matches your home's interior: First pick a focal color and then build upon that with different shades and harmonious (adjacent) hues on a color wheel.

  For a deep-magenta focal point (say, inspired by a favorite dahlia), you could work in a variety of purple and pink blooms leading to blush-tinged white petals. For a yellow-centric garden, the options could spill over into peach and apricot hues. Note that yellow and purple are complementary (opposite) on the color wheel, each making the other pop.

  Or, if your tastes are more eclectic, experiment with any bold mix of colors—there are infinite combinations to explore.
- Also important is having blooms from spring to frost—moving from ranunculus, daffodils, tulips, and peonies to dahlias, zinnias, sunflowers, and anemones. Plant a few no-fail varieties for each month and supplement those with flowers that you love (but may not thrive).
- If space is tight, prioritize highly productive plants with longer bloom times (and avoid short-lived peonies or biennial foxgloves)—and grow vertically with climbing vines for flowers and foliage. You can supplement with container plants on a patio, too.
- Plant for beautiful displays by familiarizing yourself with the basics of creating arrangements on page 348.

OPPOSITE: A classical urn peeks out from masses of flowering *Verbena bonariensis* in a garden teeming with sunflowers, dahlias, and other delights.

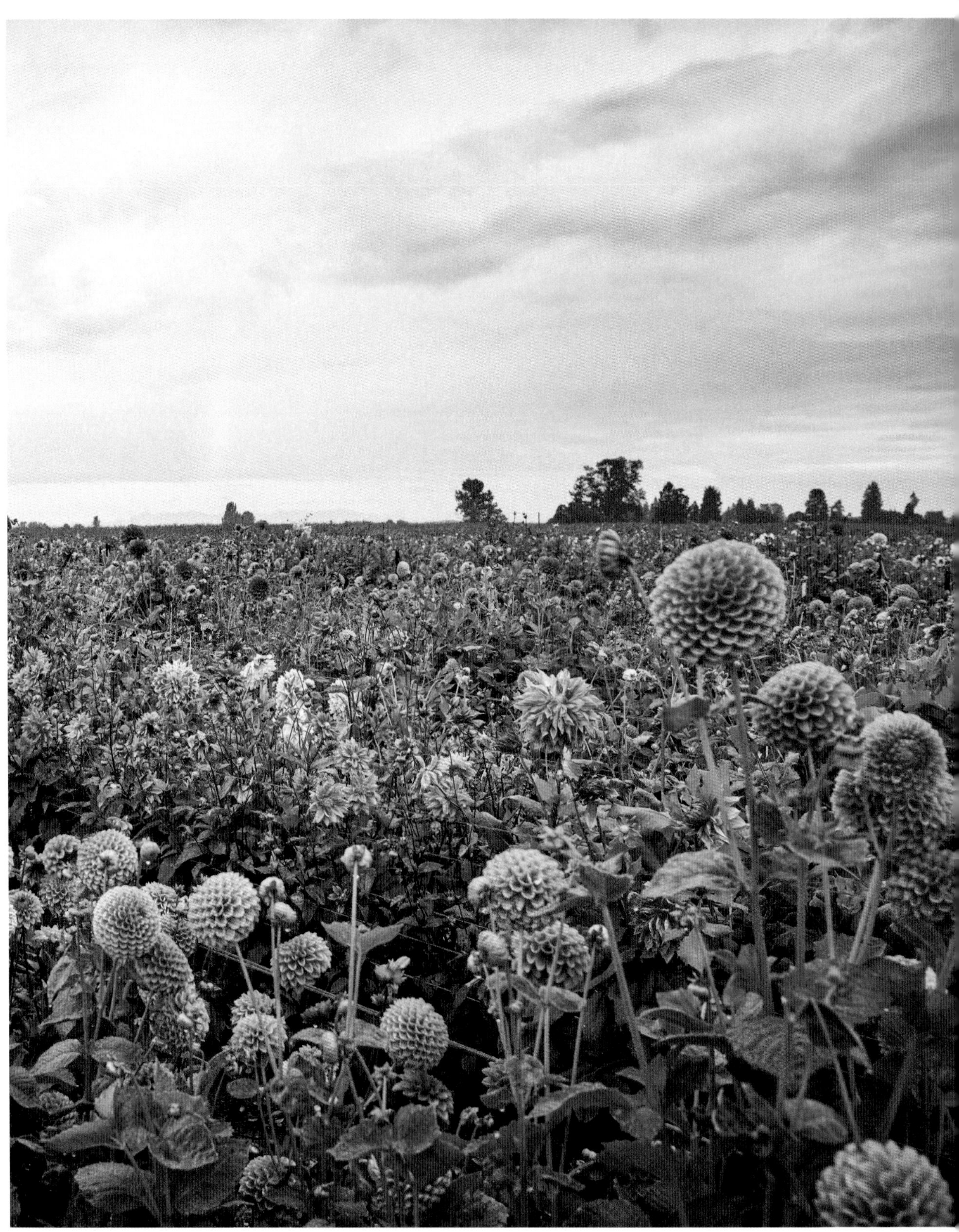

Dahlias—the Darlings of the Cutting Garden

Dahlias provide incredible color in the garden all summer long and into autumn. Their varied blooms offer endless possibilities for cut-flower arrangements, too.

Choose

Technically tubers, dahlias come in an amazing array of colors and sizes—and the size of the tuber has nothing to do with the size of the flower. Even tiny tubers can grow a bloom that reaches up to a foot in diameter.

Aim for a mix of sizes and flower heads—pompons, single flower, double flower, dinner plate–size, and so on.

Of the countless varieties growing in her fields, Erin Benzakein, founder of the famous dahlia farm Floret in the Pacific Northwest, recommends the standouts listed below. In addition, 'Beatrice', raspberry 'Sonic Bloom', and coppery 'Hy Sunton' are shown in the photo at left.

- 'Appleblossom'
- 'Mystique'
- 'Polka'
- 'Honka Fragile'
- 'Castle Drive'
- 'Café au Lait'

Tend

Dahlias are heavy feeders and benefit from monthly fertilizing with an organic all-purpose fertilizer or fish emulsion.

Stake individual plants or corral them in rows with twine. (See page 164 for more details.)

Harvest

Pick dahlias when they are almost fully open, in the morning or evening, placing them in cool water right away. Do this regularly and snip any that have faded so they don't go to seed. Go big: The more you harvest, the more they'll bloom.

Let them rest out of the sun for a few hours before arranging. Clip the stems and strip away leaves that will be below the waterline. Mix in flower food, and change the water every other day.

Overwinter

If the ground freezes in winter where you live, the traditional method is to dig up the tubers after the first deep frost, separate the clumps into individuals, and let air-dry. Store them in a cool, dry place (such as nestled in newsprint inside a shoebox or other box).

Alternatively, you can cover the entire bed with burlap, a thick layer of hay (step on it to compress), and a tarp to protect from moisture (anchor with wood stakes).

Select the site

It doesn't have to be large. Where space is limited, a mixed border or even a vegetable garden works just fine. Simply integrate your favorite cutting plants into the existing beds. If you have room, consider planting a dedicated cutting patch. Just make sure the site meets the following flower-growing conditions.

Sunlight: Most flowers are sun worshippers, so make sure the garden receives at least 6 to 8 hours of direct sunlight each day. Of course, you can plant shade-tolerant plants in a location that receives morning sun and afternoon shade; these include hellebores, Solomon's seal, bleeding heart, snowdrops, lily of the valley, Japanese anemones, lady's mantle, masterwort, and hydrangea.

Protection: Gusty winds can topple tall, top-heavy stems and take down even staked flowers. Ideally, the garden will be sheltered by your home or other structure; if not, consider erecting a wind-breaking fence or planting a hedgerow.

Soil: Rich, loamy, well-draining soil is best—either test what you have or consider growing in raised beds, where you can control the fertility and composition with a high-quality mix (see page 23). If planting in the ground, amend the soil by working in lots of organic matter.

Paths: Whether planting in the ground or in raised beds, plan for easy access by spacing the rows or beds at least 2 (preferably 3) feet apart. It would be a shame to trample on your efforts when taking the cuttings.

Watering: Make sure the site is within easy reach of an outdoor spigot for watering with a garden hose or other irrigation method.

Plant the selection

You'll want to follow the usual guidance for planting annuals, perennials, and bulbs as described elsewhere in this book, as well as these specific tips for cutting gardens.

Start from seed (if desired): This method is a cost-saving way to grow annuals and some perennials. Starting varieties that germinate faster than others will also give you the longest harvest window. Keep in mind that some perennials will not flower in their first year when started from seed (as noted on the packet). Be sure to harden off your seedlings before transplanting after the ground has thawed.

Plant in groups: Ease your cutting efforts by planting the same variety in masses so you can quickly gather the various elements of your desired arrangement. You may also want to plant in color-coordinated rows so you can better see how the various flowers will look together in a vase.

Pack tightly: You can and should practice intensive planting in a cutting garden, positioning the plants closer together than usual for a higher yield. This also helps crowd out weeds, making that task easier.

Consider the height: Grow taller varieties behind shorter ones, both for beauty in the garden as well as for access, ensuring you can clip easily without harming surrounding plants.

Jump-start growth: Give your seedlings a boost by adding an organic all-purpose fertilizer to the soil when planting (being careful to follow the package instructions to avoid overfeeding) and then watering in thoroughly.

Add stakes: Be sure to provide the necessary support to peonies, dahlias, and other top-heavy plants, as well as trellises or other structures for clematis, sweet pea, and climbing roses.

Tend the garden

The same general rules apply to cutting gardens, only more so because the flowers tend to be heavy feeders—and you will want to pay close attention to an intensive garden in terms of pruning.

WATER

A drip irrigation system or soaker hose drenches the roots but not the foliage. Most flowers prefer to be watered deeply once a week, twice during hot, dry spells.

FEED

Establish a twice-a-year fertilizing regimen in the spring and fall, with intermittent feedings every month during the growing season. (Refer to the seed packets or plant tags for more specific guidance.)

PRUNE

Deadheading spent flowers will encourage more blooms. Same for pruning roses and other flowering shrubs. Check frequently for suckers and prune those as well to direct the plant's energy toward flowering.

TROUBLESHOOT

As with perennial and border gardens, check frequently for signs of disease—these conditions can spread rapidly, especially in intensive plantings. Look for pests and remove them at once or treat them with natural solutions (as discussed on page 161).

Lilies

Although this subject tends to spark friendly debate, many gardeners declare that there is no finer plant to grow for impact in the garden or as a cut flower for arrangements than the lily. Over the years, in both the Bedford landscape and in the garden at Skylands, lilies have become true staples. They are decorative, colorful, and strong. Turn the page for a glossary of lilies in two favorite hues.

Golden Hues

Many of the varieties shown here derive their rich sunset colors from the species *Lilium henryi*.

1. *L. superbum*
2. 'Doeskin'
3. 'White Henryi'
4. 'Antequera'
5. 'Touching'
6. *L. henryi*
7. 'Gloriana'
8. *L. henryi*
9. 'Red Hot'
10. 'Lady Alice'
11. *L. leichtlinii*
12. 'Conca d'Or'
13. 'Madame Butterfly'

Blush Colors

A range of pink and red tones looks harmonious in a garden and in a vase.

1. 'Candy Club'
2. 'Tiger Edition'
3. 'Pink River'
4. 'Scheherazade'
5. 'On Stage'
6. 'Amarossi'
7. 'Black Beauty'
8. 'Maryland'

Herbaceous Peonies: Hardy Lovelies

Although their blooms are fleeting, appearing for just a few weeks, they appear in late spring or early summer when other plants are dormant—and when pollinators lack other food sources.

Most herbaceous cultivars perform well in both the garden and the vase, too. Some varieties even produce many buds on one stem rather than having one terminal bud and no or only a few side buds. All symbolize love, beauty, and happiness. Here's how to plant them so they last for decades to come.

Planning

Peonies are hardy and long-lived but do require patience—they can take a few years to settle in. Here are a few pointers to keep in mind.

Choose the plants

Because they require a dormant period, peonies do best in zones 2 to 8. In zone 8, choose early-blooming cultivars.

PICK A PALETTE

Time was when peonies came in white, pink, and crimson. Now you can find thousands of varieties in a range of shades, including yellow.

VARY THE TYPE

Herbaceous peony types range from elegant simples, with as few as five petals, to lush doubles, with hundreds. Select from the following eight forms or shapes.

- **Anemone peonies** are an early-blooming type of flower that makes for a great garden plant. They're low-growing—around 2 inches tall—and because their flowers are lighter, they usually don't require staking.
- **The single peony** is revered for its prolific blooming; these peonies look like big daisies. They do well with a bit of shade in the afternoon to protect the flowers from the heat of the midday sun.
- **The lotus peony** is another heavily blooming plant. Its flowers feature two or three layers of guard petals and need to be protected from the hot afternoon sun.
- **Chrysanthemum peonies** are many-petaled flowers, with five to ten layers of guard petals that get smaller as they approach the center. They prefer full sunshine.
- **Rose peonies** feature a strong rose-like scent and lots of petals. Their petals are larger near the outside of the flower, and the blooms are beautiful as cut flowers.
- **The golden circle** is a striking variety with big, full flowers and wonderful blooms.

Tip

To make the most of the short peony season, deadhead blooms after they finish flowering; but wait until fall to cut back the foliage.

- With their large, wide outer guard petals and tight, curly center petals, **crown peonies** are shaped like scoops of ice cream. When fully open, the guard petals fold all the way back and the flowers look like big balls in the garden.
- **Hundred proliferate flowers** contain the most petals out of any peony form—at least 100 each. They are so full that you can hardly see the distinction between guard petals and center petals. They're widely known as the best form for cut flowers.

Pick the location

Both herbaceous and tree peonies can tolerate full sun, but the flower will last longer if there is a bit of shade each day. They also prefer moist but well-drained soil in an area that's free of competing plant roots.

Plant properly

The best time to plant is generally when temperatures are mild, such as in spring or fall. When buying peony roots to plant, look for healthy, fleshy, fibrous roots (they should feel like firm carrots) and abundant eyes. As you plant, it's important to position the eyes of the root at the right depth. This varies by zone—in general, you'll want the eyes closer to the surface the warmer your climate. You can also find container-grown peony plants that are typically a few years old; plant these as directed on the plant tag, spacing them about 3 to 4 feet apart.

Stake as needed

The doubles are notorious for becoming top-heavy and require staking with peony rings or other supports (as discussed on page 164). Those with fewer petals capture less rainwater and are less likely to flop over.

Tend

Water well after planting to keep the soil moist. Established plants need only regular watering and a single annual application of low-nitrogen fertilizer.

Harvest

Peonies make great cutting flowers and are ready when buds begin to show color and feel like firm marshmallows. Harvest them in the early morning, cutting stems at an angle, and placing them in a pail of cool water as you go. Transfer to vessels filled with fresh cool water, arranging as desired. If you won't be displaying the peonies for a couple of days, you can also snip them before they are open, when hard like marbles. Then wrap them in newspaper, with rubber bands around the stem ends, and store them in the refrigerator until ready to arrange.

Peonies look lovely in sweet, single-stem displays that can be placed throughout the home, as well as in bountiful bouquets. Change the water and trim the stems daily. Opening buds will last a week or more; fully unfurled blooms, a day or two. With cut peonies, come ants: Shake them from the cut blooms, or wash them off with a gentle spray of water.

Flower Arranging 101

Knowing how to create an eye-catching mixed arrangement will help you choose what to grow in your cutting garden. Keep the three overarching display components—scale, color, and texture—in mind as you explore the following "ingredients."

Seasonal Stars (Thrillers)

These showy stems grab your attention and tend to have large, lush, round flower heads (think dahlias and peonies) or striking spiky shapes (like foxgloves or hollyhocks). Make sure you plant varieties that bloom all season long. Here are some favorites:

Spring: daffodil, tulip, rhododendron/azalea, lilac, allium, peony, foxglove

Summer: clematis, delphinium, hydrangea, lily, poppy, rose, hollyhock

Fall: dahlia, rudbeckia, sunflower, chrysanthemum

Supporting Players

Beauties in their own right, these secondary acts either complement or harmonize with the focal points.

- Plant one or more in a variety of shapes—mixing in spiky specimens (like larkspur, lupine, astilbe, Agastache, blue false indigo, gladioli, snapdragons, and salvia) with smaller flower heads (asters, pompon dahlias, zinnias, cornflowers, daisies, and cosmos).
- Plumelike flowers like lily of the valley, goldenrod, and celosia introduce yet more colors and shapes, as do multitoned bearded irises and hellebores.

Fillers

Don't underestimate the power of these additions to do more than just fill in gaps. Chosen wisely, these hard workers unite the stars and supporting players with their foliage and/or flowers.

- Lady's mantle, Queen Anne's lace, bleeding heart, love-in-a-mist, sweet pea, sweet William, variegated Solomon's seal, and sedum are popular options.
- Try adding tree and shrub cuttings, such as horse chestnut, crab apple, dogwood, magnolia, forsythia, hydrangea, and flowering quince.

Foliage

Greenery is more than an afterthought—it serves as an attractive backdrop for the flowers.

- Layering tall, sturdy stems (eucalyptus, cotoneaster tree) and softer leaves (myrtle, lemon balm) creates height and dimension, as does incorporating feathery ferns, grevillea, and ornamental grasses.
- Glossy magnolia or monstera leaves, silvery-green olive branches, and variegated hostas add visual interest.

Extras

Though optional, these elements provide a wow factor or a more subtle hint of whimsy.

- "Spillers" such as Italian ruscus, sapphire clematis, and ivy (among countless others) look lovely trailing over the side of a vase, as do branches from a weeping cherry tree.
- Ground covers like creeping thyme or phlox, wood hyacinth (bluebells), creeping blue star, and many stonecrops lend an organic, plucked-from-nature look.
- Fritillaria and columbine offer their own brand of eye candy.
- Or harvest interesting crops from your vegetable garden for extra personality.

Harvest

While most cut flowers last for about one week, there are a few easy steps you can take to increase their longevity and keep them looking prettier for longer. Read the tips and techniques below to come up with a rhythm and process that works for you. Consider choosing the vessel before you gather the flowers, so you know how long to cut the stems.

GATHER

Generally, flowers should be picked when they are just opening and out of the tight bud stage. Dahlias and zinnias are among the exceptions that are best picked when fully open. Be sure to research the right time for the specific varieties in your garden.

- It's best to cut the flowers in the early morning or at dusk when it's cool, rather than in the heat of the afternoon when the stems are more likely to wilt. Avoid harvesting when plants are wet from rain or watering.
- Bring a well-cleaned bucket filled with water to the garden to hold the cut flowers as you go. You can use multiple buckets of varying sizes and heights to organize the stems and avoid crushing them.
- Use sharp floral shears or a florist knife for tender stems, and secateurs for woody stems—dull blades will crush the stems and prevent them from taking in water. Make sure all tools are thoroughly cleaned with rubbing alcohol between each harvest.
- Cut at a sharp angle, leaving enough stem on the plant for new blooms to grow. Snip flowers with nodes (such as azaleas) just above a node to increase the plant's ability to absorb more water.
- Strip the leaves from the bottom portion of the stems (consider having an empty bucket at hand for this plant matter) and shake the stems to remove excess dirt. Place the cuttings into the bucket of water.
- Once indoors, refill the bucket(s) with fresh water. Trim all stems at a 45-degree angle—this allows them to take in more water and keeps them from sitting flat on the bottom of the vessel.
- Some plants need additional help to absorb water and retain nutrients: Cut an X on the bottom of woody stems from shrubs; dip the ends of milky stems (such as poppies, hellebores, and hollyhocks) into boiling water for 30 seconds, or sear with a flame.
- Strip any leaves, petals, and thorns that will be below water in the vessel—these can promote bacterial growth and cloud the water—but leave foliage above that line. Remove spent blossoms so the flower can focus on healthy blooms.

CONDITION

This simple process helps strengthen stems so they hold up better in arrangements. It also extends the vase life of the flowers.

- Submerge the stems in clean, tall containers filled almost to the top with cool water; woody stems prefer tepid water. Note that daffodils and hyacinths need to be conditioned in separate containers, as their natural pest repellent is toxic to other blooms. Be sure to cut these stems to their final length before conditioning.
- Florists add flower food, and you can, too—like the packets that come with store-bought bouquets. You can find this flower preservative at garden centers and florist shops.
- Place the containers in a cool area away from direct sunlight and let the stems soak up the water for at least a few hours and preferably overnight.

While you are conditioning the stems, clean the vessels that will hold the arrangements. Scrub with mild dishwashing soap and warm water or a damp sponge sprinkled with baking soda, then rinse well with warm water. For stubborn spots, fill the vessel with white vinegar above the waterline, then add baking soda and scrub with a soft-bristled bottle brush; rinse thoroughly.

- Fill the clean vessel with cool water and sprinkle in flower food before adding the flowers.
- Change the water daily, adding more flower food each time.
- Recut the stems at an angle every 3 days.
- Remove any faded blooms or moldy stems right away.
- Keep the arrangement away from direct sunlight or heat sources—the cooler the room, the longer the flowers will last.
- Also, avoid displaying floral arrangements near a fruit bowl—the emitted ethylene gas causes cut flowers to deteriorate faster.

Monthly Calendar

Gardening will be more manageable—and the results more rewarding—if you schedule the necessary monthly tasks over the course of each year. Use Martha's calendar as a guide to creating your own, adapting the seasonal chores and important dates to your specific region and garden.

March

- Order roses
- Apply ¼ cup Epsom salts to rosebushes
- Take burlap off shrubs as weather permits
- Fertilize flower beds with 0-46-0
- Top-dress flower beds with compost
- Prune raspberry canes
- Start seeds for annuals (cutting flowers) and early-season vegetables, such as sweet peas, or direct-sow in warmer regions
- Rotate houseplants to ensure even sun exposure
- Plant out cool-weather crops
- Finish pruning trees
- Do spring cleanup
- Harvest flowering branches and pussy willows for arrangements

April

- Prep soil, test, and amend as needed, and rototill
- Begin transplanting seedlings
- Turn on water for outside faucets, and set up hoses for easy watering
- Aerate and fertilize lawn (lime as needed)
- Trim, feed, and unmound roses
- Plant out more cool-weather crops
- Start mowing
- Add a layer of compost to vegetable gardens
- Edge garden beds
- Finish composting
- Take outdoor furniture out of storage and give it a good cleaning
- Set up outdoor space

May

- Organize outdoor potting supplies
- Set up peony supports in the garden for blooming peonies
- Prune flowering plants
- Cut lilacs for arrangements
- Grow potted plants
- Weed vegetable gardens

June

- Finish planting perennial beds before heat sets in
- Pick strawberries and make jam (page 333)
- Plant and stake tomatoes, eggplants, and peppers
- Plant sunflowers and any other late-summer and fall annuals
- Prune lilacs
- Deadhead perennials, like peonies—continue to do so as needed for healthy growth
- Feed roses

July

- Plant basil and new crops of lettuce, carrots, and beets
- Stake and tie dahlias, lilies, eggplants, peppers, and tomatoes
- Cut hydrangeas for displays
- Take garden tours
- Start harvesting seeds (when they are dry, not damp) and store in a labeled container for the next season
- Prune boxwoods
- Fertilize tomatoes, eggplants, and peppers

August

- Harvest vegetables
- Weed and groom herbs
- Pickle vegetables (page 310)
- Plant cool-weather cruciferous vegetables, such as broccoli and cabbage
- Order bulbs for fall planting
- Prune/deadhead flowering plants to prolong blooms, such as dahlias and cosmos
- Transplant perennials (through September)
- Turn compost

September

- Plant cool-weather greens
- Pick raspberries
- Harvest last of tomato crops; pull up and compost
- Divide and plant perennials (bearded iris, phlox, hosta, rudbeckia)
- Start planting bulbs
- Weed flower beds and deadhead faded blooms
- Aerate lawn
- Refill bird feeders
- Continue to gather flower seeds

October

- Finish planting bulbs before the first frost and the ground freezes
- Plant violas and pansies
- Plant garlic
- Dig up and divide hostas
- Cut back perennials
- Collect leaves for compost and mulch-mow; turn compost pile
- Bring tender plants inside before first frost
- Begin potting up winter flowering bulbs in greenhouse
- Turn off outside water faucets before temperature freezes

November

- Dig up and store any spring bulbs, or cover with burlap and hay
- Layer compost over cut-back perennials
- Plant indoor bulbs such as amaryllis and paperwhites for forcing, for holiday displays
- Check bird feeders and refill as necessary
- Start wrapping shrubs and boxwood in burlap
- Feed and begin pruning trees and shrubs

December

- Craft wreath from outdoor elements
- Start ordering seeds
- Visit a tree farm to pick out a Christmas tree; plant it outdoors after the holidays
- Prune any damaged or broken tree branches
- Fertilize orchids

January

- Start sowing seeds
- Plant cool-season vegetables in hotter climates
- Start winter pruning as weather permits
- Service garden equipment
- Maintain garden tools
- Touch up paint on outdoor furniture
- Care for houseplants
- Use Christmas tree branches to cover/protect delicate perennials

February

- Order summer bulbs
- Finish sowing seeds
- Continue winter pruning
- Feed houseplants and repot begonias after they bloom
- Mulch tree pits
- Enjoy flowering hellebores, snowdrops, and witch hazel

Acknowledgments

▸ Gardening has always been a passion at Martha Stewart—planting and nurturing to create something absolutely extraordinary.

Thank you to our dear friends and colleagues, who have devoted themselves to this glorious topic. May this book continue to inspire all our readers and fellow gardeners to keep digging in the dirt.

This book would not have been possible without a hardworking group, who always can be relied upon, led by editorial director Susanne Ruppert: contributing editor Evelyn Battaglia, who never fails to deliver exceptional work (and good humor), and Kim Dumer, whose knowledge of photo rights and whose dedication is unparalleled. Generous with both their expertise and their time were the gracious Melissa Ozawa and incomparable James Maikowski. Special thanks to Laura Palese for designing the beautiful layouts and to Liz Pepperell for illustrating the charming cover.

A standing ovation to all the talented photographers who contributed to this book for providing us such gorgeous gardens to visit again and again, most notably Claire Takacs, Ngoc Minh Ngo, and Caitlin Atkinson. (For a full list of the phenomenal photographers, see page 368.) Warm thanks to the Martha family, a lovely crew, who collaborated on the how-to images that grace these pages: photographer Martin D. Toub, lighting technician Charlie Hohenshilt, creative director Anduin Havens, and assistant Amelia Bowman.

Special thanks to Kevin Sharkey for his invaluable creative guidance, and Christian Martin, Patsy Pollack, Ryan Mesina, and Ryan McCallister for their keen insight. For ongoing support, thank you to Marquee Brands, namely Heath Golden, Amy Chiaro, Judith Morris, Jocelyn Santos, Sophie Roche, and Benjamin Luckadoo.

We are so pleased to be partners with Harvest/HarperCollins, collaborating with the wonderful and kind publishing family of Deb Brody, Tai Blanche, Jacqueline Quirk, Stephanie Fletcher, Mumtaz Mustafa, Shelby Peak, and Kimberly Kiefer.

Index

NOTE: *Italic page references* indicate photographs.

G

H

Q

R

Image Credits

Cover illustration: Liz Pepperell

Sang An: 260, 261, 262, 263, 321

Caitlin Atkinson: 5, 67, 124–125, 178–179, 230–231, 244, 267, 329

Christopher Baker: 97, 151, 180, 320, 339

Winona Barton-Ballentine: 157

Fadil Berisha: 85, 139

Marion Brenner: 31, 73, 79, 268, 270–271, 273, 274

Brown Bird Design: 207 (illustration)

Jennifer Causey: 70–71, 235

Jesse Chehak: 2–3, 27

Christopher Churchill: 63

Paul Costello: 203

Craig Cutler: 28, 75

Olivia Dance: 94

Victor Demarchelier: 327

Noe DeWitt: 12, 72, 112, 251

John Dolan: 101, 201, 279, 287

Tara Donne: 47

Pieter Estersohn: 134

Richard Felber: 250

David Fenton: 24–25

Kristine Foley: 104, 105, 344, 345

Roger Foley: 20–21

Don Freeman: 214

Dana Gallagher: 288

Bryan Gardner: 34, 350

GETTY STOCK: 143

Gabriela Herman: 78, 89, 152, 166, 220–221

Michael A. Hill: 292 (illustration)

The Ingalls: 243

Ditte Isager: 319

John Kernick: 298–299, 307

Frédéric Lagrange: 218

Kit Latham: 254–255

Mgmt. Design: 301

Kate Mathis: 145

David Meredith: 349

Ryan Mesina: 77

Johnny Miller: 216, 232, 296

Andrew Montgomery: 155

Martin Morrell: 60

National Trust Images / Andrew Butler: 257

Marcus Nilssen: 308–309

Ngoc Minh Ngo: 17, 38–39, 58–59, 69, 98, 122, 131, 173, 176–177, 184, 192–193, 194, 195, 196, 198, 199, 200, 224–225, 239, 241, 258, 295, 340, 352–353

Paola + Murray: 316, 335

Victoria Pearson: 57, 208–209

Eric Piasecki: 249, 289

Jose Picayo: 264, 265

Julia Rothman: 237 (illustrations)

Juliana Sohn: 6, 314–315

Seth Smoot: 37

Thomas Staub: 276–277

Martha Stewart: 174

Claire Takacs: 10–11, 13, 32–33, 42–43, 55, 61, 64–65, 83, 102–103, 129, 136–137, 165, 181, 182–183, 186–187, 188, 190–191, 211, 223, 226–227, 253, 280–281, 283, 285, 290–291, 302–303, 323, 337, 357

Christopher Testani: 311, 333

Martin D. Toub: 49, 50, 107, 109, 110, 111, 116, 123, 170

Andreas Trauttmansdorff: 168

Lennart Weibull: 115, 118

Anna Williams: 149

Elizabeth Zeschin: 90